The Third World Coalition in International Politics

The "Foreign Relations of the Third World" Series

SECOND, UPDATED EDITION

The Third World Coalition in International Politics

Robert A. Mortimer

Westview Press • Boulder and London

Foreign Relations of the Third World, No. 2

Copyright © 1984 by Westview Press, Inc.

Published in 1984 in the United States of America by Westview Press, Inc., 5500 Central Avenue, Boulder, Colorado 80301; Frederick A. Praeger, President and Publisher

First edition published in 1980 by Praeger Publishers

Library of Congress Catalog Card Number: 84-50317
ISBN: 0-86531-773-9
ISBN: 0-86531-774-7 (pbk)

Composition for this book was provided by the author
Printed and bound in the United States of America

To Mimi

Contents

Preface to the Second Edition x
Acknowledgments xii

1   Solidarity and Empowerment 1

    Note 5

2   The Spirit of Bandung, 1955-65 6

    Bandung, Symbol of Solidarity 6
    Nasser, Nehru, and Tito: The Founding Fathers 9
    Geneva and the Group of 77 15
    The Demise of Afro-Asianism 18
    Notes 22

3   Constructing the Coalition, 1966-73 24

    The First Ministerial Conference of the Group of 77 24
    Lusaka: Nonalignment Reconsidered 29
    The Activists Take Charge: Lima, Santiago, and Georgetown 33
    Back to Algiers: The Fourth Nonaligned Summit 38
    Notes 42

4   The Politics of the New International
    Economic Order, 1974-75 43

    The OPEC Revolution 44
    The Sixth Special Session 48

Energy Versus Development—The Battle of the Agenda 57
The Seventh Special Session 66
Notes 71

5   The Relationship Between the Nonaligned and the 77 74

The Group of 77 and UNCTAD IV. 75
The Threat of Disaggregation and the Fifth Nonaligned Summit. 84
The Nonaligned, the 77, and Collective Self-Reliance 90
Notes 94

6   The North-South Conference. 95

Setting Up CIEC: A Political or Technical Forum?. 96
The Group of 19 Negotiates for the Group of 77. 100
CIEC's Final Inventory. 105
Notes 109

7   The Tension of Solidarity and Dispersion, 1977–79 110

New Crises in the Third World 111
Utilizing the United Nations System 113
Cleavage in the Nonaligned Group 122
UNCTAD V: New Stress on Collective Self-Reliance. 126
Notes 130

8   Third World Power and United States Policy. 132

The United States and the Third World, 1973–79. 132
The Nature of Third World Power. 137
Notes 140

9   The Politics of Stalemate, 1979–83. 141

Blowing Smoke in Havana. 142
Punching Holes Through Smoke. 150
New Currents and the Mainstream 155
Indian Influence and the Dual-Track Strategy 162
Moderation and Rebuff 170
Power and Policy. 173
Notes 175

Appendix: Chronology of Major Third World
and North-South Conferences 179

Bibliography. 182
List of Abbreviations 187
Index 189
Titles in This Series 195
About the Book and Author 196

Preface to the Second Edition

How has the Third World coalition fared since mid-1979, when the first edition of this work went to press? Some observers were predicting in the summer of 1979 that the Nonaligned Movement would shatter on the shoals of the Havana summit. That did not happen, and in March 1983 Cuban leader Fidel Castro turned the chairmanship of the movement over to India's Indira Gandhi. On the other hand, the Group of 77 seemed seriously to be considering creation of an independent secretariat, which could have substantially strengthened its capacity as a collective actor in the international system. That has not happened either, even though the Group of 77 has remained the coalition's principal bargaining agent in the increasingly complex framework of North-South relations.

To this extent there has been a fundamental continuity in the two instruments of collective diplomacy that in the first edition I called the "backbone of the Third World coalition." The durability of these diplomatic groupings is perhaps the most striking constant in a global landscape that has been buffeted by significant changes since 1979. The coalition has had to plot its course across a field of tumultuous events that included civil war and foreign intervention in Afghanistan, war between Iraq and Iran, paralysis of the Organization of African Unity, crisis within OPEC, Israeli engagement against the Palestine Liberation Organization in Lebanon, and revolutionary and counterrevolutionary warfare in Central America. These events, among others, contributed to a resurgence of East-West tensions that risked relegation of the North-South dialogue to the bottom of the international agenda. Governmental changes in the North (Reagan, Mitterrand, Kohl) further rearranged the pattern of variables facing the Southern governments seeking a New International Economic Order.

This combination of events in North and South might well have torn the Third World coalition asunder. One might well have expected that the competing pulls of centripetal and centrifugal forces—what I called the tension of solidarity and dispersion—would have been resolved in favor of dispersion in the face of the events of the waning 1970s and early 1980s. That they were not requires explanation. The forces that underlie the survival of the Third World coalition are even more pertinent to understanding contemporary international politics today than they were four years ago.

The first edition of this work was written to provide students of international relations with a clear account of how the South had over twenty-five years forged a consequential coalition out of the enormous heterogeneity of the developing world. It focused upon the period from 1974 to 1977, which we can identify in retrospect as the first Third World drive to institute a New International Economic Order. Just after that manuscript was completed, the Havana nonaligned summit formulated a proposal to initiate a new round of talks on the all-important development issue. This was the call for a Global Negotiation. The record of the period since 1979 is in large measure the record of the diplomatic struggle to initiate the Global Negotiation. This second edition updates the status and role of the Third World coalition as it has maneuvered to launch a second drive.

The coalition has defied the predictions of its demise in spite of determined adversaries committed to the essential preservation of the existing economic order. In Chapter 9, new to this edition, I analyze the North-South debate over global negotiations and examine the political and organizational techniques by which the Third World coalition has held itself together over a period of economic recession and political turmoil. As in the original edition, I conclude this new chapter with reflections upon U.S. policy toward the compelling reality of poverty that lies at the root of the very existence of a Third World coalition.

Robert A. Mortimer

Acknowledgments

Two institutions have given particular support to this work. One is the Centre de Recherches et d'Etudes sur les Sociétés Méditerranéennes in Aix en Provence, France. The cordiality and collegiality of its research group created a perfect climate for work on this project. I wish to thank the director, Maurice Flory, for the warm welcome and complete cooperation that he extended to me, as to so many others whose research brings them to CRESM, and to express my warm appreciation to all those in the staff—library, documentation, administration—who responded to my every request.

The other is Haverford College. I am happy to thank Haverford for sabbatical leave support and for a grant to cover the costs of typing the final manuscript. I wish to express my special thanks to all those friends on the staff and in the library without whose support Haverford's teaching and research endeavors would falter. To my students, especially those in Political Science 245 who offered helpful comments on the manuscript, a further expression of thanks. I am particularly grateful to Adeline Taraborelli for her cheerfulness and professional competence in typing the final manuscript.

Haverford, Pennsylvania
August 10, 1979

Once again I wish to thank all those persons at Haverford College who have encouraged and supported my work on this updated edition. Special acknowledgment goes to Mark Bonham of the class of 1981 whose senior thesis on the Eleventh Special Session was a valuable guide to understanding that event. Adeline Taraborelli did her customary splendid job in typing the manuscript. For diligence beyond devotion, I thank Amy Mortimer, who prepared the index.

Haverford, Pennsylvania
September 30, 1983

1. Solidarity and Empowerment

Weak states never have had much say in world politics. Accordingly, the developing states of Asia, Africa, and South America have been more objects than subjects in the international system. Until quite recently, to speak of the Third World in international politics was to identify an arena of great-power competition, not an actor. Only in the 1970s has a new collective actor begun to give an active role to the Third World in international affairs.

This book is about the emergence and role of the Third World coalition that began to exercise power at the Sixth Special Session of the United Nations General Assembly in April-May 1974. This coalition of over 100 countries is as unlikely as it is unprecedented. It defies the enormous diversity of its constituent members, a body of states flung across three continents and ranging from ultraconservative to radical in their political orientation. In regard to culture, resources, population, and national regimes, these states vary greatly. Furthermore, many have been caught up in intense regional rivalries and even armed conflicts (India-Pakistan, Ethiopia-Somalia, Algeria-Morocco, Angola-Zaire, Vietnam-Cambodia suffice to illustrate that local tensions abound).

Yet there is an obvious common bond. The states of the Third World are poor. They lie on the same side of a severe international economic cleavage. As one Third World spokesperson has put it: "A poverty curtain has descended right across the face of our world, dividing it materially and philosophically into two different worlds, two separate planets, two unequal humanities—one embarrassingly rich and the other desperately poor."[1] The poverty curtain has obliged the developing states to find a means of articulating their shared interest

1

in economic development. Whatever potential power they have resides in their numbers. The challenge has been to organize a strategy of collective action.

In the early 1970s, two novel associations, the nonaligned movement and the Group of 77, began to provide a credible capacity for joint diplomatic action. These groups are neither alliances nor international organizations in the common understanding of these terms. Rather they are original responses to the peculiar situation of a large body of weak states in international politics. This study focuses on the consolidation and maintenance of these two associations, which constitute the backbone of the Third World coalition.

Long-term, large-scale collective action has rarely, if ever, been seen in international politics. The current Third World coalition is the result of two decades of political effort to mount a cohesive force. This organizational activity has been accompanied by the elaboration of a shared critique of the structures of international economic relations. What was once a mildly embarrassed protest against economic disparities has become a theory of structural dependency based upon an analysis of the terms of trade and the international division of labor prevailing between North and South. This critique questions the adequacy of free market principles and current practices of international resource transfers to produce economic development. It is the intellectual foundation for the slogan of a New International Economic Order, as articulated at the Sixth Special Session. The goal of structural change is a source of unity, but the question remains whether so heterogeneous a group of states can be expected to maintain its cohesion for very long.

The pressures of diversity and vested interests are in constant tension with the incentive to act in concert. The ideal of solidarity, which has inspired the persistent drive to build a coalition, competes with the desire to seize relative advantage, which has long been deemed the characteristic behavior of independent states in an anarchic international system. The push of solidarity versus the pull of national interests has determined the starts and halts of the gradually emerging Third World movement since 1955. It will be seen that this tension has recurred since the consolidation of the coalition as a consequential actor in 1973. The problem of fashioning solidarity out of diversity will be the central theme of this study of the Third World in international politics.

It is not surprising that a world divided into rich and poor states should reproduce the concept of solidarity historically associated with working-class movements. Yet the reality of economic cleavage does not guarantee that states can organize like workers. State interests are more complex than individual interests, and power is much more diffused throughout the state system than in an industrial relationship or even a national political system. Although the trade union analogy is far from perfect, it nevertheless remains suggestive. One might hypothesize that the poor states must develop a strategy similar to a strike if they are ultimately to exert successful pressure for change.

In any case, it was something analogous to the power to strike, namely, the power to withhold oil, that triggered the contemporary test of strength between North and South. This power was exercised by the Arab oil-producing states in October 1973 during the fourth Arab-Israeli war. Their embargo set the stage for the December 1973 decision by the Organization of Petroleum Exporting Countries (OPEC) to quadruple the price of oil. In taking this action, OPEC ushered in the politics of a New International Economic Order. This was the first time that a group of Third World states significantly altered the course of international economic relations. The OPEC move was a sudden breach in the structure of Northern economic supremacy around which the other developing states were able to rally. The exercise of oil power was at once a symbol of Third World assertion and a model of collective action.

The developing states were well aware that oil was a special case, a commodity crucial to the entire industrial economy and (in the winter of 1973-74) in scarce supply. Furthermore, the handful of petroleum-exporting states had needed years of joint consultation to build OPEC itself into an effective political instrument. The common economic interest binding the oil exporters was much more immediate than the diffuse interest of all developing states in economic development. The OPEC model, therefore, could not be directly applied to the Third World as a whole, but it was suggestive of a strategy of broader collective action that had gradually been taking shape in Third World conferences. More than the model, it was the symbol of Third World assertion that encouraged the developing states to utilize the nonaligned movement and the Group of 77 as instruments of collective pressure.

Could these more inclusive groupings develop a comparable solidarity? Could they capitalize upon the mood of economic crisis created by the oil price hikes to induce the industrial states to accept reforms in the workings of the world economy? Could they ultimately wield the threat of withholding Third World natural resources if significant changes in international economic relations were not enacted? These were the questions posed by the strategy of Third World solidarity, and they are the questions that will be explored in analyzing the evolution of the coalition since 1974.

Such a study is essentially an examination of intra-Third World, or South-South, political relations. The most important forums for these South-South interactions are the meetings of the nonaligned movement and the Group of 77. They have occurred with increasing frequency in the past few years in Algiers, Dakar, Manila, Colombo, Havana, and Mexico City. These meetings are a cross between traditional diplomatic conferences and party (or union) caucuses. Unlike sessions of the United Nations General Assembly or Security Council, these conferences are not normally open to public scrutiny, making it difficult to know just how the participating states arrive at their final public declarations. Although one would often like to know more about the internal bargaining pro-

cesses at these conferences, it is nevertheless possible to discern the general con-
tours of intra-Third World debate and to judge the overall cohesion of the coalition as it evolves from meeting to meeting.

The itinerant nature of the intra-Third World diplomatic process has been
an obstacle to a well-informed understanding of the role of the developing countries in international politics. The process appears to lack continuity in the absence of a central vantage point from which to view it. The journalist who covers
a conference in Lima is unlikely to be present at the next meeting in Belgrade,
and the quality of journalistic reporting has suffered accordingly. No previous
study has systematically followed the trail of the Third World coalition from
conference to conference. This work is designed to fill that gap and thereby provide an analysis of the internal dynamics of the Third World coalition.

These Third World conferences channel demands into the permanent
forums of the United Nations and UNCTAD (United Nations Conference on
Trade and Development), which are the principal arenas of North-South politics.
The North-South agenda has embraced such issues as decolonization in southern
Africa and the Palestinian issue in the Middle East. These issues are of central
importance for certain Third World states, but the core matters for the coalition
as a whole are economic. The study focuses, therefore, on economic issues. In
this issue-area, the North is, for practical purposes, the West, because the bulk of
the developing world's economic transactions has always been with the Western
industrial states.* Within the Western world, the United States is obviously a
crucial participant.

The rise of the Third World coalition poses policy questions for the U.S.
government. As the United States has been one of the principal beneficiaries of
the prevailing world economic system, it must assume a major responsibility for
the quality of North-South relations. The demands for a new order are largely
demands upon the United States to face the issue of economic development.
United States policymakers must make choices about the kind of global economic system that the United States wishes to defend. These choices surely
ought to turn upon values of welfare and equity—that is, upon some conception
of a just international economic order. In international politics, however, most
decisions are determined by assessments of power. The relevant variable for the
foreign policymaker is the amount of power that an international actor, whether
a nation-state or a multistate coalition, can bring to bear behind its demands.

To be sure, the issue of global poverty is of great moral significance. The

---

*East-South relations have had little salience. The East has often backed the South's
demands, but on some issues it has made common cause with the capitalist states. Rather
than distinguish West-South and East-South relations, the common usage of North-South
accurately enough denotes the international politics of rich versus poor states.

demands of the developing countries oblige us to ask in what kind of a world we wish to live. As individuals we cannot escape the ethical implications of massive inequality in the standard of living around the globe. But the basic assumption of this study is that the international system is fundamentally amoral. Distributive issues will not be decided on moral grounds. The Third World has every right to appeal to moral sensibilities, but the rich states are likely to be influenced only by power. The conceptual focus of this work is upon power, not policy, but it is hoped that the study will stimulate reflection as well upon the values that the United States should be pursuing in its relations with the Third World.

Solidarity within the Third World is not a new norm of state behavior. Rather it is a strategy of empowerment in a balance of power system. Acting together is a source of power in any political order, but the mobilization of collective action across national boundaries has always proven difficult. States by their nature are reluctant to be bound by organizational obligations. The Third World has achieved greater operational solidarity than might have been expected, but not enough as yet to force major concessions by the rich states.

As this study will demonstrate, the idea of empowerment through solidarity and collective action has endured in Third World thinking over a series of highs and lows in its practical implementation. On balance, the overall capacity to act in concert grew from 1955 through 1976. Since then, it has diminished somewhat. It would be foolhardy to assume, however, that Third World power peaked in the mid-1970s. By examining closely how the coalition has been constructed and what it has achieved, one can best evaluate its future impact upon the international system. So long as the South has compelling incentives to seek change in international politics, the strategy of solidarity will remain a factor in the balance of power.

NOTE

1. Mahbub ul Haq, *The Poverty Curtain* (New York: Columbia University Press, 1976), p. xv.

2. The Spirit of Bandung, 1955–65

The Third World coalition began to take form in 1955 in the Indonesian resort city of Bandung. The Bandung Conference was the first large-scale meeting of leaders from independent Asian and African states, and, more than anything else, the conference was a symbol of the inchoate idea of Afro-Asian unity. It created no enduring institutional relationships among developing states, but it did unleash political energies that greatly affected Third World politics in succeeding years. Over the following decade, politicians often invoked the "spirit of Bandung" as they sought to organize a more systematic framework for Third World collaboration. The first phase of Third World organizational politics ended in 1965 in a futile attempt to convene a Bandung II. The decade was one of false starts and frustrations in which the tension between solidarity and diversity was evident. Yet, by 1965, both the nonaligned movement and the Group of 77 existed in rudimentary form. This chapter analyzes the formative period of the Third World coalition, explaining why the initial Bandung formula failed, while the spirit of Bandung was preserved in new organizational forms.

BANDUNG, SYMBOL OF SOLIDARITY

The Bandung Conference captured the contemporary imagination first and foremost by its size. Twenty-nine delegations came to Bandung in April 1955. That figure is a far cry from the 120 current members of the Group of 77. Yet, at a time when the United Nations itself had only 59 member-states, this seemed a very large number. Equally impressive was the prominence of

6

many of the leaders who came to Bandung: Prime Minister Nehru of India, the senior statesman of Asian independence; Prime Minister Chou En-lai, extricating China from diplomatic isolation; Presidents Nasser and Sukarno, representatives of an emergent neutralism; and Princes Sihanouk and Faisal, traditional leaders advancing toward growing international roles alongside renowned nationalists like U Nu, Mohammed Ali, and Carlos Romulo. This combination of numbers and personalities made Bandung a notable event, however modest the concrete accomplishments of the conference.

How did it come about that 29 states should gather for such an event? To convene a body of sovereign states always requires a substantial organizational effort—an agenda must be proposed, decisions must be made about who should participate, numerous agreements must be struck merely to get any such project off the ground. In the absence of an established institutional framework, such matters may raise divisive political issues. Indeed, it will be seen that issues of agenda and membership have frequently been controversial in Third World organizing.

The primary initiative for Bandung came from Indonesia's Prime Minister, Ali Sastroamidjojo, who saw such a conference as an opportunity to shore up his own position in Indonesian politics. Sastroamidjojo persuaded his counterparts in the loose association known as the "Colombo powers"—an informal grouping of Burma, India, Pakistan, Sri Lanka, and Indonesia—jointly to sponsor a meeting of Asian and African governments. The purpose of the conference was cast in very general terms:

> to promote goodwill and cooperation among the nations of Asia and Africa . . . to consider social, economic, and cultural problems . . . to consider problems of special interest . . . [such as] racialism and colonialism . . . to view the position of Asia and Africa and their peoples in the world today and the contribution they can make to the promotion of world peace and cooperation.[1]

The project was hazily defined, but the vague hope that such a meeting might enhance the place of the new states in the international system was sufficient to get things started.

Together the Colombo powers set and applied the criteria that governed the invitations to Bandung. The basic criteria were juridical and geographic, namely, the participants were to be independent Asian and African states. Each of these apparently straightforward criteria required some interpretation. The first was stretched to include two colonies deemed to be well on their way to independence (Sudan and Ghana). The second was contracted to exclude such geographically eligible candidates as Israel, South Africa, South Korea, North Korea, and Taiwan. There were plausible political reasons for each of these membership decisions, but they confirmed the fact that who should be invited was not self-evident.* These early decisions already implied that neither geography nor political independence was an altogether satisfactory organizational concept for mobilizing the Third World.

The roster produced by these decisions can be broken down into four roughly defined cultural, regional subgroupings: the Arab world, southeast Asia, southern Asia, and black Africa. Divided accordingly, the Arab states were the most numerous: Egypt, Sudan, Libya, Saudi Arabia, Yemen, Jordan, Lebanon, Syria, and Iraq. There were eight participants from southeast Asia: Indonesia, Burma, Thailand, Cambodia, Laos, North Vietnam, South Vietnam, and the Philippines. Between these two groups of states lay Iran, Afghanistan, Pakistan, India, Nepal, and Sri Lanka. The three black African delegations were Ethiopia, Liberia, and Ghana. Finally, there were three special cases: Turkey, Japan, and China.

Each of the special cases illustrated in an extreme form the extraordinary heterogeneity of a geographically defined ensemble of states. Turkey was a member of the North Atlantic Treaty Organization and thus intricately involved in the political and military organization of Europe. Japan was a highly industrialized state, one of the world's major economic powers having little in common with the developmental needs of the rest of the Bandung participants. China was the world's most populous state whose potential national power placed it much closer to the situation of the great powers than to that of the Third World. These states were in, but not of, the Third World, a political reality that the geographic formula of Afro-Asian obscured.

This heterogeneity was only slightly less pronounced among the remaining 26 participants. The Asians and Africans present at Bandung were deeply divided in their foreign policy orientations. Several were formal members of the Western alliance system (Pakistan, Iraq, Iran, Thailand, and the Philippines), while one (North Vietnam) had a comparable relationship to the communist bloc. This cleavage dominated the actual proceedings at Bandung. Lively debates occurred between these states, and those advocating a neutralist policy, most notably India, Egypt, and Indonesia—Asia and Africa, in other words—were penetrated by the bipolar conflict that dominated international relations in the 1950s. This hindered the states at Bandung from focusing upon autonomous Third World political and economic goals.

These divisions proved to be fatal to the simple Bandung formula of an Asian-African conference. The final communique "recommended that the five sponsoring countries consider the convening of the next meeting of the Con-

---

*The Arab states would not attend a conference with Israel. South Africa was already ostracized in the non-Western world. Divided Korea posed political problems that the organizers preferred to avoid, and, as the participation of the People's Republic of China was essential to Nehru, Taiwan was out of the question.

ference, in consultation with the participating countries,"[2] but no further conference was ever successfully convened under these auspices. Although the
Bandung 26 (omitting Turkey, Japan, and China) are recognizable as the core
group of the future Third World coalition, they were destined to a lengthy
search for a more effective organizing principle than the elementary solidarity of
geography.

What did survive, however, was the aspiration to forge a common Third
World consciousness. Bandung was in essence a celebration of the wave of independence that had swept across Asia and was then cresting in Africa. The very
act of bringing together the first generation of nationalist leaders created an unprecedented sentiment of Third World change and potential. Bandung thus became the symbol of a goal. Furthermore the Bandung communique pointed to
the two principles that have remained the foundation of Third World solidarity,
decolonization and economic development.

The Bandung Conference was, then, an augur of a future protest against
the subordinate status of the developing countries in the international system. In
the following years, various leaders sought to materialize the spirit of Bandung
in more concrete terms.

NASSER, NEHRU, AND TITO:
THE FOUNDING FATHERS

As David Kimche has observed, "Bandung appears to have affected the
Egyptian leader [Gamal Abdul Nasser] most strongly of all the participants."[3]
The conference was Nasser's first substantial exposure to the larger Afro-Asian
world. It is known from his autobiographical pamphlet of 1953 that even before
Bandung Nasser thought of Egypt as part of three "circles": the Arab world,
Africa, and Muslim civilization.[4] The Bandung experience gave force to Nasser's
conviction that Egypt had an important role to play in the Third World and
added new dimensions to his own conception of neutralism as a foreign policy.
Especially after the Suez crisis of 1956, Nasser became a key figure in Third
World organizing. He shared this central position with India's Jawaharlal Nehru
and Yugoslavia's President Josip Broz Tito.

Nehru's reaction to Bandung was much more reserved than Nasser's. He
was more struck by the divisions within the conference than by any spirit of
unity. He was opposed in any case to the formation of anything resembling a
new bloc in international politics. His assessment of the conference and the
future of a Third World movement was cautiously detached. In an interview
shortly after Bandung, Nehru judged that the conference had not achieved a
great deal but added that "it may develop into something which holds together."[5]
Bandung nevertheless enhanced Nehru's own reputation as the dean of Third

World statesmen, and India's view consequently carried great weight in shaping Third World thinking.

Tito of course entered the scene through a different door. As a communist leader but a renegade from the Soviet bloc, Tito was in a unique diplomatic situation in the early 1950s. Yugoslavia's fierce desire for independence from both superpowers led him to seek out allies in Asia and Africa. Even before the Bandung Conference, Tito had begun "to establish good personal relations with Nehru, U Nu, Sukarno, and above all Nasser . . . by visits, by consistent Yugoslav support for the anti-colonial cause, and by offering such token amounts of economic and technical assistance as he could afford."[6] Tito's interest was to surround Yugoslavia with a diplomatic buffer of politically sympathetic states. Conversely, the Yugoslav system of socialism buttressed by U.S. economic aid was an attractive model for many in the developing world. By continuing to woo the developing countries, especially through regular contacts with Nehru and Nasser, the Yugoslav leader became one of the major actors in the next round of Third World organizing. His initial role was to call into question the geographic rationale of Bandung as a mobilization theme for Third World diplomacy.

None of these three was actually the first to pick up the ball after Bandung. That distinction fell ironically enough to the Asian Solidarity Committee, an organization founded principally by Asian communists in the spring of 1955 as a countermanifestation to the Bandung Conference. In December 1956, this committee reconstituted itself as Afro-Asian and proposed to Nasser (who had just emerged diplomatically victorious from the Suez crisis) that Egypt convene a Peoples' Solidarity Conference of anti-imperialist political parties. Nasser agreed, a decision that created a new form of Afro-Asian activity, much more militant in tone than its Bandung antecedent.

This activity was channeled through a new organization called the Afro-Asian Peoples' Solidarity Organization (AAPSO), which was created in Cairo in December 1957. The Cairo Conference and the AAPSO reflected a convergence of Nasserist anticolonialism and communist anti-imperialism, a "marriage of convenience" between these two political forces as one contemporary observer put it.[7] AAPSO was not officially an organization of states but rather a transnational association of political parties. The creation of AAPSO at the first Afro-Asian Peoples' Solidarity Conference served to keep the concept of Afro-Asianism alive, but gave it a different political coloration.

The significance of AAPSO was twofold. It organized a series of conferences from 1958 to 1965 that created a spate of activity around the concept of solidarity. And, although much of the stimulus behind the organization came from the Soviet Union and China, both eager to extend their ties and enhance their influence especially within Africa, it also involved Nasser much more deeply in Third World politics. Nasser was careful to keep the organizational controls in Egyptian hands. He entrusted the preparation of the Cairo Conference to his close associate, Anwar Sadat. He insisted that the secretariat of the new organization be based in Cairo, and saw to it that an Egyptian national, Yussuf Sibai, was selected as secretary-general.

The Cairo Conference thus became the second major manifestation of the Afro-Asian idea. It was much larger than Bandung, because it extended membership to colonial territories as well as to independent states. There were 44 delegations at Cairo, but many did not represent governments. Some were oppositional parties with little influence at home (for example, the Indian Communist party or the Jordanian Nasserists); others were nationalist movements, some of which would eventually be in power (the Algerian National Liberation Front) and others of which would not (the Cameroon People's Union). The most prominent newcomer, however, was the Soviet Union, represented by party delegates from its Asian regions. Similarly, Mongolia and North Korea were represented by their ruling parties.

These dual characteristics of major (communist) power involvement and nongovernmental status limited the potential of AAPSO as a vehicle for effective Third World coalition. The communist role in the organization alienated many Third World governments. Furthermore, as the Sino-Soviet split became intense in the 1960s, AAPSO meetings became dominated by polemical exchanges between these two powers. When the sessions increasingly degenerated into Soviet-Chinese diatribes, even the more radical Third World states lost interest in the organization. As AAPSO was more an instrument of ideological radicalization than of governmental decision making, it was not suitable for purposes of coalescing Third World governments.

During its heyday after the Cairo Conference, nonetheless, AAPSO did have some impact upon Third World politics. From 1956 to 1965 it organized a large number of conferences specialized according to profession (Afro-Asian doctors, journalists, lawyers, writers, and so on) or to subject matter (seminars on economics, housing, rural development, women, youth). The Executive Council of the organization met annually and there were three more plenary conferences after the Cairo meeting, held in Guinea in 1960, in Tanzania in 1963, and in Ghana in 1965. As these sites suggest, radical African states gave the greatest backing to AAPSO. It provided an additional framework for quite regular interaction and consultation for several years.

Although it proved to be largely a dead end in Third World organizing, its existence stimulated other initiatives of greater relevance.* The most important among these came from Tito, who advanced a counternotion to Afro-Asian solidarity in the concept of nonalignment. Solidarity, he contended, should be a function of political commitments, not of geographic location. Yugoslavia's

---

*AAPSO continued to function on a modest scale into the late 1970s. Indeed, Sibai remained secretary-general until 1978 when he was assassinated in Cyprus (by Palestinians hostile to Egypt's new policy toward Israel) while attending an AAPSO meeting.

policy of nonadherence to either superpower bloc meant that it shared many common concerns with other states pursuing neutralist policies. Having pursued a Third World oriented foreign policy bilaterally for several years, Tito in 1960 began to seek a regroupment. Just as the creation of AAPSO had been a maneuver to capture the energies released at Bandung, Tito's call for a conference of nonaligned states was a move to channel them in a slightly different direction.

The intensification of cold war hostilities in 1960–61 gave Tito the opportunity he was seeking. The collapse of the Soviet-U.S. summit talks over the U-2 incident, the growing tension surrounding Berlin, interventions in such states as Laos and the Congo, and U.S. pressure upon Cuba capped by the Bay of Pigs invasion—all contributed to create a sense of extreme polarization in the international system by the spring of 1961. Tito seized upon the sentiment of smouldering crisis to insist that the fundamental interest of the developing states was to act against the bloc system. The real need was to organize those countries resolutely opposed to the pressures of both camps. These states, Tito argued, were not neutral in their international commitments, but rather had a positive commitment to refuse incorporation into the dominant bipolar structure that confined expression of the interests of the developing states.

The operational criteria of nonalignment were less clear than the geographic rationale of Bandung or AAPSO. As will be seen, its working definition has evolved from conference to conference since 1962. The initial attractiveness of nonalignment lay in the possibility of regrouping a non-negligible number of states without reproducing the political divisions of the Bandung Conference or the Sino-Soviet dimension of AAPSO. As interpreted for the inaugural Belgrade Conference, nonalignment was a classic application of the organizational stratagem of reducing ranks in order to produce a more politically homogeneous grouping.

In launching the idea of a nonaligned conference, Tito's first task was to convince Nasser of its opportuneness. The Egyptian president then agreed to organize a preparatory meeting to set the agenda and in effect to determine which states met the political criterion of nonalignment. The working definition accepted at Cairo in June 1961 was that a nonaligned state pursued a foreign policy of national independence based on peaceful coexistence, supported national liberation movements, and eschewed the multilateral military alliances (North Atlantic Treaty Organization, Warsaw Pact, Central Treaty Organization, and Southeast Asia Treaty Organization) and bilateral alliances with the great powers. Only 16 of the 29 states at Bandung were deemed to meet these criteria.*

---

*Afghanistan, Burma, Cambodia, Ethiopia, Ghana, India, Indonesia, Iraq (which had withdrawn from the Central Treaty Organization after the 1958 coup), Lebanon, Nepal, Saudi Arabia, Sri Lanka, Sudan, Yemen, and the United Arab Republic (which in 1961 represented both Egypt and Syria).

Virtually half the Bandung group was left aside—on the one hand, the two Soviet allies, China and North Vietnam, and on the other, the members of the Western multilateral alliances plus South Vietnam, Laos, Jordan, Liberia, Libya, and Japan. Such an amputation was made plausible by the availability of ten new recruits. Six of these were African states that had become independent since 1955: Morocco, Tunisia, Guinea, Mali, Somalia, and Zaire (then known as Congo-Leopoldville). The seventh was Algeria, the only nonindependent state to be invited, which was represented by its provisional government-in-exile, the Provisional Government of the Algerian Republic (GPRA). The final three were Cyprus, Cuba, and of course Yugoslavia.

The composition of the Belgrade Conference of Nonaligned States in September 1961 thus was substantially different from that of Bandung. In simplest terms, it was a more radical coalition. Although far from politically monolithic, Belgrade assembled a group of governments generally more inclined to challenge the Western powers' role in the developing world. A few key issues had served to crystalize the composition of the first nonaligned conference.

One was the war in Algeria. The diplomatic ramifications of the Algerian war operated to exclude the bulk of the newly independent francophone states that had retained close cooperative ties with France. These states (including Senegal, Ivory Coast, Upper Volta, Dahomey, Niger, Gabon, Central African Republic, and Congo-Brazzaville, among others) were then loosely associated in what was called the Brazzaville Group. They had taken a conciliatory position on the Algerian war, which did not satisfy the Algerian provisional government. By contrast, Algeria's closest allies were Egypt, Morocco, Ghana, Guinea, Mali, and Tunisia, all of which except Tunisia were then associated in the rival Casablanca bloc. Both Yugoslavia and Egypt considered support of the Algerian nationalist movement a necessary condition of nonalignment, and this largely determined the African representation at Belgrade.

A similar division had emerged in Africa over the Congo crisis. Most of the Casablanca bloc states had backed the Congo's first premier, Patrice Lumumba, during the turbulent period that followed Congolese independence in the summer of 1960. The Brazzaville Group had supported Lumumba's rival, Joseph Kasavubu. The overthrow of Lumumba and his subsequent assassination had exacerbated the division of Africa into two camps. The preparatory meeting devoted considerable time to the question of whether to invite the Lumumbist faction (led by Antoine Gizenga), which was then claiming to be the legitimate government of the Congo, to the Belgrade Conference. This matter was not actually resolved at Cairo, because some states were unwilling to take a position on an issue in internal Congolese politics. This was but the first of many representational conflicts that the nonaligned movement would have to face in the future. (By the time of the Belgrade Conference, a shaky "national union" government with Cyril Adoula as premier and Gizenga as deputy premier had been formed in Leopoldville, and this government was invited to participate.)

A third key international issue centered on Cuba. The U.S. reaction against Castro's revolution had made Cuba something of a symbol of resistance to great-power intervention. Castro, like Tito, had sought Third World diplomatic support for his regime in its struggle with the United States. The decision to invite Cuba to the Belgrade Conference was the first step to include Latin America within the orbit of Third World politics. Cuban participation underlined the new conception of solidarity that was promoted at Belgrade: autonomy from the great powers in the international system.

In light of its political composition, the Belgrade Conference struck a more radical tone than Bandung. There were competing analyses as to where the developing countries should focus their efforts to change the existing system. One analysis centered on colonial issues, while the other focused upon the dangers of the cold war. The strongest advocates of the former position were Indonesia's Sukarno and Ghana's Kwame Nkrumah. They saw continuing great-power intervention or neocolonialism in Asia and Africa as the greatest obstacle to the full liberation of the new states. Nehru, on the contrary, believed that the menace of nuclear war between the superpowers was the overriding problem facing all states. The erection of the Berlin Wall in August 1961 and the Soviet announcement of its resumption of atmospheric nuclear testing on the eve of the conference convinced Nehru that cold war mediation should be the preeminent task of the nonaligned.

Tito and Nasser occupied a middle ground between these two arguments. Both were sufficiently involved in East-West politics to feel the weight of Nehru's concerns, but they also considered strong anticolonial action crucial to the growth of Third World power. They steered the conference toward a conclusion stressing the dual nature of the issues blocking Third World development. The final resolutions adopted at Belgrade pointed to both the arms race and colonialism as obstacles to peace.[8] All were able to agree upon a conception of the nonaligned states as a pressure group acting upon both blocs.

The relative importance of East-West issues in the debates at Belgrade was in one sense reminiscent of Bandung. The imprint of the cold war upon Third World deliberations was still strong, as it had been six years earlier, but it was not exactly the same imprint. At Belgrade there was a much stronger sentiment that the very structure of the bipolar system was hostile to the interests of the Third World. At Bandung each superpower had its allies, at Belgrade neither camp had committed followers. To be sure, some of the governments at Belgrade leaned toward Moscow (Cuba, Guinea) and others toward Washington (Ethiopia, Saudi Arabia), but the majority of the 25 were intent upon strengthening their collective potential and effecting some changes in the international status quo. The Belgrade Conference began to shift the conceptual center of gravity in Third World affairs toward a more autonomous conception of Third World interests.

The political regrouping effected at Belgrade in 1961 was the point of departure for a more sustained Third World organizational effort. In the economic realm, the Belgrade Conference set in motion a train of events that eventually produced the United Nations Conference on Trade and Development (UNCTAD). In the political realm, it laid the groundwork for a series of conferences that have been extremely important in the evolution of the contemporary Third World coalition. With the backing of such figures as Tito, Nehru, Nasser, Sukarno, Castro, Sihanouk, Nkrumah, Sekou Touré, Bourguiba, Haile Selassie, Bandaranaike, U Nu, Modibo Keita, King Hassan, and Archbishop Makarios,* the concept of nonalignment was securely established as a rallying point for Third World diplomacy.

GENEVA AND THE GROUP OF 77

The next few years were a period of intense but competitive organizational activity. Three lines of diplomatic action issued from Belgrade. One went toward the United Nations and led to the creation of UNCTAD in Geneva in 1964. The second followed a relatively direct path to a second nonaligned conference in 1964. The third veered toward a more radical formulation of Afro-Asianism, and reached an impasse in 1965. China was the essential force behind this third direction. For China, the Belgrade Conference represented its displacement in Third World affairs by Yugoslavia, and it sought to redress this situation by revitalizing the theme of Afro-Asian solidarity. The three paths produced a maze of diplomatic activity from 1962 to 1965.

The UN General Assembly had always been an important forum for the developing countries. Well prior to Bandung, an informal Afro-Asian caucus began to function there. After Bandung this caucus became a bit more structured, especially as its numbers grew with the entry of many new states. The arrival in 1960 of 16 more African states definitively shifted the weight in General Assembly voting to the developing world. The passage of a major statement on decolonization in December 1960, Resolution 1514 (XV), was the first widely noted manifestation of this new force within the UN system. During the General Assembly session immediately after the Belgrade Conference, the developing states followed up on an idea that Tito had advanced there: convocation of a world trade conference and establishment of a global economic organization devoted to development.[9] Although it required almost three years before UNCTAD was successfully established, the efforts toward this end were of enormous significance for the Third World coalition.

---

*All of these attended the conference with the exception of Castro, who was represented by Cuba's head of state, Osvaldo Dorticos, and Sekou Touré, who sent his foreign minister.

The crucial new variable was the introduction of Latin American states (beyond Cuba) into the Third World organizational framework. This began in July 1962 at the Cairo Economic Conference, a follow-up to the first non-aligned meeting. Convened mainly at Tito's urging to discuss issues of economic development—and thereby to mobilize political support behind the development organization proposal—the Cairo meeting reassembled the bulk of the states that had been at Belgrade plus Bolivia, Brazil, Mexico, Chile, Ecuador, Uruguay, and Venezuela.* Even more important for the future was the fact that Raul Prebisch, the Argentinian economist who was then executive secretary of the United Nations Economic Commission for Latin America (ECLA), took an active part in the Cairo deliberations. He was to become the first secretary-general of UNCTAD. Prebisch's participation was integral to the establishment of ties that would produce the Group of 77, and strengthened the interest of the Latin Americans in the development conference project.

As the proposal wended its way through UN institutional processes, other developments contributed to the expansion of the coalition. Primary among these was the May 1963 Addis-Ababa Conference at which the Organization of African Unity (OAU) was founded. The formation of the OAU at least temporarily closed the split of Africa into competing blocs. Although the OAU has never been able fully to transcend Africa's political divisions, the formation of a single continental organization did improve Africa's capacity to present a common front on such broad issues as economic development. The OAU brought into being a working group of 32 independent African states (in contrast to the 6 from Africa at Bandung or the 11 at Belgrade). By the end of 1963, the OAU and the ECLA states joined the original Asian core of Bandung to issue a Joint Declaration on their conception of the purpose of the forthcoming Geneva Conference on Trade and Development.[10] Seventy-five states supported this declaration, clearly presaging the coalescence of the South in its Group of 77.

The Geneva Conference, or UNCTAD I, which met from March through June 1964, was thus the first major forum of North-South politics. The developing countries' Joint Declaration pointed to a host of economic objectives that they hoped to achieve through the discussions in Geneva: tariff reductions, expansion of their market opportunities, stabilization of raw materials prices, provision of greater financial resources for development, and improvement of their share in the "invisibles" of trade such as shipping and insurance. All these issues were raised during the conference, but the largest question overhanging the

---

*The last four were officially observers rather than full participants, indicating that they were interested in, but not formally bound by or responsible for, the proceedings and resolutions. In all, 36 states attended the Cairo Economic Conference, the other newcomers being Kuwait, Libya, Malaya, Pakistan, Singapore, and Tanzania (Iraq and Nepal, present at Belgrade, did not attend).

three-month proceedings was entirely political, namely, the institutionalization of some kind of permanent organization devoted to the broad goal of economic development.

The Western industrial powers had agreed to the UNCTAD conference with great reluctance, and they did not wish to establish a distinct new organization of trade and development. They preferred to rely upon an instrument like the General Agreement on Tariffs and Trade (GATT, technically a multilateral treaty designed to regulate and harmonize trading relations), which had given little explicit attention to developmental issues up to then. The developing states on the contrary wanted a new agency, although they held different views as to the precise form that it should take. At Geneva they established a caucus largely to hammer out a common position on the question of institutionalization. The caucus was an organizational extension of the Joint Declaration. The group identity of the 75 was consolidated by the effort of working together to create a permanent agency.

The Western governments' bargaining position was that any new institutional machinery should be subordinate to the United Nations Economic and Social Council (ECOSOC). They further proposed equal representation of developing and developed countries on the standing committee, or, as later revised, a voting procedure by which a majority vote of the 12 major trading nations would be required on substantive decisions. In other words they sought to limit the autonomy of the proposed agency and to retain a veto by any combination of six of the industrial powers. The developing states on the contrary wanted an independent agency in which their numerical majority could be exercised. The practical question within the developing country caucus was just how much compromise was permissible in order to reach agreement with the developed countries. There were heated debates over tactics—"many feared that the nascent Group of 75 was splitting up under the strain" of achieving a common bargaining position—but the process ultimately strengthened the emerging developmental coalition.[11]

The bargain that was finally struck at Geneva reflected the economic power of the North and the numerical weight of the new Group of 77. (The 75 of the Joint Declaration lost New Zealand, but added Kenya, South Korea, and South Vietnam during the conference; since then almost 50 more states have joined the group, but the name has stuck.) The compromise produced a more elaborate agency than the West desired but less than what the militants among the developing states had aimed for. UNCTAD was institutionalized as a subsidiary organ of the General Assembly—neither an autonomous specialized agency nor an organ subordinate to ECOSOC. The voting arrangements did not include a veto, but they did involve an elaborate procedure of conciliation designed to allow decisions by consensus. The North protected its bargaining power (through the obligation to reach consensus), while the South gained a new bargaining forum.

At the conclusion of the conference, the Group of 77 released its first official statement. The gist of the declaration was that UNCTAD I had fallen short of the Group's hopes substantively as well as institutionally, but that members had achieved a new determination to work together. The Group pledged to maintain its unity as an "indispensable instrument for securing the adoption of new attitudes and new approaches in the international economic field."[12] The developing states were still far from genuine operational unity, but the establishment of UNCTAD and the Group of 77 gave the developing world new institutional and political instruments that they would put to increasing use. The emergence of the Group of 77, like the founding of the nonaligned movement three years earlier, implied a new framework for collective action. The relationship between the two groups remained to be clarified.

THE DEMISE OF AFRO-ASIANISM

At the same time that UNCTAD I was unfolding in Geneva, two meetings were held in Asia that ushered in the final phase of organizational rivalry between nonalignment and Afro-Asianism. The major partisans of nonalignment remained Yugoslavia, Egypt, and India, while the main proponents of a second Afro-Asian conference were China, Indonesia, and Pakistan. These states waged a fierce struggle to influence the future direction of the Third World movement.

For his part, Tito began to push for a second conference of nonaligned states in 1963, urging Nasser to organize such a meeting. Nasser in turn enlisted Ceylon's Prime Minister Sirimavo Bandaranaike in the project. She agreed to organize a preparatory meeting in Colombo in March 1964 at which it was agreed that the second nonaligned conference should be held in Cairo that October.[13] This series of ad hoc contacts was a way of building diplomatic support behind the project, but also reflected the absence of a permanent organizational framework. The necessity to create a special diplomatic framework for each proposed conference was one of the great weaknesses of the Third World through 1970.

Undaunted by the Colombo decision or the need to create another organizational framework, Indonesia promptly invited the major African and Asian governments to a similar preparatory conference in Jakarta in April. Sukarno was able to win approval in principle of an Afro-Asian conference tentatively scheduled for spring 1965. Several states participated in both preparatory meetings. Why were they unable to make a decisive choice between the two organizational formulas?

The competition placed a number of governments, especially African ones, in a crossfire. To several of them the optimal choice in the spring of 1964 was to keep all options open. They saw no reason totally to exclude China from a movement against imperialism and underdevelopment. While India was opposed and Egypt was cool to the idea, they did not have the means to block it. The mood of several of the other states at Jakarta was optimistic: move ahead on as many fronts as possible. The steering committee formed at Jakarta included such states as Algeria, Cambodia, Ghana, Guinea, and Tanzania that were representative of the militant wing of the Third World. They perceived Bandung II as a way of maintaining momentum—erroneously as matters turned out.

The second nonaligned conference was held as scheduled in October 1964, attended by almost twice as many states as three years earlier. From 25 at Belgrade, the number now swelled to 47 governments. Most of the new participants were black African states, many of which were in fact already independent in 1961.* The increase in participation was attributable, therefore, less to decolonization than to the diplomatic reconciliation effected by the creation of the OAU. Tito in particular was eager to see the movement grow in numbers, prevailing upon some of the more radical African states, notably Egypt, that would have still preferred to keep the nonaligned framework more selective. In practice nonalignment was redefined in 1964 to mean nonadhesion to an alliance with the United States or the Soviet Union; a defense agreement with France for example became permissible now that the Algerian war was over and Gaullist France was itself adopting an antibloc foreign policy.

This expansion diluted the ideological affinity of those present. The issue, however, had also changed over three years in such a way as to allow greater cohesion among the more diverse participants. Two major trends had marked the international system since 1961. Following the Cuban missile crisis, Soviet-U.S. hostility had begun to decline; the Nuclear Test Ban Treaty of 1963 was one of the early signs of the cold war thaw that would lead to détente. By contrast, the sharpest tensions in international politics were increasingly concentrated in the developing world: Vietnam, the Middle East, the Congo and southern Africa, Malaysia, and Cyprus. The focus of debate was shifting from the East-West conflict to the issue of intervention. Within such a context, there was some common ground for agreement: everyone was against intervention.

Intervention to be sure did not mean exactly the same thing to everyone at the Cairo Nonaligned Conference. For some it meant essentially colonialism. The presence of ten liberation movements as participants demonstrated the con-

---

*The new participants from sub-Saharan Africa were Cameroon, Central African Republic, Chad, Congo-Brazzaville, Dahomey, Liberia, Mauritania, Senegal, Togo (all independent in September 1961), Burundi, Kenya, Malawi, Nigeria, Sierra Leone, Uganda, Tanzania, Zambia, and Angola, whose provisional government the Angolan Revolutionary Government in Exile (GRAE) was admitted with full status. The other new participants were Libya (another OAU member), Jordan, Kuwait, Laos, and Syria (once again diplomatically independent). The Congo-Leopoldville was excluded, because the new premier, Moise Tshombe, was considered overly dependent upon the West by several of the other participants.

tinuing importance of decolonization as an issue. For others it included residual Western economic influence in the developing world. For some it was synonymous with Western political influence, while others feared communist subversion. In other words, the real common ground still remained quite limited, but the enlarged participation served to accredit the general concept of nonalignment as the foreign policy norm for a developing state.

To this extent, then, there was a modest drift toward the left in Third World politics. The moderates at the Cairo Conference joined the radicals in a set of resolutions that were more militant in tone than those of Belgrade—stronger insistence upon decolonization and specific condemnation of intervention by the great powers in Asia, Africa, and Latin America. The degree of emphasis upon the idea of Third World mediation between the superpowers was less. Cairo focused upon the interventionary character of the great powers, especially the Western powers whose historic and economic role in the developing world was the greater. As the Algerian leader Ahmed Ben Bella now put it, nonalignment "must take the form of an unceasing struggle . . . against every attempt to subordinate us."[14] The internal diversity of the nonaligned group became greater at Cairo, but the protest against the subordinate status of the Third World in the international system was more forcefully articulated.

The Cairo Conference represented the high point of President Nasser's influence in Third World politics. Although India had played an extremely important role in defining the 77 in the politicoeconomic context of Geneva, Indian influence was declining on other questions. Even before Nehru's death in May 1964, India's national conflicts with China and Pakistan were turning Indian diplomacy away from Third World leadership. Tito retained great influence, but his orientation remained closer to the concept of Third World mediation that the Cairo Conference began to leave behind. Nasser, on the other hand, was perfectly comfortable with the strong anti-imperialist emphasis of the second conference. In 1964 alone, furthermore, Egypt was the host country for two Arab summit conferences and the annual OAU summit in addition to the nonaligned conference. Nasser had quite successfully placed Egypt at the center of a nonaligned circle by 1964, and nonalignment had been established as the organizational focal point of Third World politics. Its organizational supremacy was not yet unchallenged, however, for Bandung II remained on the diplomatic agenda.

The projected Afro-Asian conference was China's final bid to reenter Third World politics after its effective displacement by Yugoslavia. As such, the idea was extremely controversial from the beginning. Algeria's Ben Bella took this controversy upon his shoulders in offering Algiers as the site, and the weight proved too much for him. The problem, which ultimately contributed to the overthrow of Ben Bella, was to resolve a number of extremely divisive invitational disputes.

One involved the Soviet Union, which was loathe to allow China to dominate such a conference. Insisting upon its Asian status (as within AAPSO), the Soviet government mobilized such friends as Egypt and India to exert pressure within the preparatory committee for Soviet participation. China resolutely blocked the proposed invitation. A second question involved Malaysia against whose participation Indonesia was adamant. A third involved the Congo-Leopold-ville where Moise Tshombe had become premier to the dismay of the African radicals. Algeria itself desired to exclude Tshombe, but this alienated numerous other African governments whose participation was desired. In each instance a decision one way or the other would have a boomerang effect: If a given state were admitted, others would defect; if it were excluded, others would abstain. Behind each dispute lay issues regarding the likely political tenor of the conference. As the preparatory committee labored through seven sessions without settling these disputes, the pressure became concentrated upon the host country in June 1965, when Ben Bella was toppled by Colonel Houari Boumediene.

The fall of Ben Bella affected the fate of the Afro-Asian conference just as the advent of the conference contributed to the coup d'etat. In both cases, however, there were numerous variables at play; the coup was not solely a consequence of the conference nor was it the sole cause of the failure to hold the conference. The conference exacerbated preexisting internal divisions in Algerian politics to trigger the coup. In turn the coup became a pretext to scuttle a project that had aroused widespread misgivings among many African and Asian states.

The real question posed by Bandung II was China's place in Third World politics. China represented a radical force that could not be ignored but that could not be readily assimilated either. The distinctive ideological posture that China would bring to an Afro-Asian meeting was a polarizing rather than a unifying factor. An Afro-Asian conference was therefore at once impossible without China but implausible with China. Numerous states seized upon the coup as an excuse not to send a delegation to Algiers. Some cited the mild disorder that followed the coup, others a desire not to legitimize the new regime. Behind these excuses lay the growing sense of the implausibility of such a conference.

Formally the conference was merely postponed to November, but the events of the next few months confirmed the demise of Afro-Asianism as a Third World organizing principle. Whereas the conference was implausible in June with China, it proved impossible in November without China. During the autumn of 1965, the Soviet government maintained its pressure for admission and appeared to be gaining ground; then, in October, Sukarno was overthrown in Indonesia, depriving China of its most fervent ally. China now lost its own appetite for the project. Algeria labored to save the conference, but once China reversed its own policy and requested cancellation, it was irretrievable.

The circumstantial factors provoked by the Algerian coup provided the straw that broke the back of Afro-Asianism. The underlying problem was the extreme ambivalence aroused by China. Algeria's Foreign Minister Abdelaziz

Bouteflika, who had led the campaign to salvage the conference, posed a question that pointed to the contradiction embedded in the idea of Afro-Asianism: "Can a great power, even if it represents forty-five percent of the population of Asia, impose its will upon fifty smaller countries?"[15] In calling for cancellation, China certainly imposed its will upon Algeria; the essential insight was of course that China was a great power in the geographic company of small states characterized by their vulnerability to external power. However sympathetic Peking might be to such Third World goals as decolonization and economic development, China could not be other than an imposing presence in their midst.

The collapse of the Afro-Asian conference in November 1965 marked the end of the first phase in Third World organizing. Instead of increasing momentum as the radicals had hoped, Bandung II finally had a braking effect. After several years of frequent conferences and almost uninterrupted diplomatic activity, the organizational push that began at Bandung momentarily tapered off. A period of reassessment was necessary.

The decade from Bandung to the ill-fated Bandung II was one of groping for an appropriate organizational concept for the developing states. The ideal of Afro-Asian solidarity served to launch this quest. China's desire to exert influence over the developing states and the Soviet reaction to Chinese policy ultimately destroyed Afro-Asianism. All the membership debates that plagued the preparation of the Algiers Conference reflected one or another intrusion of great-power influence into the developing world. As an organizational principle, Afro-Asianism did not address the Third World's need to act independently of great-power intervention. The alternative concept of nonalignment came closer to serving this need. At least there was no question of Chinese or Soviet participation in a nonaligned framework. Yet the nonaligned states, such as they were composed at the 1964 conference, were quite split among themselves over the issues raised by the Algiers Conference. The tensions raised by this second Afro-Asian initiative spilled over into the nonaligned group, stymieing further organizational efforts under these auspices for several years. Still the experience of 1955-65 embedded the idea of collective power in Third World consciousness. The spirit of Bandung survived the debacle of Bandung II.

NOTES

1. George McTurnan Kahin, *The Asian-African Conference* (Ithaca, N.Y.: Cornell University Press, 1956), p. 3.

2. Ibid., p. 85.

3. David Kimche, *The Afro-Asian Movement* (New York: Halsted Press, 1973), p. 82.

4. See Gamal Abdul Nasser, *The Philosophy of the Revolution* (Buffalo, N.Y.: Smith, Keynes, and Marshall, 1959).

5. Michael Brecher, *The New States of Asia* (New York: Oxford University Press, 1966), p. 210.

6. William Griffith, "Yugoslavia," in *Africa and the Communist World*, ed. Zbigniew Brzezinski (Stanford, Calif.: Stanford University Press, 1963), p. 117. A thorough study of Yugoslavia's important role is Alvin Z. Rubinstein, *Yugoslavia and the Nonaligned World* (Princeton, N.J.: Princeton University Press, 1970).

7. The expression comes from Homer Jack, *Cairo: The Afro-Asian Peoples' Solidarity Conference* (Chicago: Toward Freedom, 1958) cited in Kimche, *Afro-Asian Movement*, p. 143.

8. The text of the resolutions appears in Odette Jankowitsch and Karl P. Sauvant, eds., *The Third World Without Superpowers: The Collected Documents of the Non-Aligned Countries* (Dobbs Ferry, N.Y.: Oceana, 1978), pp. 3–8.

9. For a detailed account of the UN institutional process leading to the first UNCTAD conference, see David A. Kay, *The New Nations in the United Nations, 1960-1967* (New York: Columbia University Press, 1970), pp. 95–100.

10. The text of the Joint Declaration appears in Alfred George Moss and Harry N. M. Winton, eds., *A New International Economic Order, Selected Documents 1945-1975* (New York: UNITAR, 1978), pp. 18–19.

11. Branislav Gosovic, *UNCTAD: Conflict and Compromise* (Leiden: A. W. Sijthoff, 1972), p. 51.

12. Ibid., p. 271. The full text of this statement appears in Moss and Winton, *Documents*, pp. 32–34.

13. The official record of this meeting appears in Jankowitsch and Sauvant, *Collected Documents*, pp. 65–71.

14. *Le Peuple* (Algiers), October 8, 1964. The resolutions adopted at Cairo appear in Jankowitsch and Sauvant, *Collected Documents*, pp. 44–61.

15. *Le Monde Hebdomadaire* (Paris), October 21-27, 1965.

3. Constructing the Coalition, 1966–73

The disputes surrounding the ill-starred second Afro-Asian conference left the Third World in political disarray. Furthermore, the fall of Algeria's Ben Bella and Indonesia's Sukarno in 1965 and of Ghana's Nkrumah early in 1966 eliminated three leaders who had stimulated the organizational process in the first half of the 1960s. A period of political drift ensued. The economic imperative to organize remained no less compelling, however. In these circumstances the most likely direction in which to turn was toward the UNCTAD/Group of 77 organizational framework, and this was what happened in 1967. The Group of 77 was able to serve a specific functional purpose related to the periodic UNCTAD meetings, but this was not fully adequate to the goal of exercising autonomous Third World power in international politics. President Tito remained convinced that the instrument best suited to the larger goal was the nonaligned movement, and he renewed his efforts in this direction in 1968. For a time the two groupings operated along parallel tracks. Then they began to converge toward the landmark Sixth Special Session of the United Nations General Assembly.

THE FIRST MINISTERIAL CONFERENCE OF THE GROUP OF 77

In the period right after the Geneva Conference, the Group of 77 functioned with a bare minimum of institutional identity. As Branislav Gosovic has written, "no one was quite certain where the authoritative voice of the 77 was located."[1] In practice, the developing countries' representatives in Geneva consulted together in three regional groups—Latin America, Asia, and Africa—each of which sought a regional consensus before attempting to adopt a groupwide position. The chairman of the Latin American group initially acted as chairman of the Group of 77, while the 31 developing countries on the Trade and Development Board, which was UNCTAD's decision-making organ between plenary conferences, functioned unofficially as an executive committee of the 77.

These working procedures remained quite informal. The extreme diversity of the 77 inhibited the developing countries from creating any more elaborate institutional framework. Inasmuch as the UNCTAD secretariat itself under Raul Prebisch's direction had a strong pro-development orientation, the immediate need for more formalized Group of 77 institutions was minimal. As the time for a second plenary conference approached, however, the utility of reinforcing the identity and the authority of the Group of 77 became greater. The next stage of Third World organizing began with the decision to schedule a ministerial conference of the Group of 77, which was held in Algiers in October 1967.

The evolution from caucus to international conference was itself a rather modest step in the growth of the corporate identity of the Group of 77. Yet the importance of the politicoeconomic stakes added weight to the decision to convene such a conference. The conference would demonstrate to what extent the developing countries could coordinate their diverse economic interests into a single platform for international economic reform. At Geneva, the Group of 77 had taken form as a bargaining agent. The kind of bargain that it could hope to drive in the second round of UNCTAD negotiations, scheduled for India in February-March 1968, depended upon the degree of unified purpose it could now muster. Algeria was particularly convinced that the conference of the 77 was a critical opportunity for the developing countries to get themselves moving again as a collective force in international politics.

For Algeria the conference was a phoenix rising from the ashes of Bandung II. More than many other countries, Algeria has perceived its national development as integrally linked to international politics. During its prolonged struggle for national independence (1954-62), Algeria developed a radical outlook in which Third World solidarity and militant anti-imperialism were closely allied. For the Algerians, political independence was but a first victory in a longer term struggle against the prevailing international economic structures that reproduced much the same dependence that the Third World had known under colonial rule. Algeria had needed the diplomatic solidarity of others to achieve independence, and saw Third World political solidarity as equally necessary to break the postcolonial system of structural dependence.

Under Ben Bella, Algeria plunged deeply into the politics of Third World organizing. The Boumediene government, which came to power in 1965, did not significantly alter the general orientation of Algerian foreign policy, but it devoted attention first to domestic affairs and a national program of economic development. During the first two years of the Boumediene regime, Algeria increasingly assumed control of its oil and natural gas resources and created state enterprises in most sectors of the economy. The process confirmed Algeria's conviction that all developing countries had to achieve genuine national control over their economies. Algeria sought to inject a strong dose of its own development strategy into the first conference of the Group of 77.

This "Estates-General of the Third World," as *Le Monde* put it, was the largest Third World gathering up to that time, over 70 states sending delegations to Algiers[2] Their practical task was to synthesize three documents that had been drafted in each of three continentwide meetings, a task that reflected perfectly the regional nature of the Group of 77 at the operational level. Algeria set a tone of political militancy as a first step toward a new synthesis of Third World developmental demands.

Boumediene opened the conference with a vehement condemnation of the existing political and economic order, which he characterized as a system of vast economic disparities bequeathed by the colonial era and defended essentially by U.S. economic and military power. The developed countries, Boumediene asserted, owed their wealth to their "odious exploitation" and "pillage" of Third World resources. The war in Vietnam, he went on, was the prime evidence among other cases that the United States was determined to suppress the movement for Third World liberation. Furthermore, the evolution toward détente in superpower relations had been of no benefit to the developing countries, "imperialism having exploited the new conditions . . . to concentrate its strongest efforts against the Third World." Boumediene summed up the Algerian analysis by concluding that "the principal confrontation in today's world is between imperialism and the Third World."[3]

The economic implications of this political analysis were straightforward. Each Third World country must acquire effective control over its resources. This meant nationalization of any key sectors of the economy under foreign control; it meant the rapid formation of national personnel to take over foreign managerial responsibilities; it meant the creation of new international financial resources to replace the need for foreign private capital. Algeria was particularly interested in forcing a change in the World Bank's loaning policies that discriminated against countries emphasizing public investment. Only when the developing countries had taken the management of their own resources into their own hands, Algeria argued, would they have the power to bargain effectively over other aspects of the international economic structure.

The tone of Boumediene's speech was typical of an approach that Algeria would pursue with great energy and growing impact over the following several years. The Algerian strategy was to call into question the entire structure of North-South relations before proceeding to any specific negotiation, and to insist first upon measures that the Third World could initiate unilaterally. Fundamentally, Boumediene was saying, the problem of underdevelopment was political. On the one hand, the Third World had to acquire a clear political consciousness of the structures of dependence. On the other hand, the industrialized countries would have to show a political will to aid the Third World to change these structures. The political will of the North would turn upon its perception of the determination of the South to challenge the existing structures.

The mood of political confrontation in Boumediene's keynote address startled a number of delegations, especially among the Latin Americans. Algeria further politicized the early proceedings by discriminatory treatment of delegations from South Vietnam and South Korea, raising once again in a new guise the old question of who would participate.* Algeria was hereby treading a fine line between its own political convictions and its official responsibilities as the host government for an international conference. Although Boumediene's speech and the cavalier treatment of the Saigon and Seoul representatives caused some political tension during the first few days of the conference, the Algerians managed to set the tone of Third World protest that they desired.

The conference then settled into two weeks of deliberations in committees on specific issue areas. The three regional groups did not all have the same ideas on how to use trade policy to spur economic development. By far the most difficult problem existed between Latin Americans and Africans over the issue of preferential tariffs. The former generally opposed the special trading arrangements that existed between numerous African states and the European Economic Community (EEC), but the Africans were reluctant to sacrifice the protection that this accorded their exports. Agreement was eventually struck upon the principle of a "generalized system of preferences" applicable to all developing countries coupled with "equivalent advantages" to be extended to those giving up specialized preferences. This was understood to mean that the African associates of the EEC would be compensated in other ways for any losses suffered by surrendering their privileged access to that market.

This issue illustrated the competitive nature of the economies of many of the developing states. The same question had arisen already at the Geneva Conference where it had been the object of an ambiguous compromise. The further discussions in Algiers allowed the Africans and the Latin Americans to move closer to an understanding of each other's particular interests while working toward a common position for UNCTAD II. There were similar debates in committee to establish a list of basic commodities on which to seek general trade agreements during the New Delhi session. Those that were too controversial were eliminated at Algiers. The conference thus permitted the 77 to identify their internal differences while exploring the outer limits of what they were agreed upon.

---

*As participants in UNCTAD, South Vietnam and South Korea were automatically members of the Group of 77, but Algeria recognized neither. The Algerian authorities admitted their representatives, but "quarantined" them at the actual conference site on the outskirts of Algeirs. After token participation in the opening formalities, the two delegations withdrew from the conference.

The result of this exploration was a text called the Algiers Charter (UN Document TD/38), the Third World's first comprehensive platform on development. This document set forth an ensemble of proposals for international action in a number of sectors critical to the developing countries. The first sector had to do with trade in raw materials. Among other measures, it called for the creation of regulatory stocks of key commodities in order to avoid the extreme price fluctuations that wrought havoc in Third World export revenues. The second major sector dealt with trade in manufactured and semifinished products. Here the major demands were for the generalized system of preferences and for a more rapid transfer of technology to the developing countries. The third major issue area was development finance, essentially an appeal for a genuine commitment to multilateral cooperation in the funding of development projects. Here the Third World called for the developed countries to pledge a fixed level of development funding (1 percent of gross national product) and international action to ease the burden of Third World indebtedness (which was then approaching some $40 billion). The remainder of the document treated maritime transport and other trade "invisibles," such as insurance and freight rates, proposals to improve intra-Third World trade, and a series of special measures for the least developed countries.

The Algiers Charter was a major achievement in Third World organizing. It gave coherence to the Group of 77 by establishing an authoritative groupwide plan of action to submit to UNCTAD II. By drafting the charter, the developing countries demonstrated a unity of purpose regarding international economic reform that had not previously been seen. It allowed them to enter the second round of UNCTAD with a well-articulated position on what needed to be done to advance their economic development. The North was obliged to recognize that it faced a cohesive bargaining partner in the Group of 77. Yet the immediate impact was small; indeed, the Algiers Charter stands as a dubious monument to the resistance of the North to the South's desire for change, for, as will be seen, several of the charter's policy proposals still appear on the agenda of North-South negotiations.

In retrospect one can see that the Algiers Charter was an early formulation of the demands that would be reiterated with greater force in the mid-1970s. The document represented, as Algeria's Foreign Minister Abdelaziz Bouteflika put it at the end of the conference, "an invitation to the rich countries to join us in the battle against underdevelopment." He further expressed the hope that the New Delhi session of UNCTAD would constitute a "decisive stage in the transformation of international economic relations."[4] But the developed states did not accept the invitation and the New Delhi Conference was a decisive disappointment to the developing countries. Their preparatory efforts, both through the UNCTAD secretariat and through the ministerial conference in Algiers, had little impact upon the willingness of the industrial world to join the battle.

The Third World may well have approached UNCTAD II with undue optimism. There was little to indicate that the developed countries were pre-pared to reorganize international commodity markets or to commit large sums to developmental finance. The Western economies themselves were caught up in a serious international monetary crisis in early 1968. The fact remains that after nearly two months of negotiations in New Delhi the results were sparse and the sentiment of disillusionment strong. One accord of some import was reached—an agreement in principle on the gradual application of a generalized system of pre-ferences for Third World manufactures.* Beyond this, very little was achieved. Speaking for the 77, the head of the Ivory Coast's delegation summed up the prevailing Third World reaction: "The extent of agreement is insignificant next to the immense hope which inspired us when we came to New Delhi."[5] Algiers had pumped up hopes that New Delhi punctured. The net result was to increase the sense of cleavage between North and South.

The outcome of UNCTAD II was perceived as a major setback within the Third World. The paucity of concrete results confirmed the lack of power of the Group of 77. At best, the UNCTAD strategy was revealed as a painfully slow process. The disillusionment over UNCTAD II's results, however, spurred a new round of organizational efforts.

LUSAKA: NONALIGNMENT RECONSIDERED

There remained much internal disagreement over the best strategy by which to affirm a forceful Third World presence in international politics. Yugo-slavia and Algeria emerged as the primary contestants in a tactical debate. Tito remained fully committed to the idea of nonalignment. From the spring of 1968 on, he undertook a campaign of bilateral contacts to drum up support for another nonaligned conference.

Algeria was convinced that it was now desirable to reestablish a revolu-tionary core of the most radical Third World states. Nonalignment should stand for a militant approach to the crucial issues facing the developing states. For Algeria the U.S. intervention in Vietnam remained the burning example of im-perialistic opposition to progressive forces in the Third World. The proper gauge of nonalignment thus became a policy of uncompromising support for the Vietnamese National Liberation Front; more precisely, Algeria was moving to-ward militant anti-imperialism as a substitute for nonalignment as an organiza-tional principle. Yugoslavia, on the contrary, maintained that noninvolvement in superpower alliances and support of peaceful coexistence remained a sufficient

---

*Over the next several years, various European states enacted legislation granting such tariff advantages. The United States put such a system into application only in 1976.

measure of nonalignment and argued that the Third World's interest lay in assembling a broader rather than narrower coalition. Yugoslavia nonetheless recognized that Algerian support was critical to further nonaligned activity.

Throughout 1969 Tito worked to lay the groundwork for a third non-aligned conference, while Algeria advanced reservations as to its opportuneness. He organized a consultative meeting in Belgrade in July; a second such meeting followed in September in New York at the opening of the General Assembly session. Then, in November, Tito made a state visit to Algeria for direct talks with Boumediene, and won an Algerian commitment to participate in a further preparatory meeting, which was scheduled for April 1970 in Tanzania. The gap between the two states' approaches remained visible nonetheless during Tito's visit. The Yugoslav spoke of the proven success of the nonaligned movement as a "moral and political force" in the international system, while Boumediene declared that Algeria wanted "to reestablish its original meaning and force, and give it back its positive content."[6]

The distance between Algeria and Yugoslavia was significant but not unbridgeable. Algeria granted that the Third World needed a political vehicle alongside the economically oriented Group of 77. The difference was tactical—should they refurbish an old vehicle or design a new, more compact model? Tito's conviction that the Third World progressives ought not be retrench into a smaller more radical grouping prevailed. In acquiescing to the renovation of nonalignment, Algeria decided that the best tactic was to try to steer the available vehicle in the direction that it wanted the Third World to go.

Algeria brought its conception of "positive content" for nonalignment to the preparatory meeting in Dar es Salaam the following April. Once again underlying disagreements took the form of a membership dispute. Algeria championed the admission of the Vietnamese Provisional Revolutionary Government (GRP) to the forthcoming conference. Insisting that the nonaligned countries must take an unambiguous stand on the war in Vietnam, Algeria called for the GRP to participate with full membership rights (as the Algerian GPRA had in 1961). Yet Algeria was one of only a handful of states that had actually recognized the GRP as the legitimate government of South Vietnam. Although Yugoslavia itself was favorable to GRP participation, it was reluctant to force the issue when several other governments—notably Indonesia, Malaysia, and Laos—were opposed. The debate was complicated by the presence in the Tanzanian capital of two competing Cambodian delegations, one representing Prince Sihanouk and the other representing Lon Nol, the pro-U.S. military leader who had just overthrown Sihanouk. The preparatory conference was unable to resolve either of these membership disputes, deciding finally to refer both questions to the eventual summit conference itself. Algeria declared that the failure to admit the GRP and Sihanouk's GRUNK (Royal Government of the Khmer National Union) revealed major internal contradictions and political shortcomings within the Third World.

The Third Nonaligned Conference thus opened in the shadow of this dispute. The conference was held in September 1970 in Lusaka, Zambia, attended by 53 states, about half of which were represented by the head of state or the head of government. The membership questions dominated the final preparatory discussions on the eve of the actual summit conference. It was agreed to admit the GRP as an observer but not as a fully participating government. This compromise admitted the Vietnamese with the same status as nine other observer states (all from South America); none of the other observers, however, had desired full participation. An informal sounding was taken on the question of Cambodian representation. Twenty-one states supported the Sihanouk Delegation, seven favored admission of the Lon Nol delegation, twelve others preferred that the seat remain vacant on the gounds that the conferees could not settle an internal Cambodian matter, and the rest abstained.[7] In these circumstances, the seat was finally left vacant.

These two decisions were of course unsatisfactory to the radical wing, but at the same time it was apparent that the largest single group within the conference did favor the admission of the GRUNK delegation. Furthermore, the exclusion of the delegation representing the de facto government in Phnom Penh was a diplomatic defeat for the new Cambodian regime. The radicals could realistically anticipate a potential swing of the movement toward admission of GRUNK (and therefore presumably of the GRP as well) from the balance of forces at Lusaka. This perception encouraged the radicals to continue to use the nonaligned framework.

The final resolutions of the Lusaka Conference particularly reflected its southern African setting.[8] President Kenneth Kaunda of Zambia was strongly concerned to focus international attention upon the situations in Angola, Mozambique, Rhodesia, Namibia, and South Africa. The conference endorsed strong and detailed resolutions on these questions, calling for trade embargoes and the severance of diplomatic relations with Portugal and South Africa so long as they ignored the United Nations' resolutions on self-determination and apartheid. The resolution on South Africa explicitly condemned the United States, France, Great Britain, West Germany, Italy, and Japan for their political, economic, and military collaboration with the South African government. These resolutions attracted the greatest attention at the time, but others were more significant for the evolution of the nonaligned group.

A long Declaration on Nonalignment and Economic Progress was approved, bringing international economic issues to the forefront of the concerns of the nonaligned group. Although the Cairo Conference had also issued a statement on Economic Development and Cooperation, the Lusaka Declaration was the first to insist that "the poverty of the developing nations and their economic dependence . . . constitute a structural weakness in the present world economic order" and that "the persistence of an inequitable world economic system inherited from the colonial past . . . poses insurmountable difficulties in breaking the bondage of poverty."[9] Not only was the rhetoric regarding the international economic system becoming more militant but a strategy of implementing economic change was more fully spelled out. The declaration specified various forms of mutual planning, trade, and technical cooperation among the developing countries themselves, and set a number of systemwide goals to be met through action in the United Nations. Toward this end, it called for convocation of a second ministerial meeting of the Group of 77 in order to prepare a common Third World position for UNCTAD III, which was scheduled for 1972. The nonaligned states thus began to fix a working relationship between the two Third World frameworks. In skeletal form, the Declaration on Nonalignment and Economic Progress outlined the shape of the coming decade of North-South relations.

A further resolution was specifically devoted to the United Nations, designating it as "the most suitable forum for cooperative action by the nonaligned countries."[10] It set forth several specific political and economic objectives for the forthcoming General Assembly session, including admission of the People's Republic of China (finally achieved in 1971), adoption of what became the International Development Strategy (Resolution 2626 [XXV], and progress toward international agreement on the use of the seabed as a source of revenue for national developmental purposes (one of the key issues once the Law of the Sea Conference got underway). As in the case of the economic declaration, the Lusaka resolutions were not the first to call for systematic coordination by the nonaligned states at the United Nations, but they expanded upon the means by which this should be achieved.

Not only should this occur through regularized mutual consultation at the United Nations and in its specialized agencies but also, a further resolution declared, through the overview of a "chairman." This latter resolution reflected a debate of crucial organizational significance: To what extent should the nonaligned movement institutionalize its activities? Most of the states at Lusaka were not prepared to create a permanent secretariat or other formal institutions as some states proposed. The majority preferred the much looser framework of periodic summit conferences, however cumbersome the process of convening them might be. Permanent institutions carried unwelcome financial implications, but they further implied a measure of organizational control that most of the states participating in the conference were reluctant to grant to any organizational center. Yet a few states pressed the argument for a permanent organizational base, at the minimum in the form of a permanent bureau or a standing committee. While no such institution was in fact approved at Lusaka, the desirability of greater continuity between summit meetings was granted in the resolution just cited. It then went on to "entrust" Zambia's Kaunda, as the presiding officer of the conference, "with the function of taking all necessary steps to maintain contacts among member States [and] ensure continuity."[11]

As skimpy as these organizational concessions were, they nevertheless served the cause of the diplomatic activists eager to keep the nonaligned framework functioning after Lusaka. Although Kaunda himself did not seek to exercise the role of chairman very actively, others seized upon the resolution encouraging continuity to keep the nonaligned group in operation. The Lusaka Conference thus provided a forward thrust that was to transform the nonaligned framework from an irregular gathering of heads of state into a predictable cycle of regularized contacts. The resuscitation of nonalignment at Lusaka was first and foremost a tribute to Tito's perseverance. The subsequent organizational thrust of the 1970s was attributable to a core group of states unwilling to see the nonaligned mechanism wind down again as it had after Cairo.

THE ACTIVISTS TAKE CHARGE:
LIMA, SANTIAGO, AND GEORGETOWN

The nonaligned activists were the same states that had been ready at Lusaka to establish some kind of permanent body. Drawn mainly from the more radical states, they included Algeria, Cuba, Guyana, Iraq, Tanzania, and Yugoslavia. These states took the initiative over the next few years to guarantee more sustained mutual interaction. They began by calling a consultative meeting at UN headquarters in September 1971. Virtually all the states that had been at Lusaka attended this meeting, most represented by its Foreign minister or UN ambassador.* This meeting allowed the nonaligned group to reformulate its objectives for the 1971 session of the General Assembly in light of the past year's developments. Most significantly from an organizational point of view, the consultative meeting approved convocation of a ministerial-level meeting to be held in the summer of 1972, and established a preparatory committee to organize this new meeting.

This decision had two noteworthy effects. In fixing another meeting for the near future, it definitively accelerated the pace of nonaligned organizational activity. The decision meant that the nonaligned states would meet shortly after the conclusion of UNCTAD III, scheduled for April 1972. In light of the fact that a conference of the Group of 77 preliminary to UNCTAD III was already on the agenda for November 1971, this new undertaking suggested an emerging conception of a division of labor between the Group of 77 and the nonaligned. The former as the inclusive grouping of developing states should formulate a common Third World bargaining position for the North-South negotiation taking account, to be sure, of the Lusaka Economic Declaration. Then, after

---

*The opening of the General Assembly each fall increasingly has become the occasion for a round of diplomatic contacts by foreign ministers from developed and developing countries alike. This provides an opportunity for high-level consultation with a minimum of extra arrangements or expense. There were, for example, 26 foreign ministers from nonaligned states at the United Nations when the meeting was held.

UNCTAD III, the nonaligned states would meet to assess the results and analyze the political implications of the UNCTAD negotiation in the context of the overall international situation. The nonaligned group was drafting a scenario that implied its own larger political role alongside the Group of 77.

Second, the appointment of a preparatory committee created a body that virtually fulfilled the practical function of a nonaligned standing committee. This minor organizational coup by the activists favoring institutionalization was carried out by simply renewing the mandate of the preparatory committee that had been formed a year and a half earlier at Dar es Salaam to prepare the Lusaka meeting.* By reactivating a preexisting group, the organizational activists acquired in 1971 the equivalent of what they had been unable to get in 1970. The existence of such a body facilitated the transition from one conference to the next.

The preparatory committee eventually chose Georgetown, Guyana, as the site for the ministerial conference. The choice reflected a desire to project the idea of nonalignment into the Western Hemisphere. Some Latin American states attended the first three nonaligned conferences as observers, but only Cuba had itself fully associated with the movement. In 1970 three former British colonies—Guyana, Jamaica, and Trinidad and Tobago—attended the Lusaka Conference. The coming to power of the Salvador Allende government in Chile and the Juan Velasco government in Peru added two new regimes that identified strongly with the concerns of the African and Asian states. Indeed, the entire next round of North-South politics was scheduled to take place in South America, as Peru was the site of the next Group of 77 conference and Chile was the host country for UNCTAD III. The selection of Georgetown was a further step in the integration of the South American continent into the Third World coalition.

The Lima Conference of the Group of 77 was in large part a reaffirmation of the position articulated four years earlier in Algiers. The Lima Declaration explicitly reiterated "the principles and objectives set forth in the Algiers Charter, which retains every bit of its relevance and which ought to serve as the guideline in the quest for positive international cooperation."[12] It went on to charge that the lack of progress since the 1967 meeting was caused by the unwillingness of the developed countries to give up an "anachronistic" and "irrational" international division of labor, and their failure to make the political commitment necessary to create a more equitable system of international economic relations. Although the 77 drafted a comprehensive proposed Program of Action for submission to UNCTAD III, the conference was subject to an underlying political malaise.

---

*The composition of this preparatory committee was Algeria, Burundi, Ceylon, Egypt, Ethiopia, Guyana, India, Indonesia, Iraq, Malaysia, Morocco, Senegal, Sudan, Tanzania, Yugoslavia, and Zambia. At the 1972 meeting, its term was extended up to the 1973 summit.

The fundamental problem at Lima was to come to terms with the impasse in North-South relations since UNCTAD II. Inasmuch as the Algiers Charter had barely affected the attitude of the industrial powers, what was the best strategy with which to approach UNCTAD III? For some of the developing countries, the need now was to propose those limited measures that appeared to have the greatest chance of acceptance. For others the need was to articulate a much more radical critique of the entire structure of international economic relations. In light of these conflicting approaches, the debates in committee were more tense in Lima than in Algiers. As there was less confidence in the utility of achieving a common front, the clashes between moderates and militants were more heated.

The Lima Conference did not raise the high hopes that had characterized its predecessor.[13] Where Algiers had been a conference of rising expectations, Lima was one of troubled stocktaking. This difference reflected in the final analysis a more realistic attitude regarding the prospect for rapid change in North-South relations. To both militants and moderates alike, it was clear that the Third World faced a long haul. By meeting once again, however, the developing states confirmed their intention of using the Group of 77 as an instrument in North-South politics. The practice of consultation became further established, and the Group of 77 became a more familiar tool.

UNCTAD III differed from UNCTAD II in much the same way that Lima differed from Algiers. It raised fewer hopes and it ended less in disillusionment than with a heightened sense of the intractability of the situation confronting the Third World. The conference met in Santiago in April and May 1972. During five weeks of deliberations, the 3,000 delegates inched along toward the scantiest of agreements. The principal elements in the Group of 77 position remained stabilization of commodities prices, better access for manufactures to the markets of the rich countries, and an increase in the international resources available for development. They proposed to establish a link between the creation of international monetary liquidity in special drawing rights (SDRs) and developmental credits. They also proposed a new liaison arrangement between UNCTAD, GATT, and the International Monetary Fund (IMF) to give the developing countries a greater say (through UNCTAD) on both international monetary and trading issues. None of these proposals was approved.

From the Third World perspective, the conference was a dismal failure. Aside from a vague agreement to create a special aid program for the 25 most disadvantaged countries, the various contentious issues were referred back to committees and study groups. The United States in particular insisted that institutions such as GATT and IMF (where the Third World had even less influence) retain their traditional decision-making power, and led the opposition to the SDR link. United States policy also impeded any progress in the area of preferential treatment for Third World manufactures, because the United States lagged behind the other industrial powers on implementation of the General System of Preferences approved at UNCTAD II. Although it was apparent in

Santiago that some of the industrial states were more sympathetic than others to the Third World proposals, the North as a whole stood by the status quo. Eight years after Geneva, four years after New Delhi, the South had yet to achieve a significant breakthrough on international economic relations.

The stalemate at Santiago had an impact upon the Georgetown meeting of the nonaligned group. One should note that the Georgetown Conference began less than three months after the conclusion of UNCTAD III. The timing contrasted sharply with the situation that prevailed after UNCTAD II. On that occasion there had been no comparable Third World follow-up—more than two years passed before the Lusaka Conference or even the Dar es Salaam meeting took place. In effect there was no concerted Third World response after UNCTAD II. By 1972, the level of organization of the Third World group was considerably higher. The timing factor was one measure of the growing strength of the coalition.

In the wake of Santiago, the Georgetown meeting was a ready opportunity to mobilize a more radical posture on the issues facing the Third World in the summer of 1972, and it marked a political triumph for the radical states. First Georgetown approved the admission of the Vietnamese GRP and the Cambodian GRUNK as full participants.* Three states—Indonesia, Malaysia, and Laos—walked out of the conference in protest over this decision, but they did not definitively break their ties with the group. This membership victory for the advocates of a more militant conception of nonalignment was mirrored in the further acts of the conference.

Both the political and economic declarations basically embodied the arguments that states like Algeria had been defending for some time. According to the Georgetown Declaration, the evolution toward superpower détente was commendable but had been of little benefit to the Third World. Progress toward decreased tensions in Europe was inadequate, they declared, unless the process was extended into the various crisis areas in Asia, Africa, the Middle East, and Latin America. On each of a series of conflicts involving Third World states, the Georgetown document endorsed a more militant position than previously adopted; for example:

Indochina: support of the programs of the GRP and the GRUNK;

Africa: a pledge to support decolonization by considering "ways and means of establishing a method of providing systematic finance, armaments, and training, for the Liberation Movements of Africa";

----

*In a final compromise on this ever divisive issue, their admission was characterized as provisional until ratified by the next summit. This "ratification" did occur at the 1973 meeting.

Middle East: not only condemnation of "the continued occupation of Arab Territories by Israel" but also explicit support for the Palestinians' "recovery of their national rights";

Latin America: support of the Chilean, Peruvian, and Panamanian governments in their disputes with the United States.[14]

These stands revealed the growing influence of the radical wing within the non-aligned movement.

The resolutions on economic policy showed this same leftward evolution. The conference adopted an Action Program for Economic Cooperation, which stressed cooperation among the nonaligned themselves such as to implement the ideal of "self-reliance both in and among developing countries."[15] The theme of self-reliance, which was most prominently associated with Tanzania's Julius Nyerere, connoted a strategy of autonomous socialist development free of foreign capital; now the term began to acquire greater international salience. Although the Lusaka Economic Declaration had already made reference to cultivating the "spirit of self-reliance," the Georgetown documents went on to spell out the letter of the new law, linking it particularly with the complete exercise of sovereignty in the economic realm.

In this vein, Algeria set forth its 1971 decision to nationalize all foreign oil companies as a model of a policy of self-reliance. "The road of Third World economic emancipation," Foreign Minister Bouteflika contended at Georgetown, "does not run through UNCTAD," but rather through direct Third World initiatives to reclaim control over their own economic resources.[16] This could be achieved so long as the developing countries backed one another in such initiatives, and this the new Action Program pledged them to do.* It also "denounced the practices and activities of transnational corporations, some of which violate the sovereignty of developing countries," and characterized economic threats and pressure as "an act of aggression" against the developing world.[18] It called for the establishment of further raw materials producer associations (like OPEC) and instituted a committee to examine the effects of private foreign investment in the developing states. In all these ways the Georgetown statement articulated a much sharper critique of the existing international economic order than previous nonaligned or Group of 77 documents.

---

*Nonaligned Countries emphatically affirm that the complete exercise of permanent sovereignty over their natural resources and the direct control of strategic economic activities . . . are vital to economic independence. Nonaligned Countires therefore agree to grant their unstinting support to other developing countries which are struggling for the full and effective control of their natural resources and those strategic economic activities under foreign control."[17]

The results of UNCTAD III, the Action Program stated, "showed once again the crisis international cooperation" was experiencing. This crisis created by the intransigence of the North required the developing countries to count upon their own means, but these still included the Group of 77 as a pressure group in international negotiations. The document reiterated the nonaligned group's support for the proposals in the Lima Declaration. The nonaligned would continue to "encourage every effort to strengthen the unity and coordination of the Group of 77" in order ultimately to force a change in the policy of the developed countries.[19]

What emerged from the Georgetown Conference, therefore, was a two-tiered strategy: a more radical conception of self-help as the foundation for more effective pressure in North-South negotiations. The nonaligned movement was seen to operate at the more fundamental level, radicalizing national policies as component parts of a collective policy of self-reliance. Their own growing economic clout would in turn reinforce the Group of 77.

The overall political orientation of the Georgetown resolutions clearly reflected the influence of the nonaligned radicals. So did the final decision taken there, which was to schedule the next summit for September 1973 in Algiers. Georgetown raised Algeria to a level of organizational influence comparable to that exercised by Yugoslavia, or Egypt, or India in earlier periods. The Algerians for their part were prepared to make the fourth summit conference a major event in Third World politics.

BACK TO ALGIERS:
THE FOURTH NONALIGNED SUMMIT

Having worked to shape a more radical orientation, Algeria was now determined to marshall an ever larger number of states under the banner of non-alignment. It mounted a vigorous campaign to turn out a large and high-level attendance. Algerian diplomats were sent to most Third World capitals in July 1973 to discuss the conference and to urge participation by the heads of state themselves. A further round of contacts followed in August, when most of the ministers in the Algerian government undertook similar missions.

As a result Algeria succeeded in gathering 75 states in Algiers compared to the 53 at Lusaka.* Even more significant was the fact that 54 states were repre-

---

*The new participants included three former Latin American observers (Argentina, Chile, and Peru) and the two delegations in dispute at Lusaka (Cambodia and South Vietnam). Several were African states that had stayed aloof from previous meetings: Ivory Coast, Dahomey, Niger, Upper Volta, Gabon, Gambia, Madagascar, and Mauritius. Saudi Arabia (present at the first meetings but absent at Lusaka) returned with four of its Persian Gulf

sented by the chief of state or head of government, over twice the number that had attended the previous summit. Tito, Gandhi, Sadat, Senghor, Sihanouk, Nyerere, Bourguiba, Makarios, Castro, Qaddafi, Kaunda, Gowon, Mobutu, Bandaranaike, Faisal, Assad, Haile Selassie, Houphouet-Boigny—virtually every Third World figure of grand international reputation was present in Algiers, giving the Fourth Nonaligned Conference a diplomatic significance of the order of the Bandung Conference 18 years earlier.

Bandung had summed up the aspirations of the first generation of independence. Algiers gave the highest political sanction to the radical critique of postindependence international structures that had been gradually emerging since Bandung. From this perspective, the Algiers summit was the culmination of the forces set in motion at Bandung. Algiers largely restated with the additional authority of the heads of state what had already been said at Georgetown. From a different perspective, just as Bandung had unleashed new energies in Third World politics, Algiers became the point of departure for an unprecedented burst of Third World diplomatic action. The difference between Bandung and Algiers was that there was a much stronger commitment to organizational continuity at the latter. This commitment was largely vested in the host country itself, which had already demonstrated its capacity for diplomatic activism and which was determined to use the nonaligned framework as an instrument of Third World assertion.

The intellectual focus of the Algiers meeting was to analyze the implications of détente for the Third World. The advantages of détente were the reduction of superpower tension and the emergence of a multipolar distribution of power in the place of the postwar bipolar order. Yet, according to Bouteflika as he opened the preconference meeting of foreign ministers, "the advantages of détente are far from reaching into the regions to which we belong."[20] Boumediene followed in his keynote address by distinguishing détente from full-fledged international cooperation. Insofar as the Third World remained subject to colonial-style wars, "vassalization," economic aggression, and political intervention, the Algerian leader asserted, détente looked very much like superpower "pretension to reign over the world."[21] This argument found its way into the final Political Declaration, which reiterated "peace is far from being assured in all parts of the world" and that "as long as colonial wars, apartheid, imperialist aggression, alien domination, foreign occupation, power politics, eco-

---

neighbors (Oman, Qatar, Bahrein, and United Arab Emirates); Burma also returned after a long period of self-enforced diplomatic isolation, while Bangladesh and Bhutan were new Asian participants. Finally, Algeria backed and won admission of Malta after some debate over the British military base there, which the Maltese government pledged to close down by 1978—the earliest that it considered economically feasible.

nomic exploitation and plunder prevail, peace will be limited in principle and scope."[22]

Algeria had been one of the first to argue that détente had been no boon for the Third World. The resolutions adopted at Algiers fully affirmed this analysis, and its corollary, "the need for more resolute action by the nonaligned countries."[23] Still the breakdown of the bipolar structure was a positive opportunity for the Third World if it could organize itself into one of the power centers in a new multipolar system. Boumediene presented Algeria's conception of the nonaligned movement as a "pole of attraction" around which the Third World should coalesce for more resolute action. The key to such a coalition, Algeria argued, lay in permanent institutions. Institutionalization would enhance Third World power by assuring that the nonaligned movement function as a reliable source of Third World pressure and initiatives.

On this point, the activists won a half-victory. They proposed that the member-states create a permanent secretariat. This idea was not accepted, but the conference did regularize the role of the former preparatory committee in the form of a 15-member Bureau.* This was the first time that a summit conference entrusted ongoing activities to some standing group, in effect ratifying but also amplifying the practice since 1971 when the preparatory committee had been exhumed. The decision was indicative of the growing influence of the diplomatic activists who now had the rudiments at least of a permanent organizational apparatus.

The responsibilities of the Bureau included the tasks of making preparations for the fifth summit and for an interim conference of foreign ministers, coordinating the activities of the nonaligned governments particularly at the United Nations, making recommendations regarding the future establishment of a permanent secretariat, and supervising the implementation of the Action Program for Economic Cooperation adopted during the conference. This mandate was clearly more substantial than that of the previous preparatory committee, and, even more crucially, Algeria was willing to see that it was carried out. The conference gave Boumediene the coordinating role that it had entrusted to Zambian President Kaunda three years earlier. Boumediene was prepared to interpret the powers of this office broadly and to use his position as acting president to infuse new activism into the nonaligned framework.

The composition of the Bureau was Algeria, Cuba, Guyana,* Kuwait, Liberia, Malaysia,* Nepal, Peru, Senegal,* Somalia, Sri Lanka,* Syria, Tanzania,* Yugoslavia* and Zaire. (The seven starred countries were holdovers from the preparatory committee.) The political dosage remained roughly the same. Cuba, Syria, and Peru replaced Burundi and Iraq as radicals, and Liberia replaced Indonesia as a conservative representative; among the centrists Kuwait, Nepal, Somalia, and Zaire replaced Egypt, Ethiopia, India, Morocco, Sudan, and Zambia.

The distance traveled from Lusaka to Algiers could be measured on several scales. The first was a steady evolution to the left in the content of the political and economic resolutions. The second was the progress toward greater organizational continuity expressed in more frequent meetings and an interim Bureau. The third was the heftier political weight of the movement as measured by the sanction of over 50 heads of government. On all these counts, the Algiers Conference marked a new level of Third World political cohesion. After foundering in the second half of the 1960s, the Third World finally acquired organizational substance. The nonaligned movement now provided an operational framework, however modest, for the ideal of solidarity.

There remained enormous differences within the group to be sure. Some member-states certainly leaned toward the Soviet Union and China, others toward the United States and Western Europe. Libya's President Muammar Qaddafi had a point in contending that one could count the truly nonaligned states on the fingers of one hand. Yet in full cognizance of this residual diversity, the Third World was emerging as a separate pole in international politics. Neither Henry Kissinger, who took exception to the "alignment of the nonaligned" (against the United States and the West), nor Leonid Brezhnev, who warned the conferees against dividing the world into rich versus poor (rather than progressive versus imperialist), was terribly satisfied with the overall orientation of the conference. C. L. Sulzberger of the *New York Times* acknowledged that "the so-called Third World is gradually edging into its own."[24] Jean Lacouture of *Le Monde* viewed the militance and the coherence of the final resolutions as a major success for the movement and the host country, questioning only whether Algeria had "the means to exploit this success and to instill its own dynamism to the whole of the movement."[25] It soon became evident that Algeria would use what means it had to keep the nonaligned movement active.

From Algiers in October 1967 to Algiers in September 1973, both the Group of 77 and the nonaligned movement had greatly reinforced their corporate identity. The Algiers documents offered a slightly new formulation of the relationship between the two: "The Heads of State or Government recommend that nonaligned countries should act as a catalytic force in the Group of 77 in order to increase the effectiveness and solidarity of the developing countires."[26] This conception of the nonaligned movement as catalyst, as a group within a group, completed the process by which the two tracks of Third World collective diplomacy converged to arrive at the Sixth Special Session. Algiers capped the efforts undertaken five years earlier by Tito to recharge the nonaligned movement. Building upon Lusaka and Georgetown, the Algiers summit consolidated the Third World coalition on the eve of a critical new phase in North-South relations. The tortuous itinerary from Bandung to Algiers finally produced a political and organizational infrastructure that enabled the Third World to respond promptly and coherently to the international crisis opened by OPEC's first major blast at global economic structures.

NOTES

1. Branislav Gosovic, *UNCTAD: Conflict and Compromise* (Leiden: A. W. Sijthoff, 1972), p. 272.

2. *Le Monde* (Paris), October 8-9, 1967.

3. *El Moudjahid* (Algiers), October 11, 1967.

4. *El Moudjahid*, October 26, 1967.

5. *Le Monde*, March 28, 1968.

6. *El Moudjahid*, November 6, 1969.

7. The tally is recorded in Odette Jankowitsch and Karl P. Sauvant, eds., *The Third World Without Superpowers: The Collected Documents of the Non-Aligned Countries* (Dobbs Ferry, N.Y.: Oceana, 1978), p. 151, and was reported in *Le Monde*, September 9, 1970. Although no formal breakdown of the vote was announced, one can ascertain from the account in *Le Monde* and the official resume that the vote was essentially as follows: for Sihanouk's GRUNK: Algeria, Central African Republic, Congo-Brazzaville, Cuba, Guinea, Iraq, Libya, Mali, Mauritania, Somalia, South Yemen, Sudan, Syria, Tanzania, Uganda, Yemen, and Yugoslavia; for the Lon Nol government: Botswana, Lesotho, Swaziland, Liberia, Laos, Malaysia, and probably Indonesia; to leave the seat vacant: Afghanistan, Egypt, Ghana, India, Kenya, Kuwait, Morocco, Togo, Tunisia, Singapore, Sri Lanka, and Zaire.

8. The texts of the Lusaka resolutions appear in Jankowitsch and Sauvant, *Collected Documents*, pp. 80-113.

9. Ibid., p. 85.

10. Ibid., p. 104.

11. Ibid., p. 106.

12. *Documents d'Actualité Internationale* (Paris), no. 14, April 1-7, 1972.

13. *Le Monde*, November 9, 1971.

14. The full texts of the Georgetown resolutions are in Jankowitsch and Sauvant, *Collected Documents*, pp. 432-74.

15. Ibid., p. 449.

16. *El Moudjahid*, August 11, 1972.

17. Jankowitsch and Sauvant, *Collected Documents*, p. 450.

18. Ibid., p. 447.

19. Ibid., p. 448.

20. *El Moudjahid*, September 3, 1973.

21. Ibid., September 7, 1973.

22. The complete resolutions appear in Jankowitsch and Sauvant, *Collected Documents*, pp. 189-281. The citation is from p. 193.

23. Ibid., p. 195.

24. *New York Times*, September 9, 1973.

25. *Le Monde*, September 8 and 11, 1973.

26. Jankowitsch and Sauvant, *Collected Documents*, p. 237.

4. The Politics of the New International Economic Order, 1974–75

Three related events in the last three months of 1973 ushered in a critical phase in North-South relations. The first was the war launched by Egypt and Syria against Israel's position in the occupied territories of Sinai and the Golan Heights. The second was the embargo decreed by the Arab oil-exporting states in an effort to pry Europe, Japan, and the United States away from support of Israel. The third was the decision of the ensemble of Third World oil exporters to raise the price of oil fourfold. The intensification of the conflict in the Middle East and the exercise of "oil power" by the OPEC states created a political and economic crisis in the international system of profound consequence for the developing world as a whole.

Throughout 1974 and well into 1975, there was a period of intense international maneuvering in response to the new situation. The price and the supply of oil were questions of great importance to the industrial powers. The U.S. government promptly initiated a campaign to pressure the OPEC governments to reduce the price of oil. The latter sought to defend their political autonomy and their financial gains. The majority of the developing states, that is, those that had to import oil for their energy needs, found themselves in a politically ambiguous position. On the one hand, their own economies would be hard hit by the quadrupled price of oil. On the other, they saw a positive precedent in the revaluation of a raw material by a group of developing states. The key political question for the Third World in early 1974 was whether the OPEC offensive could be turned to the advantage of the broader body of developing states.

The real novelty of the situation created by the OPEC price action was the saliency suddenly accorded to an issue in North-South relations. For the first time developing states were major actors in a systemwide international crisis. This unprecedented situation was a test of the capacity of the emerging Third World coalition to respond coherently to a crisis in which their interests were centrally implicated.

This chapter examines the action of the Third World states from January 1974 through September 1975, the period of intensive systemic attention to the international economic crisis. This period embraced the Sixth and the Seventh Special Sessions of the General Assembly, as well as a host of other international conferences that were part of a prolonged diplomatic struggle to define a new balance of economic power in the wake of OPEC's financial coup. For the rich states, the goal was to minimize the blow to the existing international economic structures. For the Third World, the stakes were to achieve a political breakthrough regarding the principle of a New International Economic Order.

THE OPEC REVOLUTION

Throughout the crisis, the developing states used the instruments of collective diplomacy that they had been shaping over the previous several years. They particularly drew upon the political infrastructure created during the Algiers Conference. By virtue of its acting presidency of the nonaligned group, Algeria played a critical role in organizing a cohesive Third World position. The Algerian role was all the more important because the country was a member of OPEC. It is pertinent to review briefly the emergence of OPEC as a crucial Third World actor before analyzing the events of 1974-75.

The spectacular price hikes of fall 1973 were the culmination of a series of political and economic developments that transformed OPEC in the early 1970s. The organization was founded in 1960 by Venezuela, Iran, Saudi Arabia, Iraq, and Kuwait shortly after the oil companies cut the price of oil for the second time in 18 months. Until 1960, the major Western oil companies controlled the international oil market thanks to their capital, their technological expertise, and their distribution activities. The formation of OPEC was the first step toward the mutual defense of the interests of the producer states. During the 1960s, the organization provided a forum for the exchange of ideas and the gradual coordination of the national policies of the states toward the companies. As much as anything else it was a joint learning experience by which the exporter countries acquired access to the technical and financial domains of a complex industry.

Over the course of the decade, other states joined the organization—Libya, Indonesia, Algeria, Nigeria, Qatar, Abu Dhabi—so that, by 1970, the members of OPEC produced 90 percent of the world's oil exports. Parallel to this growing organizational strength occurred some key political developments, most notably the overthrow of the Libyan monarchy in September 1969. The accession of a group of radical military officers led by Muammar Qaddafi to power in Libya was the catalyst for a process of rapid change from 1970 to 1973. It permitted the consolidation of a radical front within OPEC composed of Iraq, Algeria (which had joined the organization only in 1969), and Libya, and it set in motion a process of negotiation that produced the first general increase in oil prices in 13 years.

The new Libyan regime was militantly pan-Arabist and was willing to take risks to establish the country as a leader in Arab affairs. It was also quick to capitalize upon certain bargaining advantages presented by the particular Libyan situation. Libya's oil economy was relatively young, having grown enormously during the 1960s in large measure through the investments of "independent" oil companies.* The Libyans calculated that these smaller companies were more vulnerable to political and economic pressure than the "majors" that controlled the Persian Gulf resources, especially at a moment when the shutdown of the Suez Canal enhanced the value of Libya's oil, which was directly available in the Mediterranean. The new government esteemed furthermore that Libya's financial situation was satisfactory enough to allow a momentary cutback in production without grave consequences.[1]

In this perspective, the Libyans singled out an independent company, Occidental, which had limited sources of supply outside Libya for special attention. Invoking legislation that allowed them to decree production cutbacks for purposes of conservation, the Libyans demanded a number of revisions in the terms of their contract with Occidental. By progressively closing the tap, they built up economic pressure that Occidental could not resist, and in September 1970 the company capitulated to Libya's demands. The posted price rose from $2.23 to $2.53, increasing Libyan revenues per barrel by about 30 percent.† These same terms were then promptly extended to the other companies in Libya. The successful Libyan operation was itself a pebble tossed into the sea of the international oil economy, but the ripples quickly reached other shores.

They touched first at Caracas, Venezuela, where OPEC held its semiannual meeting in December 1970. The Caracas meeting fixed a set of goals, the general

---

*The term "independent" is applied to the numerous smaller Western companies that operate in the international oil industry with the "majors" known familiarly as the "seven sisters": Exxon, Mobil, Standard Oil of California, Texaco, Gulf, British Petroleum, and Royal Dutch/Shell.

†The international oil economy was based upon a complex combination of royalty payments, taxes, and pricing arrangements that had nothing to do with the cost of production of a barrel of oil. It is possible to follow the evolving gains of the producer states without entering in detail into this complex system. In simplified terms, the key element was the posted price, a figure above the actual selling price that served as an index for the calculation of royalties and taxes. One can thus compare posted prices or the actual government revenues in measuring the course of change.

objective of which was to extend the advantages acquired by Libya to the ensemble of the exporter countries. These included a higher tax rate, an alignment
of the posted price everywhere on the highest price being practiced in any OPEC
country, and an across-the-board price increase. It was agreed that the Persian
Gulf states would present these demands to the oil companies, which themselves
formed a negotiating consortium of 23 corporations. This joint negotiation, the
first of its kind, was held in Teheran, Iran, in January and February 1971. In
mid-February the companies accepted the OPEC propositions and the posted
price of oil in the Persian Gulf climbed to $2.18, an increase of about 20 per-
cent, which meant an increase in producer-state revenues of some 27 cents per
barrel (roughly equal to the Libyan increases).

The Teheran negotiation was a major turning point in the international oil
economy. For the first time the producer states acting together had significantly
increased their revenues. Market factors clearly had played a role, for demand
was high during this period, but the political factors—Libya's hard-nosed bargaining, the growing pressure of the radical front within OPEC, and the adoption of
a common posture at Caracas—were preeminent in bringing about this change.
Analysts of the Teheran decisions have pointed out that the companies acceded
to the OPEC demands with minimal resistance, and that the settlement was not
altogether contrary to U.S. interests.* These points are well taken and guard
against hasty conclusions regarding a major shift of power toward the producer
states. The fact remains that a new relationship more favorable to the OPEC
countries was definitely emerging as the political will to challenge the status quo
grew stronger.

The situation continued to evolve rapidly. Shortly after the Teheran
accord, Algeria, which had already nationalized the smaller oil companies in the
Sahara, proceeded to nationalize 51 percent of the remaining foreign holdings
(namely, the larger French companies) and the entirety of the natural gas fields
and pipeline facilities. The Algerian action prompted a similar move in Libya
(51 percent participation), while Nigeria took over 35 percent participation in
the companies operating there. With these governments serving as a vanguard,
the Persian Gulf states set a goal of 20 percent national ownership, which became an official OPEC objective. Throughout 1972, negotiations over the participation issue dominated the relations between the majors and the Gulf coun-

---

*Relative to Europe and Japan, the United States long imported a small proportion
of its oil. Indeed through 1970, the price of U.S. oil was higher than that imported from
the Third World by Europe and Japan. The 1971 increase was thus more costly for Europe
and Japan than for the United States whose industrial productivity thus became more competitive. At the same time it was already apparent that U.S. import needs were going to
grow dramatically in the 1970s (the winter of 1970 having seen the first "mini-energy crisis").
It was in the interest of the companies that these imports enter the United States at roughly
the same price as domestic oil so as not to destabilize the existing U.S. price structures.[2]

tries. In the meantime a separate agreement was struck in January 1972 to raise prices again by about 10 percent to compensate the producers for the devaluation of the dollar. Yet another such revaluation was applied in June 1973. On all these fronts, the producer states were gradually taking greater charge of their economic situation; their strength vis-a-vis the Western companies—and hence Northern economic power—continued to grow.

The trend toward higher prices and greater national control encouraged also a more radical stance among the Arab states regarding the use of oil for political leverage—the "oil weapon." In the spring of 1973, the U.S. State Department's principal energy expert, James Akins, called attention to some 15 instances of threats to withhold oil in the context of the Arab-Israeli conflict.[3] In itself, the idea was not new, partial embargoes having existed briefly in 1956 and 1967 (the Suez crisis and the Six Day War). These had been quite ineffectual, however, in the presence of Western control over marketing and technology. Akins was correct to warn that application of the oil weapon was becoming a more consequential threat in light of the political and economic changes underway in the Arab world and the oil industry.

Throughout the period leading up to the October war, the demand for oil continued to boom, and so did the demand for higher prices or, in other words, for a revision of the Teheran accord. A new round of negotiations between OPEC and the companies was scheduled for October to discuss such an increase. This meeting began as scheduled two days after the outbreak of the war, but the companies requested a recess to study the new demands. A week later the Persian Gulf states unilaterally raised their prices. The era of negotiated agreements abruptly came to an end, as the largest producer countries, Saudi Arabia and Iran, effectively declared their independence in the realm of pricesetting.*

On the following day the Organization of Arab Petroleum Exporting Countries (OAPEC, founded in 1968 as a kind of stepsister to OPEC and including such modest Arab producers as Egypt, Syria, and Bahrein along with the seven Arab members of OPEC) met to take the embargo decision. The embargo was directed at countries considered to be supporters of Israel: the United States, its European allies, and Japan in particular. Each OAPEC state decreed a 5 percent production cutback and threatened the companies with further sanctions if they delivered Arab oil to the embargoed states. The actual embargo was of limited duration, but it was sufficient to destabilize an already tight market and more importantly to raise the specter of major oil shortages. The willingness of the OAPEC states to wage a form of limited economic warfare was an ominous precedent for the target countries. As the hot war raged along the Suez Canal

---

*The Gulf countries fixed the new price at $3.65 per barrel. This figure translated into a posted price of $5.11 (up 70 percent from $3.00) or into government revenues of $3.05 as against $1.77 (up some 72 percent).

and in the Golan Heights, the lines of a broader politicoeconomic international crisis were being drawn.

The events of October led directly of course to the December price increases that completed the revolution in the international oil economy. The major producers, most notably Iran, watched the market price of oil climb to unheard of heights during the scramble for supplies set off by the embargo. Iran and the other Persian Gulf producers took the lead in setting a new posted price at $11.65, roughly four times the figure at which it had stood at the beginning of October.* In the following weeks, the other OPEC countries aligned their own prices with reference to the new Persian Gulf standard. Not only had the era of negotiation with the companies ended but so had the age of cheap oil.

The cumulative impact of embargo, price hikes, and unilateral OPEC decision making constituted the first major blow against the international economic structures that had long prevailed between the developing and the developed states. Coupled with the nationalizations and participation agreements of the previous few years, these moves represented the first consequential implementation of the idea of Third World control over Third World resources. The OPEC decisions were a concrete expression of the demand for economic change that had been articulated in Group of 77 and nonaligned documents since 1967. As 1974 began, industrial powers and developing states alike reacted to these new economic and political variables. The former sought to stabilize and if possible redress the situation, while the latter sought to capitalize upon the mood of crisis to transform other sectors of North-South relations. The politics of the New International Economic Order were underway.

THE SIXTH SPECIAL SESSION

The U.S. government was the first to react to the larger December price increases. For some time the United States had been suggesting the formation of an organization of the major industrial oil importers. President Richard Nixon announced in January that the United States was inviting the industrial powers to meet in Washington to confer on energy policy and to consider the creation of such an organization. The idea of a "consumer cartel" or a "counter-OPEC" was not well received by France, which disliked the prospect of the industrial powers lining up behind the United States to face down the OPEC states. To

---

*This raised the revenue of the producer countries from approximately $1.75 per barrel on October 1 to $7.00 per barrel (400 percent); prior to the Teheran accord, government revenues had been about $1.00 per barrel. The figures are approximate in that they reflect an average of a variety of specific prices fixed according to the grade and the location of the various crude oils.

distinguish its attitude from Washington's, France proposed that the United Nations serve as a forum for a discussion of energy issues open to all states. At this point, Algeria proposed a special session of the General Assembly, not on energy but on "raw materials and development." The Algerian move was designed to defend OPEC's interest by placing the issue in a broader context, but it also served to shift the diplomatic initiative back toward the Third World. By defining the agenda in terms of development rather than energy, the Algerian proposal rallied the Third World behind OPEC and forced discussion of the overall economic condition of the developing countries. The issue was not the price of oil, the Third World was saying, but rather the economic situation of all those countries that depended heavily upon the export of their raw materials for their sustenance.

In proposing the special session, Algeria's Boumediene formally invoked his capacity as "President in Office of the Nonaligned Countries." A few days later, Algeria announced that the new nonaligned Bureau would meet in Algiers in mid-March to discuss the rapid evolution of global economic matters and other issues. About the same time the Algerian ambassador at the United Nations organized a consultative meeting of the nonaligned states' UN representatives to mobilize support behind the proposal. Algeria thus took the lead in putting the nonaligned framework to work in the new political context.*

The idea and eventually the convocation of the Sixth Special Session for April 1974 served to channel diplomatic activity in the direction desired by the developing states. First, however, in February the Washington Conference on Energy was held, attended by the 13 major Western industrial powers.† All of them except France agreed to create a new instrument to coordinate their own energy policies, the International Energy Agency (IEA), which was actually inaugurated in November 1974. Nevertheless, the conference only partially fulfilled U.S. hopes. The United States was seeking to arrange a prompt showdown between oil consumers and producers, but the other industrial states did not endorse this approach. Instead, they insisted that the final communique "welcome the initiative" of the UN Special Session; until then, the United States had expressed reservations regarding the opportuneness of such a session. The February meeting made it clear that the economic partners of the United States were not prepared for the kind of confrontation that Washington envisaged and preferred

---

*Algeria also convened a special session of the OAU in January 1974 to explore ways by which to cushion the blow of the higher prices upon the African oil importers. Within OPEC itself, Algeria pushed for the creation of a special development fund for Africa. On all these scores, Algeria demonstrated its particularly keen awareness of the problem of maintaining solidarity between the OPEC states and the rest of the Third World.

† Belgium, Canada, Denmark, France, West Germany, Ireland, Italy, Japan, Luxemburg, the Netherlands, Norway, the United Kingdom, and the United States.

to explore more accommodating avenues. The proposal for a special session on a broader spread of issues than oil alone opened up such an avenue.

France's desire to create a network of European-Third World relations independent of U.S. influence was an important force in orienting its Common Market partners away from a pronounced confrontation. France's distinctive position in refusing to join the IEA was a legacy of the Gaullist policy of opposition to the "two hegemonies," Soviet and U.S. Even after the death of de Gaulle's successor, Georges Pompidou, in April 1974, France continued to pursue a distinctive role that made it one of the centers of diplomatic initiative in North-South relations. The fact that France and Algeria remained especially closely attuned to one another was a factor in shaping French policy. Algeria was not in the least averse to echoing Gaullist pronouncements about a Europe independent of U.S. pressure. Algeria reacted with particular vehemence to the U.S. project of regrouping the consumer states in a countercartel. Boumediene assumed an unmistakably Gaullist tone when he declared in an interview to *Le Monde* that the United States was seeking to herd the other industrial states into a policy of confrontation: "If the Europeans bend under the American big stick," he warned, "they will pass once again to the sidelines of history."[4] The alternative to U.S. hegemony, he asserted, was a Europe "open to its neighbors" in Africa and the Arab world. The alternative to a confrontation over oil was cooperation in development to which the Third World was summoning the industrial states by the proposal for a UN special session.

In this first round of, diplomatic maneuvers, then, OPEC managed to deflect the initial U.S. reaction to the price increases. Assuming its familiar role as the political organizer, Algeria articulated a hostile response to the "big stick" (not only the Washington Conference but also Defense Secretary James Schlesinger's statements regarding the possible use of force if the industrial world should be "paralyzed" by OPEC and OAPEC policies; later Secretary of State Kissinger revised the metaphor from paralysis to "strangulation"). This hostility was communicated to Europe especially via France, and thereby influenced the outcome of the Washington Conference at which the United States was unsuccessful in winning support for an OPEC-consumers confrontation. Instead, the diplomatic itinerary was turned toward the United Nations, a victory in agenda setting at least for the Third World.

In preparation for the Sixth Special Session, the developing countries relied upon both nonaligned and Group of 77 institutions and texts. Algeria consulted the members of the nonaligned Bureau before requesting that the session be convened. Boumediene's diplomatic note to Secretary-General Kurt Waldheim cited several paragraphs from the resolutions of the Algiers Conference in defense of his argument that the real crisis at hand was not over energy but over development. The texts of the eventual New International Economic Order (NIEO) resolutions adopted at the conclusion of the session drew considerably upon the Economic Declaration and the Action Program for Economic

Cooperation previously approved at the Algiers Summit. In the middle of March, the newly instituted nonaligned Bureau met to reaffirm the cohesion of the nonaligned group as the Special Session drew near.

This first meeting of the Bureau revealed some of the persistent organizational ambiguities of the nonaligned movement. Although the Bureau had 15 members, 17 states officially attended the meeting, while 21 others participated with the status of observer. The two additional full participants were India and Mali. The former, it was explained, was included by virtue of its position as president of the political commission at the previous summit, while the latter had served as rapporteur during the summit conference. This de facto expansion of the Bureau was more realistically attributable to the fact that India, as one of the largest Third World oil importers, was especially hard hit by the price hikes and thus it was essential to associate India fully in the elaboration of a common Third World policy. Mali in turn was one of the 25 poorest countries whose economies were threatened by devastation by the rising cost of imports. The additional representation of so many observer states was explained as the manifestation of a desire to keep the activities of the movement open to all member-states. The Bureau, in other words, was not to be construed as a closed executive organ but rather as a collective interim agent. This conception of an open Bureau reflected the distrust of a potentially oligarchic secretariat that had always existed in the nonaligned group. The fact that there were more observers than official participants at the first Bureau meeting testified to the limits of its executive function.

The purpose of the March Bureau meeting in any case was more to re-mobilize than to exercise executive authority. It was designed to demonstrate that the nonaligned states were working among themselves to resolve the adverse consequences of higher oil prices, and more importantly to demonstrate that they were agreed upon the need for a "thorough structural change of [international] economic relations."[5] The Bureau set forth a broad outline of the issues that the Sixth Special Session should address: amelioration of the terms of trade for raw materials exporters, participation of the developing countries on equal terms in reform of the international monetary system and in multilateral trade negotiations, the rising price of capital goods, for food crisis, development finance, and transfer of technology. It did not seek to draft the precise document to be submitted to the Special Session. This activity was in fact already underway at the United Nations; the nonaligned Bureau recommended that this preparatory work continue "both within the nonaligned group and within the Group of 77." The latter reference suggested that the Group of 77 was the most appropriate Third World organ for common action during the Special Session. The nonaligned meeting was thus more a political prelude to the session than a decision-making forum. The nonaligned group—here operating through its effectively enlarged Bureau—remained a catalyst and a mobilizer inside the larger Third World framework.

Having built political support for the Special Session project through non-aligned channels, the operational framework now shifted to the Group of 77. As will be recalled, both the Lusaka and Georgetown declarations had explicitly assumed an ongoing working relationship between the two groupings. Inasmuch as the General Assembly session was of course a UN forum, the more inclusive group was the logical one to organize the drafting of a Third World position paper. In practice, the familiar activists took the lead—Algeria, India, Yugoslavia—in association nonetheless with at least one significant newcomer, Iran, whose growing prominence within OPEC gave its voice weight. They drew heavily upon the ideas previously advanced in nonaligned and Group of 77 declarations in drafting what became the NIEO resolutions.

While the developing countries retained the diplomatic initiative, they sought as well to create a positive climate for the session by inviting the developed countries to collaborate with them in the planning phase. Only the United States declined to participate in this planning process. The U.S. ambassador to the United Nations, John Scali, described this apparent diffidence as a policy of "constructive waiting," but it was quite clear that the United States was not at all enthusiastic about the prospect of General Assembly approval of new principles of international economic relations.[6] Through its abstention, the United States sought to minimize the significance of the forthcoming session, which Scali midway through March characterized as an "amorphous glob." The submission of the Third World proposals in early April gave definite form to the upcoming debate. United States skepticism notwithstanding, it became apparent that the Third World coalition had succeeded in focusing high-level diplomatic attention upon the event.*

This attention was not really surprising, for this was the first time that the General Assembly had ever convened specifically to discuss the issue of development. The recent exercise of oil power had dramatically introduced a new variable in North-South relations, the full consequences of which were far from clear in the spring of 1974. In these circumstances virtually everyone except the United States saw the Sixth Special Session as an opportunity to take stock of the course of change and to begin to plot a new international response to development. Both symbolically and substantively the session commanded political attention. The international system was facing a new kind of crisis, and the Third World was claiming a role in international crisis management that only the United States was trying hard to ignore.

---

*This was manifested by the attendance of numerous major power foreign ministers, including those of France, West Germany, and the Soviet Union, or comparable officials (for example, China's Vice-Premier Teng Hsaio-ping, Britain's Minister of State David Ennals), as well as a large number of Third World foreign ministers and a few Third World heads of state, most notably the convenor, Houari Boumediene. Given this array of personalities, Secretary Kissinger had little choice but to make an appearance as well.

The U.S. posture of "constructive waiting" was the other side of the coin of the Washington Conference. The United States wanted to organize an anti-OPEC coalition, and preferred to operate outside UN institutions precisely because these lent themselves to a show of Third World unity. The General Assembly was the preferred forum of the developing countries because it could register one of their few sources of power, the fact of numbers. The very idea of the Special Session in effect represented a clash between their voting power and U.S. economic power. The United States could afford its show of lone indifference, because it knew that real economic change could come about only with its acquiescence—no matter what the General Assembly might resolve. The United States counted upon its economic power as an eventual countervailing force with which the developing states would have to reckon before substantive international action on the energy/development crisis could be taken.

Still General Assembly resolutions carry a certain weight in influencing relations among states, and diplomatic isolation is never a comfortable situation. Third World voting power was therefore not a negligible factor in shaping the overall international response to changing economic conditions. Furthermore, while the United States could assume a hard line, many of its Northern allies, more dependent than the United States on their trade with the Third World, were inclined to be more conciliatory. The developing countries thus judged that the moment was ripe to articulate forcefully their conception of the policies necessary to break the vicious circle of underdevelopment.

The expression "a new international economic order" had appeared unobtrusively in chapter 7 of the Economic Declaration of the Algiers Nonaligned Summit. The twin resolutions submitted by the Group of 77 to the Special Session picked up this term as the essence of the Third World claim to a right to economic development. In formulating its position, the Third World coalition followed its recent practice of coupling a declaration with an action program (as had been done at the Georgetown and Algiers meetings).

Resolution 3201 (S-VI), the Declaration on the Establishment of a New International Economic Order, called for an order

> based on equity, sovereign equality, interdependence, common interest and cooperation among all states irrespective of their economic and social systems which shall correct inequalities and redress existing injustices, and make it possible to eliminate the widening gap between the developed and the developing countries.[7]

The text then observed that 70 percent of the world's population accounted for but 30 percent of the world's income, and that the crisis in the global economy since 1970 (anterior to the oil price increases) had had its most severe repercussions upon the developing states. These states were now demanding an "active, full, and equal participation . . . in the formulation and application of all decisions that concern the international community." The declaration enumerated the fundamental principles of a new order, reiterating at the outset the basic political rights of sovereign equality, self-determination, noninterference, equity, and participation. It went on to cite a series of economic principles: full permanent sovereignty over natural resources and all economic activities within a state; the right to nationalization; regulation of the activities of multinational corporations; an equitable relationship between the prices of Third World exports and imports; international monetary reform to ensure an adequate flow of real resources to the developing countries; and facilitating the role of producer associations. In a word, the declaration summarized the major themes that the developing countries had progressively elaborated since the 1967 Algiers Charter.

Resolution 3202 (S-VI), entitled Program of Action on the Establishment of a New International Economic Order, spelled out the policy implications of the principles set forth in the declaration. This companion text was divided into ten sections, each of which began with the phrase "All efforts should be made," which could be construed as an exhortation or even a normative obligation, but not as a statement of intent. The first section treated numerous raw materials issues, including measures for the recovery, exploitation, and marketing of resources by the producer countries themselves, including producers associations; a link between the prices of imports and exports (implying some system of indexation of commodities prices); and the creation of a system of buffer stocks to guarantee more stable commodities prices and improvement of the system of trade preferences for developing country exports. For the most part these were of course matters that had been raised without success at UNCTAD II and UNCTAD III. This was equally true of many of the other measures discussed in the succeeding sections: Third World participation in talks on reform of the international monetary system; increasing the net transfer of real resources, in part through a link between the issuance of SDRs and grants to development; debt renegotiation; efforts to stimulate industrialization; and the transfer of technology. The proposal to "formulate, adopt, and implement an international code of conduct" to regulate multinational corporations was a concern emphasized in nonaligned documents (more than in Group of 77 platforms) as was the chapter on assistance in the exercise of sovereignty over natural resources. Both groupings had regularly called for special measures in favor of the least developed countries, which was the subject of the final chapter of the Program of Action. The ensemble of ideas and policy goals was familiar. The function of the NIEO resolutions was to give greater saliency to these long unsatisfied Third World grievances.

Neither the letter nor the spirit of these texts was congenial to the U.S. government. Once the Third World draft texts were circulated, the United States abandoned its "constructive waiting" by characterizing the proposed resolutions as overambitious, unspecific, and unlikely to be adopted without revision. The clash between the U.S. and Third World positions was well illustrated by the speeches delivered during the Session by Kissinger and Boumediene.

The latter, as initiator of the session, gave the equivalent of a keynote address for the Third World. His central point was that the developing countries considered the existing economic order "as unjust and outmoded as the colonial order from which it originated," because "all the command levers of the world economy are in the hands of a minority of highly developed countries . . . [which] determines by itself the distribution of world resources as a function of its own hierarchy of needs."[8] The decisions taken by the oil-exporting countries were a step toward Third World control over certain of these levers of command. Now the industrial powers must grant as a general principle the right of the developing states to exercise control over their natural resources; otherwise there could be no cooperation at all between North and South. For its part, the Third World was demonstrating its "categorical refusal of the passive role to which the existing system seeks to reduce the immense majority of peoples." The question before the international system was whether the developed states were now willing to cooperate in a serious endeavor to promote Third World economic development.

Kissinger, on the contrary, saw nothing fundamentally wrong with the existing international economic system. He pointed instead at Third World political attitudes. The problem was not a global cleavage between North and South, but rather the Third World's adoption of a "politics of pressure and threats."[9] Indeed, Kissinger contended, the "notion of the northern rich and the southern poor has been shattered" by recent events (presumably OPEC revenues). A Third World strategy of banding together for radical change could only endanger the prospect of Western technical and financial assistance. The secretary of state simply ignored the items in the proposed resolutions other than to criticize producer associations and commodities agreements.

The gap between Boumediene's and Kissinger's conceptions could hardly have been greater. They were diametrically opposed on the basic rules of the game of North-South economic (and political) exchanges. Each demanded a fundamental revision of the other's position. For Boumediene, structural change was a prerequisite for North-South cooperation; for Kissinger, cooperation was feasible only if the Third World exhibited political moderation.

So long as the prevailing system was not seriously challenged, the United States was disposed to cooperate. This was the gist of a counterproposal to the NIEO resolutions that the United States introduced as the Special Session drew toward its scheduled conclusion at the end of April. The U.S. proposal set forth some specific aid commitments that the United States was willing to make, but otherwise barely addressed the issues raised in the Group of 77 draft resolution. The U.S. text could not be plausibly defended as a revised version of the resolutions that had been under discussion for the previous three weeks; rather it appeared suspiciously like an attempt to buy them off. The Third World delegations did not appreciate this ploy, and promptly tabled the U.S. counterproposal. Upon the subsequent adoption of the NIEO resolutions essentially as originally drafted by the Group of 77, Ambassador Scali was moved to protest against a Third World "steamroller."[10]

Notwithstanding Scali's talent for memorable phrases, the Sixth Special Session was neither an amorphous glob nor a steamroller. Rather it was an opportunity for the developing states to focus attention upon their analysis of what was at stake in the systemic crisis opened by the OPEC price action. Periods of crisis frequently serve to raise consciousness of social or political problems. The Third World previously had not been able to force the issue of development to the very top of the international agenda. Convocation of the Special Session achieved this goal. What the Third World had previously achieved, however, was sufficient organizational cohesion to exploit the session to its fullest potential. It was this growing diplomatic force that the United States encountered.

The Sixth Special Session carried out two of the tasks that international organizations can perform in world politics: the provision of information and the formation of general norms. The presentation and adoption of the NIEO resolutions conveyed a political message about the evolution of Third World thinking that the developed states had been reluctant to receive. It set forth some norms that were bound to influence further discussions of the international economic system. The Third World was perfectly well aware that General Assembly resolutions have no binding effect, but they exercised their majority power in the interest of systemic consciousness raising.

The passage of the NIEO resolutions established neither a new order nor even a new idea. But they gave a new rhetorical force and political salience to the Third World's longstanding claim of a right to development. As the British ambassador to the United Nations put it, the new texts obliged everyone to reassess existing global economic relationships. They represented a declaratory act on the part of the developing states by which all states were summoned to turn to the task of development. The resolutions documented the severity of the cleavage between North and South, making it more difficult to ignore poverty as an issue in international politics. All of this was positive so far as the Third World was concerned. The Special Session had a further impact upon the dynamics of Third World organizational activity. As an undeniable manifestation of the Third World's ability to act cohesively in the face of a systemic crisis, it strengthened the resolve of the developing states to maintain concerted pressure upon the system.

Politically, therefore, the Third World emerged from the Special Session with a clear mobilizational theme—the New International Economic Order—and a strong sense of unity. They exhibited during the session a sense of political confidence that carried over into the succeeding period. The challenge before the Third World coalition now was to transform the exhortations of the NIEO resolutions into concrete acts. The developing states harbored no illusions about the difficulty of this task, but they emerged from the Special Session with the political will to persevere.

ENERGY VERSUS DEVELOPMENT—THE
BATTLE OF THE AGENDA

Perseverance took the form of a sustained diplomatic campaign in four different arenas over the year that followed the Special Session. Some of this follow-up activity occurred at the next regular session of the General Assembly and in other UN institutions, notably the United Nations Industrial Development Organization (UNIDO). A second effort was carried out in the nonaligned framework. The third was within OPEC to guarantee the OPEC-Third World relationship. Finally, a critical battle was engaged in a new arena created by a French initiative that eventually produced the Conference on International Economic Cooperation (CIEC). The necessity to act coherently on a variety of fronts indicated that North-South relations were entering a more intense phase, which constituted a further test of the Third World's political and organizational capacities.

The essential objective of the Third World in the aftermath of the Sixth Special Session was to initiate some kind of process of implementation. This could only be a long, demanding task, given the existing international economic structures and the distribution of power that lay behind them. It implied multilateral North-South negotiations, individual and collective initiatives by the developing states, the eventual creation of new international institutions (for example, in the field of commodity trade regulation), and persistent political pressure to give weight to the interests of the Third World. The General Assembly was the logical place to renew the pressure, and the twenty-ninth session from September through December 1974 was particularly tumultuous.

The normal rotation of the Assembly presidency had brought the office around to an African state, and the OAU had designated Algeria's Foreign Minister Bouteflika as its candidate. With Bouteflika as presiding officer and the Third World generally in an assertive mood, the stage was set for political fireworks. The detonator, however, was in the hands of the North. A conciliatory attitude toward Third World interests would defuse tensions, while an intransigent stand promised to be explosive. As the session opened, considerable attention was focused on the possibility of a more accommodating U.S. policy after the resignation of President Nixon.

The new president, Gerald Ford, chose the opening of the General Assembly for his first major address on foreign affairs. Ford, however, had no intention of changing policy. He simply pushed the detonator by informing the Assembly that the United States still considered the energy question to be the essential problem of the international economy. The consumer nations, he declared, were confronted with "production restrictions, artificial pricing, and the prospect of ultimate bankruptcy," a scenario for global disaster in which OPEC would be victimized along with everyone else. In a further speech on energy a few days later, Ford reiterated his fear of global depression and the "breakdown of world order and safety" if OPEC did not relent. Secretary Kissinger, also addressing the General Assembly, pursued the same line of attack in enunciating a new law of political dynamics: "What has gone up by political decision can be reduced by political decision." Neither Ford nor Kissinger referred to the NIEO resolutions at all, unless by allusion when the former warned the General Assembly against the "tyranny of the majority."[11] Whether the new president was Nixonian or Madisonian, it was quite clear that he was not initiating a new policy toward the Third World.

So long as the United States remained fixed upon the priority of oil, there was no chance for serious consideration of the Third World propositions for structural economic reforms. The virtual refusal to acknowledge the existence of the NIEO resolutions was particularly galling to Algeria's Boumediene, who summed up the sentiment of Third World frustration in a diplomatic note to Secretary-General Waldheim:

> The majority of the developed countries have, in the final analysis, learned nothing from the debates of the Special Session and persist in wanting to regulate the problems . . . outside the framework of the principles enunciated in the Declaration.[12]

The Third World reaction was to mount a political campaign in the General Assembly to reassert its own determination to be recognized.

Three issues epitomized this campaign. The first was South Africa. The Third World coalition voted to reject the credentials of the South African delegation on the grounds that it was not representative of the black majority of that country. On the basis of this vote (98-23-14), Bouteflika suspended South Africa's participation in the Assembly proceedings (in the past, other presiding officers had interpreted such votes as rebukes to apartheid but not as a warrant for exclusion from the Assembly). The second issue was another perennial question, the Arab-Israeli dispute. Here the Assembly voted (105-4-20) for the first time to allow the Palestine Liberation Organization (PLO) to present its point of view directly to the General Assembly. Bouteflika chose to accord PLO President Yasir Arafat all the honors normally reserved for visiting heads of state to the dismay of Israel and its supporters. Both these matters were of course long-standing sources of tension; in each instance the Third World insisted upon exercising its majority in ways that the U.S. government strongly disapproved.

The third issue involved adoption of a document entitled Charter of Economic Rights and Duties of States. This text was a Third World initiative, first proposed by Mexico's President Luis Echeverria at UNCTAD III in 1972. A working group composed of both developed and developing states met on four occasions in 1973 and 1974 to draft a document designed to serve as a basic code of international economic conduct. For the developing states, the project constituted an attempt to define a body of legal norms that would protect and assist the poor states in their developmental efforts. By the summer of 1974, agreement had been reached on numerous provisions, but the most controversial matters remained under dispute. These included first and foremost nationalization and indemnification policy, producer associations, and preferential trade agreements—in other words, the gut issues of North-South relations.[13]

The question before the developing states became whether or not to push the document through to a vote. The Group of 77 decided to force the question, judging that continued discussions were unlikely to advance the state of agreement very much further. The 77 composed a draft that incorporated all the points of agreement reached by the working group, and added their propositions on the issues in dispute. This draft was then submitted to the developed states for comment, and revised to take account of some of their objections. At this point the developing countries incorporated the text of the charter into General Assembly Resolution 3281 (XXIX), while most of the industrial states urged a continuation of the drafting negotiations. The United States argued for reconsideration of the proposed text on the grounds that "an agreed Charter would be preferable to one that was meaningless without the agreement of those countries which might be small in number but whose significance in international economic relations could not be ignored."[14] This clash over the adoption of the charter was indicative of the stalemate in North-South relations at the end of 1974. Those small in number were little moved by the economic ideas of those large in number. For the latter, the charter represented an additional increment of legitimization for change; for the former, it was a further reason to defend the economic status quo.

The passage of the charter resolution was then another showdown between voting power and economic power. The December vote was 120-6-10. Joining the United States in opposition were Belgium, Denmark, West Germany, Luxemburg, and Great Britain, while most of the other industrial states abstained.* The notion that the charter was "meaningless" without the consent of the economically powerful was consistent with the unyielding attitude that the United States had adopted at the beginning of the session. The Third World determination to place its preferences on the record rather than to negotiate fruitlessly was consistent with the mood of Third World assertiveness that characterized the entire twenty-ninth session. As at the Special Session eight months earlier, the Third World continued to use the United Nations as a vehicle to deliver a message about the need for new norms supportive of development. By the same token, the developing states conveyed information about their political cohesion, namely, that the coalition was holding solid in pursuit of some kind of breakthrough in North-South relations.

---

*Austria, Canada, France, Ireland, Israel, Italy, Japan, Netherlands, Norway, and Spain.

"Solidarity" from the point of view of the Third World was "tyranny of the majority" from the point of view of the U.S. government. Ambassador Scali reproached the Third World again for the exercise of its majority, warning that the offended minority "may in fact be a practical majority, in terms of its capacity to support this organization and implement its decisions."[15] Such veiled threats merely raised tensions higher and higher. By the end of 1974, the mood of North-South confrontation was stronger than ever.

The problem was not a tyrannical majority riding roughshod over a beleaguered West as Scali would have it. It was the urgent need to address seriously and directly the Third World protest against its economic condition. The repeated demonstrations of Third World unity during the 1974 General Assembly session made it clear that the developing states were determined to maintain a common front in the face of Northern intransigence on the energy/development issue.

For the Third World it was critical that this show of unity remain visible outside the General Assembly also. As the West, and particularly the United States, continued to focus upon oil, OPEC remained at the very center of the confrontation. Whatever its condemnation of OPEC's collective policies, the United States retained close relations with various OPEC members, most notably with the biggest producer state of all, Saudi Arabia. The extensive role of U.S. oil companies in the development and management of Saudi Arabia's enormous resources coupled with the Saudi monarchy's fervent anticommunism had effected an intricate network of political and economic ties between the two states. The Saudis furthermore were awash in petrodollars, which were flowing in much more rapidly than the country's administrative infrastructure could absorb. Much of this wealth was being promptly recycled in the West, which made the Saudis more receptive than ever to Western cries of alarm. Given Saudi Arabia's weight within OPEC councils, the organization was far from immune to U.S. pressure for a cutback in prices. The more radical OPEC members were sensitive to the potential consequences of internal division. They further feared that a crack in OPEC ranks would bring about the disintegration of the larger Third World coalition.

By the same token, the OPEC governments had to be attentive to their relations with the Third World oil importers. They could not rule out a Third World backlash so long as there was little concrete progress in North-South relations. Without evidence that the OPEC gains could be transformed into more general Third World gains through the kinds of measures envisaged in the NIEO resolutions, the emergence of a countercurrent was always possible. The idea of some kind of "tripartite" forum on energy—that is to say, OPEC, Northern consumers, and Southern consumers—was in the air during autumn 1974, and the OPEC radicals viewed this as a maneuver to divide the Third World coalition.*

---

*The idea was first suggested by Saudi Arabia's Oil Minister Cheikh Zaki Yamani in

Conversely, a renewed show of support for OPEC by the Third World oil importers would not only undermine the tripartite strategy but also shore up OPEC's internal unity. A dual imperative thus was emerging for OPEC by the end of the year: maintain its own cohesion and reinforce the OPEC-Third World common front.

Once again Algeria took the lead in defining a strategy capable of achieving these goals. The Algerian government proposed an unprecedented OPEC summit conference. It sought to close ranks within OPEC by reconfirming at the highest level that the OPEC states would defend their own policies as the vanguard of a larger Third World movement for economic development. Saudi Arabia was cool to the proposal, arguing that a summit would escalate tensions, but eventually concurred. The summit conference was scheduled for March 1975, shortly after two other Third World conferences already on the diplomatic calendar for February. The combination of these three meetings provided a political framework suitable to the evolving diplomatic situation.

The first of these three conferences was a nonaligned initiative that had been organized to permit definition of a common strategy on raw materials. The nonaligned group extended invitations to all the developing countries, in effect transforming the forum into a Group of 77 meeting; the practical collaboration between the two Third World groupings was thereby further accentuated.* This joint conference, held in Dakar, Senegal, approved a motion introduced by Algeria affirming the solidarity of the Third World oil importers with their OPEC brethren. The Dakar Declaration insisted upon the principle of addressing raw materials issues globally, that is to say, the inadmissibility of discussions on oil alone. Indeed, the central theme of the Dakar Declaration was the desirability of the creation of additional Third World producer associations, not only to ensure equitable commodities prices but to enhance the general bargaining power of the developing countries. By setting forth OPEC as a model, the Dakar Declaration was a politically significant reassertion of Third World cohesion.

A week after the raw materials conference, the second meeting opened in Algiers. This was a Group of 77 conference organized in accordance with the practice of meeting to prepare for UN negotiations. In this instance the meeting was directed toward the second general conference of UNIDO, which was

---

August 1974. A more concrete proposal was then advanced in October 1974 by the new French President Valery Giscard d'Estaing. Giscard viewed the proposed conference as a more conciliatory alternative to the U.S. approach of grouping the Northern consumer states into a bloc. Yet the sole focus on energy issues and the notion of three representative groups made it suspect to states like Algeria.

*Sixty-eight states officially participated, of which 57 normally attended nonaligned meetings. Another dozen from the ranks of the Group of 77 were present as observers. The overall participation was thus actually less than at the September 1973 nonaligned summit, but nevertheless substantial.

scheduled for March 1975. The issue of industrialization was somewhat peripheral to the ongoing maneuvers on oil and raw materials, but it was unquestionably a major component in the perspective of a NIEO. The Algiers meeting therefore served notice that the developing countries continued to hold the Sixth Special Session resolutions as the point of departure for their expectations regarding industrial development.

The Group of 77 adopted a platform for the UNIDO general conference that constituted a test case of Northern intentions. The Group set as its critical objective the transformation of UNIDO into a specialized agency with a statute equivalent to that of UNESCO or the World Health Organization. Since its creation in 1966, UNIDO had remained an extremely modest institution without the financial resources or the organizational autonomy necessary to achieve much impact. In other words of its executive director, Abdelrahman Khane (an Algerian who had formerly served as secretary-general of OPEC and who had only recently assumed the UNIDO post at the time of the Group of 77 conference), the organization had "done too many little things in too dispersed a fashion."[16] The platform adopted in Algiers called for UNIDO's renovation in the following terms:

> The new division of industrial activities envisaged in the New International Economic Order should permit all the developing countries to industrialize with the aid of an effective international institution. . . . It is therefore necessary to enlarge the attributions and field of activities of the UNIDO and . . . to develop substantially its autonomy and resources. . . . Toward this end, it is recommended that UNIDO be transformed into a specialized agency.[17]

The insistence upon the NIEO resolutions and upon the creation of effective developmental institutions demonstrated that the Third World coalition intended to maintain its pressure upon the North in every available forum.*

After these two conferences and on the eve of the OPEC summit, President Giscard d'Estaing announced that France was inviting a group of representative states to a "preparatory meeting for an international conference on energy problems." The participants were to be the United States, the European Economic Community (as a single delegation), Japan, Saudi Arabia, Iran, Algeria, Venezuela, India, Brazil, and Zaire. Of the Third World invitees, Saudi Arabia

---

*During the general conference in Lima a month later, the Group of 77 stood by the platform adopted in Algiers. There was considerable effort to reach consensus upon a revised version of this document, but the issue of upgrading the institutional status of UNIDO remained a stumbling block. Unable to reach consensus, the conference proceeded to a vote. The developed states attached numerous reservations to various provisions of the Lima Declaration and several abstained in the final vote. Only the United States voted against the document (82-1-7).

(which in fact had proposed exactly this list of countries several months earlier) and Iran immediately announced that they would attend the preparatory meeting. This was the diplomatic situation as the OPEC summit opened in Algiers on March 4, 1975.

The political task of the summit was to define a position that could reconcile Saudi Arabia's desire for a more conciliatory stance toward the North with Algeria's concern to make OPEC the spearhead of the Third World. Algeria was ready to modify its position on prices so long as OPEC forcefully defended the larger concept of the New International Economic Order. Similarly, Algeria accepted the utility of a dialogue with the industrial countries so long as this was not limited to "energy problems" as the French proposal stipulated*—for Algeria the definition of the agenda remained crucial. Algeria would make a gesture toward the Saudi conception of global solidarity in return for a firm reiteration of OPEC solidarity with the other developing countries.

This blending of Saudi and Algerian concerns underlay the communique issued by the OPEC heads of state at the conclusion of their meeting. Their statement began by emphasizing that "the basic premises of this declaration belong in the context of the decisions taken at the Sixth Special Session of the United Nations General Assembly." The heads of state vigorously defended OPEC's pricing policies, but they nevertheless "declared themselves ready to negotiate the terms of a stabilization of the price of oil." They agreed to the principle of an international conference of developed and developing countries, but affirmed that "the agenda of such a conference can in no case be limited to the issue of energy." Other appropriate agenda items were specified to include raw materials, reform of the international monetary system, and international cooperation in behalf of development. OPEC pledged its own financial support to various developmental measures, insisting however that parallel to these OPEC commitments "the developed countries must contribute to the progress and development of the developing countries" through the "complete implementation of the Program of Action adopted by the United Nations General Assembly at the Sixth Special Session." The summit document concluded that:

> The sovereigns and heads-of-state solemnly agree to commit their countries to initiatives designed to open the way to a new era of cooperation in international relations. It is up to the developed countries . . . to respond to the initiatives of the developing countries.[18]

---

*A previous OPEC ministerial meeting had already issued a declaration to this effect, but it was not at all clear on the eve of the summit that Saudi Arabia and Iran, having accepted the French invitation, felt bound to insist upon this point.

The communique met the summit's political goals. It alleviated Saudi fears that OPEC was on a dangerous collision course with the West. Both the position on prices and the willingness to enter into a negotiation process gave satisfaction to the Saudis. At the same time, Saudi Arabia associated itself with Algeria's foremost political concern, namely, that the negotiation extend beyond the single issue of energy. These understandings cemented OPEC's internal unity, while the commitment to the NIEO program unequivocally placed OPEC on record in behalf of structural economic change, reinforcing the larger OPEC-Third World front. The combination in rapid succession of the Dakar nonaligned conference, the Algiers 77 conference, and the OPEC summit gave the Third World fresh diplomatic momentum that forced North-South relations to a new plateau in the following months.

The turning point came shortly after the preparatory meeting that France organized in April 1975 as the first step toward a new North-South forum. As indicated above, President Giscard d'Estaing was seeking to break the stalemate that had existed since the end of 1973 by virtue of U.S. insistence upon oil and Third World insistence upon development. Giscard's move was a diplomatic gamble. In inviting the key actors to meet "to fix the date, the composition, and the agenda of a [future] conference," Giscard was betting on the dynamics of such a meeting to bring pressure on both the U.S. and Third World delegations to settle upon a formula capable of initiating a dialogue.[19] Giscard lost his gamble, but did not completely lose his shirt.

The preparatory meeting rested upon a diplomatic ambiguity that France hoped to manipulate into a settlement. The precise formulation of the nature of the eventual conference to be prepared was as follows: "a conference . . . to examine the problems of energy to which are linked numerous aspects of international economic relations." This wording satisfied the United States in designating "the problems of energy" as the appropriate subject. In leaving the door slightly ajar regarding other "aspects of international economic relations," the phrase at least implied the possibility of examining a broader agenda. Giscard presumably calculated that the Third World oil importers (represented by India, Brazil, and Zaire), which like the North were also feeling the pinch of oil prices, could be persuaded to support the concept of a conference in which energy issues would have the highest priority. In turn, the United States would agree to the inclusion of other issues on the agenda. In practice, both sides proved less willing to compromise than Giscard anticipated.

The United States pursued an unbending policy of energy first. Just before the preparatory meeting opened, Assistant Secretary of State Thomas Enders declared that the industrial states were participating in Paris in order to "hasten OPEC's demise." His colleague, Under Secretary of State Charles Robinson revised this remark with a less inflammatory formulation of U.S. aims, but he observed that the meeting had "more than enough to handle with the energy problems."[20] The preparatory meeting ran for nine days without any significant change in the U.S. position, which steadfastly remained "energy first." The United States did accept the addition of other matters to the proposed agenda, but stood by the notion that energy issues must be preeminent. The political question became whether the seven developing states would acquiesce to this condition.

The developing states negotiated as a single unit throughout the nine days. Neither the OPEC non-OPEC distinction nor internal OPEC differences came into play to undermine this common front. Both sides altered their initial bargaining positions somewhat as the EEC delegation labored to narrow the gap between the U.S. and Third World conceptions of a suitable agenda. The initial draft agenda proposed by the Third World group called for a discussion of raw materials, energy sources figuring as one item among others, whereas the first Northern proposal did not explicitly designate raw materials as a subject at all. The Third World submitted a revised draft in which energy became the first of five equally important topics to be treated by the future conference. Upon U.S. insistence, the industrial states proposed further revisions, the effect of which was to accord the highest priority to the topic of energy. The developing states refused to accept these modifications, pointing out that the intent of their proposal was to establish "an agenda which would permit the conference to give equal attention to the problems interesting the developed and the developing countries."[21]

The mutual determination of the United States, on the one hand, and the seven Third World representatives, on the other, to stand by their divergent emphases brought the meeting to an impasse. The talks ended without agreement, a diplomatic setback for France, a deadlock so far as the United States was concerned, but something of a victory for the Third World coalition. So far as the developing countries were concerned, the stakes in Paris were the durability of the coalition as it had stood since the Sixth Special Session. The head of Zaire's delegation declared, for example, "certain industrialized countries came to this preparatory meeting thinking that they were capable of imposing an agenda and dividing us, but I am pleased to see that we were and remain united." Algeria's delegation leader made the same point: "The front of developing countries resisted every attempt to cut the group of seven in two. The efforts to 'trilateralize' the conference thus failed."[22] To the extent that the developing countries perceived the Paris talks as a challenge to their solidarity, the stalemate was a diplomatic victory for them.

The Third World representatives in Paris wielded a power that was new for the developing countries. The forum was different from the United Nations, and their stand had an immediate impact that General Assembly resolutions lacked. They were able to exercise the kind of blocking power that had previously been the province of the industrial states. The power of the seven was rendered credible by the political groundwork laid at the Dakar and Algiers conferences. Their refusal to yield thwarted French and U.S. objectives, and shifted the pressure for accommodation back toward the United States. In turn, the United States began to question the assumption that the coalition would crack under pressure.

The U.S. decision makers drew the conclusion after Paris that "the conservative members of OPEC were going to join the radical ones in bidding for the political leadership of the Third World."[23] Not only had the U.S. hard line failed to crack OPEC or the Group of 77 but it also had encouraged the predominance of the radical wing of the coalition. As Roger Hansen has written, "As long as the United States responded negatively to almost all developing country requests in almost all international conferences, the moderates within the Group of 77 had no hand to play."[24] Kissinger now concluded that this was counterproductive. It was in the U.S. interest to allow the moderates to reenter the bidding.

About a month after the collapse of the Paris talks, Kissinger declared that "Our thinking on the issue of raw materials . . . has moved forward."[25] The United States was now ready to envisage an international conference to discuss a broad range of North-South issues. Such a conference could be organized, as the Third World had proposed, into three or four commissions of equal status. This shift in U.S. policy opened the way to the North-South Conference, which eventually got underway in December 1975. More generally it constituted the first major turning point in North-South relations since the oil revolution.

The Third World succeeded, therefore, in bringing about a change in U.S. foreign policy in the spring of 1975. The U.S. policy shift was tactical, to be sure, but it was attributable to a coherent Third World strategy of solidarity. The durability of the Third World coalition placed the United States in a diplomatically untenable position from which it was obliged to retreat. The Third World triumph, limited as it was to an essentially procedural issue—the agenda of North-South negotiations—was nevertheless of considerable significance. It was the first time that the joint action of the developing countries had effected such a change. It pushed North-South relations to a new plateau by virtue of the explicit recognition that the international economic crisis entailed the entire issue of the relationship between rich and poor.

THE SEVENTH SPECIAL SESSION

The power to stalemate a conference, even the power to shape the agenda, was not equivalent to the power to effect structural change in the international economic system. The developing countries recognized that innovations in international trade and augmentation of the flow of developmental resources implied negotiated agreements with the North. Once the United States indicated its willingness to show a new "understanding for the concerns of the developing world," the Third World coalition faced some tactical decisions.[26] How should it respond to the U.S. overture? What constituted a reasonable test of U.S. intentions?

Kissinger's declarations directly concerned the Paris negotiation, but the more imminent forum was the Seventh Special Session of the General Assembly, which was scheduled for September 1975. Like its predecessor, the Seventh Special Session was a Third World initiative but, contrary to the Sixth, it had been inscribed on the diplomatic calendar for some time. The idea for a session "exclusively devoted to the problems of development" originated at the Algiers Nonaligned Summit and was approved by the General Assembly in December 1973.* After 18 months of heated confrontation on development issues, the session now loomed as a major event in North-South relations.

The nonaligned Bureau passed the preparations for the Seventh Special Session on to the Group of 77. This approach was consistent with the division of labor between the two Third World organizational bodies, the Group of 77 customarily laying the groundwork for specific North-South bargaining encounters. At the same time, the nonaligned group scheduled a conference of foreign ministers to be held in Lima just before the UN session. The Lima meeting was to act upon numerous issues before the nonaligned group, including examination of the position to be defended at the Special Session.

In preparing the session, the Group of 77 worked at the level of regular Third World delegations in Geneva and New York without recourse to a special conference. The developing countries considered that the string of recent conferences on development sufficed to allow the drafting of a suitable Third World position paper. In August 1975 they submitted an Exposé of the Position of the Group of 77, which shortly became the basic working document of the Seventh Special Session. This text set forth once again the major Third World proposals regarding international trade, developmental aid, monetary reform, and other matters. The document nonetheless was drafted with great concern for the sensibility of the United States on several key issues. It did not, for example, refer to such themes as sovereignty over natural resources, the promotion of producer associations, or control over the activities of multinational corporations. It reflected an undeniable effort to strike a relatively moderate tone so as to encourage a conciliatory attitude in the North.

This Group of 77 document was the first sign of a redistribution of influence within the Third World coalition. After an extended period of leadership by the more radical wing of the coalition, a new consensus was forming in the center. Many Third World states strongly desired a period of détente in North-South relations after the long period of tension. The moderates, whose margin of maneuver was slim during the period of U.S. intransigence, now enjoyed some

---

*The citation is from the resolutions of the Fourth Nonaligned Summit. The relevant General Assembly text is Resolution 3712 (XXVIII) of December 17, 1973, which specifies that the session should examine "world development and international economic cooperation."

diplomatic leeway again. To some extent, the jurisdiction of the Group of 77, in which such states as Iran, Brazil, the Philippines, and Pakistan (none of whom was a member of the nonaligned group) had a major voice, contributed to the moderation of the position paper. Both the more inclusive membership of the Group of 77 and its more specific function as a negotiating agent partially explained the tone of the Third World document, but the fact remained that the new wind from the United States was trimming the sails of the radicals. The resurgence of the moderates was confirmed during the session itself.

Despite the relative moderation of the Group of 77 Exposé, there remained considerable distance between it and the U.S. position as unveiled by the new U.S. ambassador, Daniel Patrick Moynihan, on the opening day of the Special Session. The much awaited new look took the form of an ensemble of concrete proposals that Moynihan distinguished from the "slogans" and "sterile discussion" regarding a New International Economic Order. These measures included the establishment of an expanded compensatory financing facility within the International Monetary Fund to protect the developing countries against drastic fluctuations in their export receipts; various methods of improving the access of the developing countries to Western capital markets and technology and a pledge to increase the funds of the World Bank's International Finance Corporation; commitments to negotiations on tariff reductions and other measures to facilitate Third World trade; programs to ensure global food supplies and augment agricultural production; the creation of producer-consumer associations for each basic commodity and support for a World Bank effort to increase raw materials production; and specific attention to the needs of the poorest countries, notably through increased financial support to the International Development Association. The ensemble of proposals and financial commitments impressed many Third World delegations as a substantial step toward progress.

Other delegations, however, were skeptical, pointing out that the U.S. statement ignored several key Third World proposals and remained very comfortably within the institutional and conceptual bounds of the existing economic order. The Group of 77 paper, they observed, included proposals for an internationally regulated Integrated Program of Commodities (which went well beyond compensatory financing), for indexation of raw materials prices, for a link between the issuing of SDRs and developmental credits, for a commitment to 1 percent of gross national product as developmental aid, and for debt alleviation, among other ideas. As negotiations got underway to narrow the distance between the two policy statements, a debate occurred within the Third World coalition as to the nature of an adequate agreement.

The more radical states argued in essence that the industrial powers "had not offered enough substantial measures to correct present and past injustices."[27] The moderate states responded, as Secretary-General of UNCTAD Gamani Corea later summed it up, that there was "quite a change of atmosphere" in the U.S. attitude that the Third World would be mistaken to ignore. The United

States in turn eased the way to agreement by reorganizing the presentation of its policy paper so as to conform to the six headings of the Group of 77 document. This made it clear that there was little disagreement regarding four headings: science and technology, industrialization, food and agriculture, and reorganization of the United Nations' social and economic structures. The sticking points still concerned major issues, but the will to come to agreement was stimulated further by this gesture. The radical states were obliged to accept the emerging consensus in behalf of an accord.

The final accord as expressed in Resolution 3362 (S-VII) was more symbolic than substantive, for the parties in large measure agreed to disagree on the thorniest issues. This was true, for example, with regard to a fixed percentage of gross national product for aid, the link between SDRs and development finance, and indexation, to all of which the United States lodged formal reservations in the final meeting of the negotiating committee. On other key issues, the text of Resolution 3362 was more tentative than the original Group of 77 draft, promising the *study* of ideas (like the Integrated Program of Commodities) that the Third World had proposed for *implementation*. Diverse editorial changes made the text more acceptable to the United States; for example a reference to the "obligatory character" of an international code for the transfer of technology was deleted, and the reference to a conference on debt alleviation "in 1976" became "as soon as possible." In addition to these specific reservations and revisions, the United States further declared that it had not changed its position on the NIEO resolutions,* the Charter of Economic Rights and Duties, and the Lima Declaration (on UNIDO). Lest there be any misunderstanding, the U.S. delegate specified that the United States "cannot and does not accept any implication that the world is now embarked on the establishment of something called 'the New International Economic Order.'"[29]

The resolution on Development and International Economic Cooperation as unanimously adopted by the General Assembly was the fruit of a dual compromise designed to clear the diplomatic air. It was evidently a compromise between North and South. The industrial states, as led by the United States, made political commitments to act upon a number of problems raised by the developing states, even if the commitment in some instances was solely to study the issue. The developing states accepted numerous revisions of their proposals in order to make agreement possible. Both sides esteemed that the moment had arrived for a breath of détente in their relations. The second compromise was within the Third World coalition. The multiple reservations, dilutions, and

---

*The preamble of the proposed resolution referred to "the New International Economic Order." According to Thomas Enders, the United States tried for eight hours to change "the" to "a." No wonder that the final negotiating committee meeting ended at 3:50 A.M. on September 16, less than 12 hours before the regular General Assembly session was scheduled to begin.[28] (Frank, "U.S. Takes Steps").

deletions effected upon an already moderate Group of 77 document amply explain the misgivings of the more ardent proponents of a new order. They wanted agreement upon radically different structures, not an ensemble of aid pledges. They could see, however, that the political tide was running against them, and they acquiesced to the moderates' strategy. The Third World endorsed the amended resolution as a way of testing U.S.–and Northern–intentions.

Whatever the dissatisfaction of the Third World radicals, the Seventh Special Session was an advance in North-South relations. It was the culmination of the campaign opened by the oil offensive of 1973. The Third World had gained the ground that it had–namely, a genuine recognition of the existence of a development crisis–through solidarity. By the spring of 1975, the North could feel the cutting edge of a solidarity painstakingly honed by Third World conferences and other forms of collective advocacy. The commitment toward the resolution of certain Third World grievances taken at the Seventh Special Session, limited as it was, was the result of the pressure mounted through solidarity.

The solidarity was mobilized largely under the leadership of the radical wing of the Third World coalition. Solidarity cuts both ways, however. The emergence of the moderates toward the end of this period illustrated perfectly the double-edged nature of the weapon of solidarity. It now cut against the radicals, who had little choice but to regroup behind the moderates for the sake of maintaining the common front. The distribution of political influence within the coalition varied according to the overall international conjuncture, and the U.S. policy shift gave the moderates a firmer grip upon how solidarity was wielded.

The Seventh Special Session originated in a nonaligned initiative to terminate two years later under the auspices (insofar as the Third World was concerned) of the Group of 77. The whole process from September 1973 to September 1975 further developed a division of labor between these two Third World groups. The course of events unfolded in a manner consistent with the notion expressed at the Algiers Summit that the "nonaligned countries should act as a catalytic force in the Group of 77."[30] The nonaligned movement contributed to precipitate situations between North and South that created negotiating instances that were the province of the Group of 77.*

This functional differentiation of course had political ramifications, the

---

*Such a division of labor was particularly apparent on the eve of the Seventh Session when the nonaligned foreign ministers, meeting as foreseen in Lima, took no action regarding the session other than to declare that "the nonaligned countries will coordinate their action with the other developing countries."[31] The political significance of the failure to endorse (or otherwise cite) the Group of 77 paper that was concurrently being submitted at the United Nations is open to speculation. It is difficult to ascertain from the accounts of the Lima Conference whether there was a detailed review of the document, but the evidence suggests that there was not. It is clear that the conference devoted much of its

moderates being relatively more influential in the Group of 77 than in the non-aligned movement. It was, however, less the political difference between the two groups than the functional distinction that came into play. As a majority within both groups believed that an agreement should be struck after the evolution in U.S. policy, the Group of 77 carried out this task.

The Seventh Special Session was a milestone in North-South relations, marking the end of a period that demanded a sustained organizational effort on the part of the developing countries. The tandem operation of the nonaligned movement and the Group of 77 enabled the Third World to carry out a diplomatic action that was remarkably coherent in light of the enormous diversity of the developing states. Each organizational apparatus made a distinctive contribution, the former serving as a mobilizer and the latter as a bargainer. Together they gave the Third World an operational capacity in the international system that was definitively registered at the Seventh Session.

A milestone in North-South relations, a landmark in Third World power, the Seventh Special Session remained nonetheless a way station. As Gamani Corea observed, it "resulted essentially in an agreement to negotiate."[32] What Jahangir Amuzegar called the "spirit of the Seventh Special Session" remained to be solidified in the subsequent rounds of bargaining, and this constituted the real test, not only of Northern intentions but also of the durability of Third World power.[33]

NOTES

1. A recurrent theme in Qaddafi's speeches was that the Libyan people had lived for 5,000 years without oil and were ready to do without oil revenues if their national rights were not respected. For a detailed analysis of Libya's key role in the politics of oil, see Hubert Breton, "Le pétrole libyen au service de l'unité arabe?" *Revue Française de Science Politique* 22, no. 6 (December 1972): 1256-75. A useful and more general account is Ruth First, *Libya, The Elusive Revolution* (Baltimore: Penguin Books, 1974), which treats oil policy in chapter 10.

2. One of the earliest analyses to make these points was Taki Rifai, "La crise pétrolière internationale (1970-1971), Essai d'interprétation," *Revue Française de Science Politique* 22, no. 6 (December 1972): 1205-36. The entire number is devoted to the politics of oil.

3. James Akins, "The Oil Crisis: This Time the Wolf Is Here," *Foreign Affairs* 51 (April 1973): 462-90.

attention to other matters (notably a divisive debate over a proposed resolution recommending the expulsion of Israel from the United Nations). It appears nonetheless that there was insufficient enthusiasm to endorse the document but also insufficient support to tamper with it in favor of more radical formulations. The muteness at Lima foreshadowed the divergence between moderates and radicals at the special session itself.

4. *Le Monde*, February 5, 1974.

5. The citation is from the final document of the Bureau meeting, which appears in *Review of International Affairs* 576 (April 5, 1974). Among the specific decisions taken to resolve tensions within the group itself were the designation of a working group of oil importers (Guyana, Sri Lanka, Liberia, and Nepal) to explore means of cushioning the blow of higher prices with the nonaligned members that were oil exporters, and the appointment of a committee to draw up the statutes of a nonaligned solidarity fund.

6. *New York Times*, March 18, 1974.

7. The texts are found in UN Document A/9559, or the 1974 UN *Yearbook*, or Alfred George Moss and Harry N. M. Winton, eds., *A New International Economic Order, Selected Documents 1945-1975* (New York: UNITAR, 1978), pp. 891-900.

8. *Le Monde*, April 12, 1974.

9. *New York Times*, April 16, 1974.

10. *Department of State Bulletin*, May 27, 1974. One should note that the resolutions were adopted without a formal vote, while those states that had reservations about one or another part of the texts were allowed to place these on the record. Most of the developed states voiced some reservations, those of the United States being the most extensive.

11. *New York Times*, September 19 and September 24, 1974.

12. *El Moudjahid*, December 31, 1974, quoting a diplomatic note of October 2, 1974.

13. A thorough account of the drafting of the charter has been presented by the chairman of the working group, Jorge Castaneda, Mexico's ambassador to the United Nations in Geneva, in his article "La Charte des Droits et des Devoirs Economiques, Note sur son processus d'élaboration," *Annuaire Français de Droit International*, 1974, pp. 31-56.

14. *United Nations Yearbook*, 1974, p. 393. The text of the charter appears on pp. 403-7.

15. *New York Times*, December 7, 1974.

16. *El Moudjahid*, February 16-17, 1975.

17. *El Moudjahid*, February 20, 1975.

18. *El Moudjahid*, March 7, 1975.

19. The citation is from the official letter of invitation as published in *Le Monde*, March 4, 1975.

20. *New York Times*, April 8, 1975. In fact the two U.S. diplomats continued to strike different blows during the conference. For Philippe Simonnot of *Le Monde*, Robinson was the "velvet glove" covering Enders' "iron hand." April 29, 1975.

21. The account of the negotiations is based upon a report by Philippe Lemaitre in *Le Monde*, April 20-21, 1975. The citation is from a declaration made by the developing states as reported in *El Moudjahid*, April 17, 1975.

22. *El Moudjahid*, April 17, 1975.

23. The citation is from an interview with Assistant Secretary Enders as reported in Richard S. Frank, "Economic Report: U.S. Takes Steps to Meet Demands of Third World Nations," *National Journal Reports* 7, no. 43 (October 25, 1975): 1481. It is worth recalling the broader international political context of spring 1975. United States policy in Indochina was crumbling to pieces; the situation in southern Africa was changing rapidly as Mozambique approached independence and the struggle for power in Angola intensified. In these circumstances the trend toward radical leadership in North-South politics was particularly distressing to Washington.

24. Roger D. Hansen, "The 'Crisis of Interdependence': Where Do We Go from Here?" in *The U.S. and World Development: Agenda for Action, 1976* edited by Roger D. Hansen, p. 58. (New York: Praeger, 1976).

25. *New York Times*, May 14, 1975.

26. The phrase is from Kissinger's speech of May 13, 1975, ibid.

27. *New York Times*, September 14, 1975. The report named Algeria, Iraq, Libya, Mexico, Syria, and Venezuela "as leaders of the militant faction."

28. Frank, "U.S. Takes Steps," p. 1484.

29. United Nations Document A/AC.176/SR3 as found in *Official Documents of the General Assembly, Seventh Special Session* (Proceedings of the Special Committee).

30. Odette Jankowitsch and Karl P. Sauvant, eds., *The Third World Without Superpowers: The Collected Documents of the Non-Aligned Countries* (Dobbs Ferry, N.Y.: Oceana, 1978), p. 237.

31. *Review of International Affairs* 611 (September 20, 1975), p. 37.

32. Gamani Corea, "UNCTAD and the New International Economic Order," *International Affairs* 53 (April 1977), p. 179.

33. Jahangir Amuzegar, "The North-South Dialogue: From Conflict to Compromise," *Foreign Affairs* 54 (April 1976): 547-62.

5. The Relationship Between the Nonaligned and the 77

By 1975, the nonaligned group had established a regular rhythm of activities: Bureau meetings in the spring, plenary conferences at the end of the summer, occasional ad hoc sessions as circumstances demanded. The practice of an acting presidency provided an adequate means by which to initiate group action on relatively short notice. Modest as these organizational arrangements were, they enabled the nonaligned movement to function as an recognizable actor in the international system.

By comparison, the Group of 77 had a much more amorphous organizational identity. As Jon McLin observed in 1976:

> Although it now has a dozen years of history behind it and a current membership of 110 governments plus the Palestine Liberation Organization, it has no headquarters, secretariat, long-term leadership, or regular staff.[1]

Until 1974 its activity was almost completely derivative from that of UNCTAD, and the Group of 77 was little more than another expression to designate the developing countries.

The intensification of North-South politics in 1974–75 enlarged the operations carried out under the mantle of the Group of 77. The expansion of negotiating tasks led some states to propose more elaborate institutional arrangements for the Group. These organizational issues implied larger political questions regarding the nature of the relationship between the nonaligned group and the 77. The possibility that a more structured Group of 77 might displace the nonaligned grouping as the prime mover in Third World affairs led to some subtle jockeying for political influence within the Third World coalition in 1976. This chapter analyzes the evolution and interaction of the two Third World groupings in the period following the Seventh Special Session.

The future organizational character of the Group of 77 was but one of a number of matters bearing upon the cohesion of the Third World coalition in 1976. Another had to do with Third World participation in the Paris Conference on International Economic Cooperation (discussed in detail in Chapter 6), which began at the end of 1975. The developing countries needed to develop a strategy that would take account of both this new forum and such established channels as UNCTAD whose fourth plenary session came up in May 1976. They sought to pursue this two-tracked negotiation with the North during a period marked by a resurgence of intra-Third World political clashes. Such issues as Western Sahara, the Lebanese civil war, and the struggle for power in Angola all wrought tensions that undermined the credibility of a united Third World presence in international politics. Furthermore, internal strains within OPEC became more pronounced during this period under changing market conditions and constant political pressure. The tendency toward dispersion remained a constant variable with which the coalition had to cope.

THE GROUP OF 77 AND UNCTAD IV

It is necessary first to look more closely at the Group of 77. How did an organization without headquarters, secretariat, staff, bureau, or acting president manage to maintain itself? The answer lay of course in its symbiotic relationship with the United Nations Conference on Trade and Development, an organization founded, after all, because of Third World pressure for development. One will recall that the developing countries first operated under the guise of such a grouping during the preparations for UNCTAD I. Since then the de facto headquarters of the Group of 77 has been in Geneva, the seat of UNCTAD, and its working members have been the regular diplomatic delegations accredited to UNCTAD by the developing countries.

By the same token, UNCTAD personnel have for practical purposes fulfilled the functions of a secretariat for the Group of 77. To be sure the professional personnel of UNCTAD are international civil servants whose job is to serve the needs of all the organization's member-states. Yet the organization itself has been described as an interest articulator for the developing countries,[2] and its secretary-general has always been from a developing country.* Given the pur-

---

*As mentioned in Chapter 2, the first secretary-general was Raul Prebisch of Argentina. He was succeeded by Manuel Perez Guerrero of Venezuela in 1969. Since 1974, Gamani Corea of Sri Lanka has held the post.

poses of UNCTAD, it was natural for the developing countries to rely upon its administrative staff to prepare background papers, documentation, and eventually proposals for their use. No separate staff was required to allow the Group of 77 to operate as a kind of caucus within UNCTAD.

Within this ready-made administrative framework, the Group of 77 merely named a chairman to provide a minimum of leadership. The practice has been to rotate the chairmanship among the three regional groups—Asia, Africa, and Latin America—on a quarterly basis. The regional groups, which have never surrendered their separate identity within the larger grouping, also select chairmen of their own. The chairman of the entire group and the three regional chairmen constitute a bureau of sorts, but the four chairmen are essentially convenors and coordinators. In effect, this provides an informal circle of leaders, "men such as Ambassadors Hortensio Brillantes of the Philippines, Akporode Clark of Nigeria, Kenneth Dadzie of Ghana, Peter Lai of Malyasia, Gabriel Martinez of Argentina, and Herbert Walker of Jamaica."[3] These diplomats based in Geneva have been the effective animators of the Group of 77, all the more so because the Group has rarely convened at a higher political level. In contrast to the nonaligned movement, there has never been a summit meeting of the Group of 77; as has been seen, there were only two ministerial-level meetings from 1964 to 1974— Algiers in 1967 and Lima in 1971.

The 77 has created one standing subsidiary group, the Group of 24 on International Monetary Affairs, which operates in Washington (seat of the International Monetary Fund and the World Bank), and issue-specific ad hoc working groups in Geneva. It also formed a preparatory committee in 1975 and again in 1978 as the plenary sessions of UNCTAD drew near. This committee structure (as constituted in mid-1978) is shown in Figure 5.1. This elaboration of specialized subgroups in Geneva has, since 1975, refined the operational capacity of the Group of 77, but the entire operation has remained dependent upon the organizational infrastructure of UNCTAD.

Although its main base of operations has been Geneva, the Group has reproduced itself in other diplomatic centers where it has adapted its organizational practices to local circumstances. In New York, for example, the chairman holds office for a year, and subgroups have been established prior to the special sessions to draft position papers; the Group's meetings are frequently closed to UN secretariat personnel, contrary to the practice in Geneva. These variations reflect different political situations in the two sites, but they illustrate as well the absence of a standardized organizational practice. The activation of further "chapters" in Rome (seat of the Food and Agriculture Organization) and in Paris (seat of UNESCO) has not been accompanied by the creation of any organ of centralized direction. McLin reports that "there is remarkably little communication among the 'chapters' in various cities except through national channels, and personal rivalries . . . put obstacles even in the way of that."[4] The

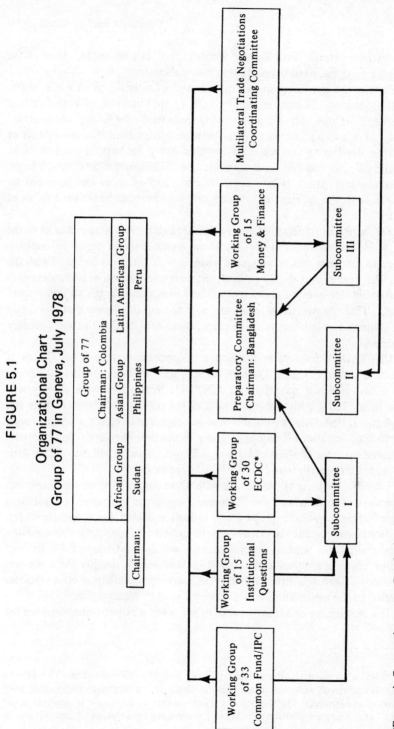

FIGURE 5.1

Organizational Chart
Group of 77 in Geneva, July 1978

Group of 77			
Chairman: Colombia			
	African Group	Asian Group	Latin American Group
Chairman:	Sudan	Philippines	Peru

Working Group of 33 Common Fund/IPC

Working Group of 15 Institutional Questions

Working Group of 30 ECDC*

Preparatory Committee Chairman: Bangladesh

Working Group of 15 Money & Finance

Multilateral Trade Negotiations Coordinating Committee

Subcommittee I

Subcommittee II

Subcommittee III

*Economic Cooperation among Developing Countries.
Source: Adapted from chart prepared by UNCTAD secretariat.

Group in other words resembles an umbrella that can be raised wherever the developing countries need to coordinate their policies.

Despite the proliferation of chapters and of activities in its name, therefore, the Group of 77 has functioned with a bare minimum of organizational apparatus of its own. More than an entity unto itself, the Group has operated virtually as a component part of the universal international organizations of which the developing countries are member-states. Its very originality as an international actor has lain precisely in its *lack* of differentiation from the larger structures within which it has acted. For a group of states characterized by economic need, the sparseness of Group of 77 institutions has made a virtue of necessity.

Yet, as the call upon the Group of 77 became more frequent thanks to the Third World offensive of 1974-75, some member-states began to question whether an umbrella was an adequate weapon with which to do battle with the North. The notion that the 77 could profit from the creation of an autonomous secretariat and/or a more elaborate political directorate began to make some headway. This organizational proposal was one of the issues that the Third World addressed as it began to make preparations for UNCTAD's fourth plenary conference.

UNCTAD IV loomed as the first real opportunity to test the "spirit of the Seventh Special Session." Contrary to the Paris Conference, which was something of an unknown quantity, the UNCTAD institutions were already well broken in by 1976. Although the results of the previous conferences were less than glorious, UNCTAD presumably had the capacity to effect a breakthrough in North-South relations if any negotiating forum did. The developing countries thus geared up their established Group of 77 procedures in order to define their priorities for this fourth round of UNCTAD negotiations.

They began their consultations with three continentwide meetings, and then proceeded to Manila in the Philippines to approve a groupwide negotiating position.* This two-tiered preparatory process reflected the economic differences from one continental subsystem to another. It also acknowledged the political reality of a residual regional identity within the Group of 77. Each of the three subgroups nevertheless arrived in Manila with roughly the same preoccupations. There was little difficulty in reaching a consensus on a platform that reflected the major Third World concerns as of February 1976.

The developing countries agreed to set forth a rather comprehensive list

---

*Each of these preliminary meetings took a slightly different form. The African meeting was organized under the auspices of the Organization of African Unity at the level of ministers of commerce. The Council of the Latin American Economic System met to define the Latin American position. The Asian governments organized an ad hoc meeting in Jakarta.

of policy objectives in the Manila Declaration and Action Program while focusing in practice upon three or four major issue areas for intensive discussion at UNCTAD IV. The comprehensive list enumerated 17 issue areas, all of which had been raised in the running debate of the past two years. The crucial issues were the longstanding question of international commodities policy, the more recent problem of Third World indebtedness, and the multifaceted matter of international transfer of technology. Alongside these substantive matters was a key institutional matter, the future status of UNCTAD itself, which they wished to see recognized as the authoritative international instrument for negotiation on NIEO issues. It was further understood within the Group of 77 that commodities policy would be pursued as the make-or-break issue at UNCTAD IV. Radicals and moderates alike considered action on commodities an urgent and essential component of a new economic order.

A major political concern at Manila was to define the relationship between the Group of 77 and the newly created North-South Conference. Only 19 developing countries were participants in the Paris dialogue.* It made political sense to assure the 77 that the 19 was adequately representing the interests of the larger body of developing states, and it made organizational sense to co-ordinate Third World action in the two forums as effectively as possible. Toward this end, the chairman of the Paris Group of 19, Manuel Perez Guerrero of Venezuela, attended the Manila meeting. As a former secretary-general of UNCTAD (from 1969 to 1974), Perez Guerrero enjoyed the confidence of the 77 as a whole and was especially well suited to serve in this capacity. He delivered a report to the Manila conferees on the early phases of CIEC, and explained that the first joint action of the 19 developing states had been to submit a List of Subjects for Discussion, which was inspired solely by the Platforms of the Group of 77 at the Sixth and Seventh Special Sessions. In turn, the Manila meeting directed that its current Declaration and Program of Action should serve as further guidance for the Third World representatives in Paris.

Beyond these political understandings, it was decided to establish a formal liaison mechanism between the 19 and the 77. The liaison group was to sit in Geneva under the chairmanship of Ambassador Brillantes of the Philippines. It brought together the states that composed the conference bureau in Manila plus the members of the Paris 19 that were not included in that bureau. The 77 directed that the liaison group should "transmit to the Group of 19 such informa-

---

*The 19 Third World participants in CIEC included the 7 that attended the preparatory meetings (Algeria, Brazil, India, Iran, Saudi Arabia, Venezuela, and Zaire) and 12 additional states chosen by the three regional groups: Argentina, Jamaica, Mexico, and Peru; Cameroon, Egypt, Nigeria, and Zambia; Indonesia, Iraq, Pakistan, and Yugoslavia (selected by the Asian group of which it was formally a member, and which already had three representatives among the original seven).

tion and views as the Group of 77 in Geneva or in New York may deem necessary for a more effective participation of the Group of 19 at the Paris Conference."[5] This liaison arrangement was important to intra-Third World relations, but it was also construed to strengthen the hand of the 19 vis-a-vis the North. As one member of the 19, Yugoslavia, interpreted the decision to create the liaison group,

> Manila confirmed that the member-countries of the Group of 19 are as a whole the mandatories of the Group of 77. . . . This not only heightens the responsibilities of the Group of 19 but also strengthens their bargaining power.[6]

A second internal issue discussed at Manila concerned the creation of new Group of 77 institutions. The strongest support for this idea came from the Asian group, and most notably from states like the Philippines, Pakistan, and Iran, which did not belong to the nonaligned group. The Group of 77 was diplomatically more important for these states, and most Asian states relied heavily upon UNCTAD processes in the absence of a regionwide political-economic organization. The Asians proposed the establishment of a permanent secretariat, while the host government proposed to exercise an interim presidency along the lines of the practice in the nonaligned group. The Filipinos likewise proposed an interim committee to be composed of the states that served as the bureau of the conference. The rationale of this package of proposals was to accord the Group of 77 greater autonomy from the UNCTAD secretariat and a short-term decision-making capacity comparable to that of the nonaligned group.

The proposals ran into both political and financial objections. The latter were perfectly straightforward. To staff and operate an independent secretariat would cost considerably more than the symbiosis with UNCTAD (whose secretariat was financed out of the regular UN budget). Many states were unconvinced that the additional investment would yield proportional dividends. The interim presidency and committee did not involve significant costs, but here less overt political misgivings came into play. Such institutions would largely duplicate those of the nonaligned movement—and toward what end? The potential for a future rivalry between two such bureaus was not lost upon the major actors of the nonaligned group. Having long persevered to win approval of the nonaligned Bureau, these states were comfortable with the existing organizational situation. The partisans of Group of 77 institutionalization had to settle for a working group to study the matter of a secretariat further. Nor was an interim committee approved, although the liaison group was a variation on this theme.

While the proposals for institutional development were soft-pedalled, another decision did point in the direction of a more active Group of 77. Manila called for a further conference of the Group of 77 on Economic Cooperation

Among Developing Countries, and suggested the establishment of some permanent apparatus in this domain. Intra-Third World cooperation was a perennial theme of Third World policy declarations, but the Group of 77 heretofore had operated almost exclusively in terms of North-South negotiations. The decision to reconvene the Group of 77 in the near term (September 1976) in order to discuss South-South economic projects broke new ground and implied new activities within the 77 framework. This meeting, scheduled for Mexico City, was later instructed to review the recommendations of the working group on new institutional arrangements.

The trajectories traced toward Paris-Geneva and toward Mexico City were indicative of the growing complexity of the diplomatic process that the developing countries needed to manage. Both North-South and South-South relations contained new variables that the Group of 77 had to take into account in mounting a coherent collective diplomacy. The Manila Conference was able to handle a wider range of problems than its predecessors without undue difficulty, and it set a heavy future agenda for the Group of 77. Its main trajectory was nevertheless aimed toward Nairobi and UNCTAD IV, where the developing countries wanted to see significant agreements on commodities and debt.

The commodities policy proposals endorsed by the Group of 77 at Manila had been taking form over the previous 18 months in Geneva. The UNCTAD secretariat had devised a scheme that had two integral components, a Common Fund and an Integrated Program of Commodities (IPC). The central concept of the IPC was the establishment by international agreement of stocking arrangements for 18 basic agricultural and mineral commodities that provide about 80 percent of the developing countries' export revenues (oil excluded). These buffer stocks would be accumulated in times of glut and sold off during times of shortage in order to eliminate drastic fluctuations in raw materials supplies and prices. The prices of these resources would be established by reference to a market basket of manufactured products in order to improve the terms of trade of the developing countries and to protect them against erosion through inflation. An integrated network of supply and purchase commitments for the ensemble of commodities would be worked out; this feature was essential to allow the developing countries to pool their bargaining power in the discussion of each particular commodity. The Common Fund, for which a total operating capital of $6 billion was advanced, was simply the financial organ that would buy and sell the buffer stocks. The goal of this dual mechanism, Fund and IPC, was not only to ensure more stable export revenues but also to shift much of the power of price determination from the Western commodities exchanges to the producer countries through international agreement. The stakes, in other words, were far from negligible.

The debt issue was also of great importance to the Group of 77. Third World external indebtedness had long been rising steadily, only to explode in 1974 and 1975 under the multiple impact of inflation in the industrialized world, declining terms of trade for their raw materials exports, and the increased cost of oil.* The annual trade deficit of the non-oil-exporting developing countries soared from about $12 billion in 1973 to $45 billion in 1975. Service payments alone cost some $11.5 billion in 1975, more than the total received in aid that year. The Group of 77 called upon UNCTAD IV to initiate a process of debt relief by convening a special international conference on debt to examine such measures as cancellation for the poorest countries and moratoria or rescheduling for others in financial straits.

These policy decisions of the Group of 77 largely determined the agenda for UNCTAD IV. Secretary-General Gamani Corea sought to maximize the possibility of agreement in Nairobi by revamping the working procedures of the conference. Nairobi was to run for four weeks rather than eight, to carry a more selective agenda, and above all to move promptly into specific negotiations in predetermined negotiating groups. Furthermore, Corea arranged a special session of UNCTAD's permanent Trade and Development Board with the intent that this might serve as a prenegotiating session. Yet, despite Corea's efforts to streamline the quadrennial conference, UNCTAD IV did not travel much faster or farther than its predecessors.

Instead of advancing directly into a detailed examination of the IPC-Common Fund as Corea and the Group of 77 hoped, the conference ran headlong into a roadblock in the form of a U.S. counterproposal. Secretary of State Kissinger attended the opening sessions in order to unveil the United States' "own comprehensive approach to commodity issues," which differed substantially from the plan set forth in the Manila Declaration.[7] The U.S. scheme called for a new institution called the International Resources Bank, the purpose of which was not to finance and manage buffer stocks but to encourage new public and private investment in raw materials production. The plan completely lacked the integrated character of the IPC, stressing instead the U.S. preference for a case-by-case approach to commodity agreements. The practical effect of the U.S. counterproposal was to serve notice that the United States was opposed to the Fund and integrated approach—an attitude shared to varying degrees by several other Northern countries. The hopes for a definitive negotiation on the Group of 77 plan were derailed at the outset, and the conference remained virtually immobilized for three and a half weeks.

The Group of 77 stood by its plan with a minimum of wavering.† The

---

*Third World debt stood at $9 billion in 1956. It rose manageably to $38 billion by 1965, then more alarmingly to $119 billion by 1973 (that is, before the quadrupling of the price of oil). By 1976, it was over $150 billion.

† The developing countries divided on the best tactic by which to dispose of the U.S. plan, which was not considered a satisfactory alternative. Some wanted to vote it down, while others preferred to let it wither away so as to avoid a sharp Third World-U.S. con-

industrial states were more divided. The Netherlands and the Scandinavian countries were ready to support an interventionary mechanism along the lines of the proposed Common Fund. France assumed a key mediatory role in accepting the principle of a fund while arguing that it should be constituted only after several precise commodity agreements had been negotiated. These specific commodity agreements would presumably each entail certain financing arrangements of their own; the central fund, France argued, could evolve later as a kind of umbrella covering the ensemble of specialized funds and facilitating transfers among them. The French position took account of the U.S. willingness to consider case-by-case commodity accords while acknowledging the Third World's insistence upon a central fund. For the Group of 77, however, the priorities remained reversed: agreement upon an international financing mechanism, then negotiation of the commodity accords.

The laborious search for an acceptable compromise ground on to the final days of UNCTAD IV—a far cry from Secretary-General Corea's overoptimistic scenario of a streamlined negotiation. Diplomatic ingenuity ultimately snatched a last-minute victory from the jaws of defeat, but again the outcome bore little resemblance to the hopes that the UNCTAD secretariat and the Group of 77 had vested in the conference. The resolution voted in the closing hours at Nairobi looked quite like the proposal in the Manila Declaration, but it was in fact little more than a timetable of future negotiations.

The key to the agreement was a dual commitment to reconvene no later than March 1977 in order to negotiate on a Common Fund and to commence preparatory meetings on diverse commodities accords in the meantime. The developing countries read this as a validation of the concept of the Common Fund. The developed countries reasoned that everything would turn on the results of the preliminary discussions on specific raw materials. In effect, the Third World order of priorities was reversed, but the developing countries did get the commitment to an international conference on the Fund itself. They interpreted the resolution to mean that the product-by-product negotiations were not a precondition to the elaboration of the statutes of the Fund in March 1977. The U.S. delegation, on the contrary, declared that its participation in the March conference would depend on the results of the preliminary commodities

---

frontation. The former had their way, but the majority of developing states abstained or took a diplomatic stroll during the vote, which was 33-31-34 against the International Resources Bank (several of the 33 being communist rather than Third World votes).

There were some substantive differences within the Group of 77 as well. Some states proposed that certain commodities be exempted from the IPC (for example, Brazil and Colombia re coffee and Chile re copper). A few better off debtor states (for example, Brazil and Mexico) had reservations about the impact of a general rescheduling of debts on their own creditworthiness. These strains did not undermine the overall pressure of the Group of 77 behind its proposals.

meetings.* The fragility of the agreement was apparent, but it saved UNCTAD IV from an ignominious fate.

The deliberations regarding the debt issue led to a similar indecisive outcome. The creditor countries never accepted the proposed special conference on debt relief. They did accept to respond multilaterally by a "rapid and constructive examination of individual requests" with a view to prompt measures of relief. The resolution went on to invite appropriate international organs to determine before the end of the year how future international lending could be made more flexible, and it requested the Trade and Development Board to follow up on the measures actually taken when it met in 1977. The language of the resolution presumed a genuine commitment to immediate and longer term debt relief policies, but preserved the Western insistence upon its own control of individual decisions.

These last-minute compromises managed to get the North-South train on the tracks again, at least insofar as the Common Fund still appeared attainable somewhere down the line. The Group of 77 weathered the trip through UNCTAD IV in reasonably good shape. Its cohesion maintained the pressure on the opponents of the Common Fund, and produced the final decision to schedule the further meeting. Indeed, the Third World coalition successfully exploited the divisions among the Northern countries in order to keep the commodities proposals at the center of North-South relations. The ability to function effectively as the Group of 77 was reconfirmed, but the capacity of the 77 to effect structural change remained unproven.

THE THREAT OF DISAGGREGATION AND
THE FIFTH NONALIGNED SUMMIT

Despite the common front of the developing countries at Nairobi, new elements of disaggregation were coming to the fore in 1975–76. Bilateral conflicts were of course a constant variable in intra-Third World relations, but those that erupted during this period were especially severe. The perennial problem of managing the interplay between particularistic interests and common interests aggravated the residual cleavage between moderates and radicals.

One of these conflicts grew out of Angola's accession to independence. The internal struggle for power between the two major guerrilla organizations, Agostino Neto's Popular Movement for the Liberation of Angola (MPLA) and Holden Roberto's Angolan National Liberation Front (FNLA), split Africa into

---

*The resolution included the notion that prices should be reviewed periodically to take account of inflation. Both Great Britain and West Germany expressed explicit reservations regarding indexation. Again the tenuousness of the agreement was evident.

two camps. The involvement of Cuba and Zaire, each backing a different claimant to power, exacerbated tensions between the Third World (and great-power) partisans of each formation. (The subsequent incursions into Zaire's Shaba province in 1977 and 1978 by rebels trained in Angola were a prolongation of this competition.) A second conflict with far-reaching diplomatic ramifications broke out over Western Sahara. Morocco and Mauritania partitioned this former Spanish colony while Algeria armed and gave sanctuary to the Polisario Front, which claimed independence for the territory. Each side sought diplomatic support in Africa and the Arab world while the region became the theater of a hit-and-run desert war. Third, the civil war in Lebanon, in which the Palestine Liberation Organization and Syria were deeply embroiled, was another harshly divisive issue. Syria's military advance deep into Lebanon in 1976 was a blow to the Palestinians and their allies on the Lebanese left, which brought Iraq, Egypt, Libya, and Algeria into conflict with Damascus. The cumulative effect of these three trouble spots was a political malaise that could only weaken the collective action of the developing countries.

A similar process of disaggregation was occurring during this period within OPEC. Each OPEC ministerial conference occasioned a strenuous debate between advocates and opponents of price increases. In September 1975, Saudi Arabia yielded to the majority and accepted a 10 percent increase; the following May, Iraq, Libya, Venezuela, and Nigeria were unable to win a further increase. By the end of 1976, it proved impossible to reach a consensus. The majority approved a price increase that Saudi Arabia and the United Arab Emirates refused to apply. These differences within OPEC, the symbol of Third World power, were symptomatic of the difficulties within the larger coalition. Economic, strategic, ideological, or other—divergent interests illustrated again the Sisyphean nature of the enterprise of Third World solidarity.

Yet if the endeavor was Sisyphean, certain barriers against a backslide had been erected. Foremost among these was the nonaligned framework. The nonaligned movement had assumed a regular cycle of meetings since 1973. Largely eclipsed by the activities of the Group of 77 from mid-1975 through mid-1976, the nonaligned group reappeared just as the Nairobi Conference closed. First a Bureau meeting and then the fifth summit conference were held; although these sessions bore the mark of the intragroup disputes, they nevertheless demonstrated the durability of the nonaligned group as an actor in the global system.

At the Bureau meeting, held early in June in Algiers, both Western Sahara and Lebanon caused trouble. Algeria clashed with Senegal and Zaire (allies of Mauritania and Morocco) on the Sahraoui question, and the PLO and its allies called for a condemnation of the recent Syrian military operation in Lebanon.*

---

*Syria was able to head off a direct condemnation, but a compromise resolution declared that "responsibility for solution of the Lebanese crisis rests with the Lebanese them-

Both conflicts flared up again during the summit conference in Colombo, Sri Lanka, two months later. The Western Sahara question in particular was the subject of a long debate in committee in which numerous states aligned behind each camp, while a third group of states labored to work out a compromise declaration.* The tensions generated by these and other bilateral disputes weighed heavily upon the fifth nonaligned summit.

What was the political significance of the summit in these conditions? It was essentially to demonstrate that large areas of consensus existed over and above the local conflicts. President Tito placed his authority as the founding father of the movement behind the argument that the nonaligned states could "respect genuine divergences of interests" and "turn solely toward that which we hold in common."[8] It was not necessary to pretend that total harmony existed to maintain the nonaligned movement as an instrument of collective diplomacy. Tito granted that the internal disputes weakened the movement, but insisted that they need not paralyze it. The Colombo summit emphasized the issue areas in which common action was plausible, and manifested a strong political will to increase the organizational efficacy of the nonaligned group.

Each nonaligned summit had been larger in number and more profuse in its declarations than its predecessor. Colombo extended both these trends. It assembled 85 fully accredited participants, 10 more than the previous summit. Of the states present in Algiers, all except Chile, banished after the coup against Allende, participated at Colombo. Eight of the new members had achieved their independence in the interim—aside from Angola, Mozambique, and Guinea-Bissau, they were island mini-states: Cape Verde, the Comoros, the Maldives, the Seychelles, and Sao-Tomé and Principe. Panama, an observer state in 1973, and the PLO, present as a liberation movement in 1973, now participated as full members. The final new member was North Korea, whose participation raised Western eyebrows and the perennial question of the criteria of nonalignment.

The entry of North Korea was tied up with the evolution of events in Indochina. The defeat of the pro-Western government in Saigon led shortly to the reunification of Vietnam. The membership accorded earlier to the GRP in effect devolved upon the Hanoi government, which desired to associate itself with the larger Third World movement.† North Korea presented roughly the

---

selves." The Algerians won a resolution affirming the right of the Sahraouis to self-determination (*Review of International Affairs* 629 [June 20, 1976] : 16).

*The compromise took note of a recent OAU decision to hold a special conference on the issue, and expressed the hope that this would lead to a just and durable solution. From the Algerian point of view, this had the merit of calling the status quo into question, but it was a much more neutral formulation than that of the Bureau meeting and was therefore tolerable to Morocco and Mauritania.

† During the period between the end of the war and reunification, both the GRP and North Vietnam sent delegations to the Lima nonaligned conference.

same characteristics—ideologically within the Soviet sphere of influence, geographically bordering China, interested in giving a Third World orientation to its foreign policy. From the point of view of the nonaligned movement, the relevant criterion was not ideology but foreign military bases; none of the Asian communist governments (Cambodia, Laos, Vietnam, or North Korea) had such bases. Well prior to North Korea's request for admission, the nonaligned movement had already adopted resolutions calling for the withdrawal of foreign troops from South Korea. The admission of North Korea did not indicate any dramatic shift in the political orientation or conceptual criteria of nonalignment, therefore; rather it was the final ramification of the earlier debates over the war in Vietnam and the admission of the GRP.*

The documents approved at Colombo covered political, economic, and organizational matters. For the most part, they reaffirmed familiar policy positions on the standing international issues, but they also revealed a distinct concern for the future role of the nonaligned movement within Third World affairs.

The Political Declaration was representative in this regard. It presented a tour d'horizon of the international political situation—Europe and the Mediterranean, southern Africa, the Middle East, Cyprus, Southeast Asia, Korea, Latin America, the Indian Ocean, disarmament, the United Nations—and then devoted a distinctive subsection to the subject of Politics and Economics. Here one found the following argument:

> It is incontestable that there is an integral connection·between politics and economics, and it is erroneous to approach economic affairs in isolation from politics. . . . The importance given to economic affairs does not diminish the importance given to political affairs at Nonaligned meetings.[9]

What inspired this quasi-epistemological observation in the midst of a listing of current issues? Its point was surely to defend the continuing political relevance of the nonaligned movement in relation to the Group of 77 at a moment when the latter was assuming a greater role in Third World politics. Economic change implied political change, and the nonaligned movement was the privileged instrument of Third World political pressure.

The Economic Declaration in turn reflected the same political concern. Although it saluted the "highly constructive role" of the Group of 77, it insisted upon the economic contribution of the nonaligned movement. Each organization had had a positive impact upon the other: "The economic content of the Nonaligned Movement has influenced and in turn has been influenced by the

---

*The Korean delegation at Colombo nevertheless strained the limits of consensus. It insisted upon a strongly worded condemnation of U.S. policy in South Korea, which drew formal reservations from about a dozen states.

articulate and dynamic organization of the Group of 77." The nonaligned movement would "strengthen its solidarity with the Group of 77," but it would also maintain its own role as an economic innovator. The declaration concluded by recalling the economic initiatives of the nonaligned conferences:

> The Belgrade summit paved the way for the establishment of UNCTAD. The Cairo summit called upon the international community to restructure the world economy in a manner conducive to the urgent economic development of the developing countries. At the Lusaka summit, nonaligned countries pledged themselves to actively cultivate the spirit of self-reliance; the initiatives stemming from the Algiers summit launched the nonaligned countries on a path of asserting that spirit of self-reliance through their collective bargaining strength based upon the right of permanent sovereignty over natural resources and economic activities, the development of producers' associations and the proclamation in the United Nations of the New International Economic Order.

In brief, the nonaligned movement laid claim to an economic raison d'etre of its own in addition to its key political role.

The companion Action Program for Economic Cooperation was largely devoted to South-South economic relations in accordance with the notion of collective self-reliance. As such, it was destined as much for the forthcoming Mexico City Conference as for the future economic activity of the nonaligned group. At the same time it demonstrated that the nonaligned movement already had launched a modest program of horizontal cooperation among the developing states. There were numerous projects in various stages of development—for example, the statutes for a Council of Producers Associations were being drawn up, an Information Center on Transnational Corporations had been set up, a center for scientific and technical cooperation was under study, and working groups on a host of other forms of cooperation were at work. Although little had been fully implemented,* they established further nonaligned credentials in the realm of Third World economic cooperation on the eve of the Group of 77 conference.

The Colombo meeting also adopted a Decision Regarding the Composition and the Mandate of the Bureau of Coordination, a document critical to the future organization of the nonaligned group. This text drew upon the practical experience of the past three years to codify the functioning of the Bureau,

---

*The most advanced of these projects was the Solidarity Fund, which was, however, a cause of minor embarrassment. Approved in principle in 1975, its convention had been ratified by only 21 states at the end of 1976, well short of the 40 necessary for it to begin operations. The gap between aspirations and cash commitments was evident; the project appears to have been financially overambitious.

which had proven its utility as an instrument of interim decision making and organizational continuity. The document instructed the Bureau to meet at least once a year at the level of foreign ministers and "with regular continuity at the level of the permanent representatives of the nonaligned countries at United Nations headquarters in New York, in principle once a month." Beyond these scheduled meetings, the Bureau was authorized to meet in emergency session when "special crisis situations . . . directly concerning the nonaligned countries" should occur, and "if need be to recommend any action which should seem appropriate."

These directives enlarged the operational authority of the Bureau, and attested to the desire of the nonaligned group to exercise a permanent presence in international decision making. The Bureau was also to serve as the organ of coordination and supervision of ongoing projects and as the preparatory organ for plenary conferences. The Decision specified that Bureau decisions should be taken by consensus as was the practice at the plenary level. Furthermore, it codified the practice of open meetings: Not only were all Bureau meetings open to all nonaligned states but non-Bureau members could even request that the Bureau be convened. Clearly, the intent was to authorize a smaller representative group of states to act in behalf of the entire group rather than to create an exclusive executive body. The Bureau gave the movement greater operational flexibility without significantly limiting the prerogatives of any member-state.

The membership of the Bureau was enlarged from 15 to 25 in order to ensure its political representativeness; taking account of the de facto situation since the first Bureau meeting (that is, the addition of India and Mali), there was an effective increase of eight states. The Decision established a fixed geographic distribution for the 25 seats as follows:

Africa:	12 seats (up from 7 in the first Bureau)
Asia:	8 seats (up from 6 in the first Bureau)
Latin America:	4 seats (up from 3 in the first Bureau)
Europe:	1 seat (unchanged)

The new Bureau included 11 holdovers (Algeria, Liberia, Tanzania, Zaire, India, Sri Lanka, Syria, Cuba, Guyana, Peru, and Yugoslavia*) and 14 new members (Angola, Botswana, Chad, Guinea, Niger, Nigeria, Sudan, Zambia, Bangladesh,† Indonesia, Iraq, PLO, Vietnam, and Jamaica). All the major political tendencies

---

*The departing members, therefore, were Mali, Senegal, Somalia, Kuwait, Malaysia, and Nepal.

† Afghanistan made a determined bid for this seat; it was finally agreed that Bangladesh would serve for 18 months and then yield the seat to Afghanistan for the second half of the term.

remained represented. The tilt of the original Bureau toward the radical end of the nonaligned spectrum also remained, no major radical state being dropped and such states as Angola, Guinea, Iraq, and Vietnam being added—plus the PLO. The practice of an acting presidency was retained, the office shifting from Algeria to Sri Lanka as the host country of the fifth summit.

The enlargement of the Bureau and the codification of its mandate contributed significantly to the organizational sturdiness of the nonaligned movement. The decisions marked a consensus on the value of such an organ, and at the same time laid to rest the question of a permanent secretariat. The Bureau was deemed both a necessary and a sufficient instrument of coordination and continuity. The new mandate strengthened its institutional legitimacy and the operational capacity of the movement as a whole. The technical problems of managing a large coalition of states were largely solved. The question now was whether the political problems would prove manageable; otherwise the wheels of the nonaligned apparatus could spin without getting anywhere.

THE NONALIGNED, THE 77, AND COLLECTIVE SELF-RELIANCE

The Colombo Conference thus improved the organizational coherence of the nonaligned movement in spite of the severe political tensions within the group. The immediate consequences of this organizational renewal were apparent the following month when the Group of 77 held its conference on Economic Cooperation Among Developing Countries. The positions adopted at the nonaligned conference strongly influenced the proceedings of the Group of 77 conference. The proximity of the two meetings provides an excellent opportunity to compare the active membership of the two formations.

Eighty-six states attended the Group of 77 conference, virtually the same number that attended the nonaligned conference. Yet there were in fact 20 states in Mexico City that were not at Colombo; although the overlap was sizable, the difference was also noteworthy. Most of the new participants fell into the two categories that had always distinguished the 77 from the nonaligned: Latin America and Asian alliance members.* On the other hand, there were 19 states

---

*The majority were Latin American states: Bolivia, Brazil, Costa Rica, Dominican Republic, Ecuador, El Salvador, Guatemala, Haiti, Honduras, Mexico, Nicaragua, Uruguay, and Venezuela; five fell in the second category: Iran, Pakistan, the Philippines, Thailand, and South Korea. The two others were each mavericks of sorts: Rumania, a Warsaw Pact member seeking to pursue a Third World oriented policy similar to that of Yugoslavia, and Malawi, the only member of the OAU that systematically boycotted the nonaligned meetings. Note that the ratio of nonaligned states to other developing states was roughly the

that attended the Colombo Conference but failed to attend the one in Mexico City, despite the fact that they were members of the Group of 77. Most of these were small countries with limited diplomatic means;* the fact that they chose to attend the former meeting while passing up the latter presumably indicated a judgment as to the relative importance of the two meetings. The more general political conference exercised the greater drawing power for these states. The variation in the composition of the two meetings illustrates nicely the slightly different character of the two Third World groupings; yet one would expect that the common core of 66 states participating in both meetings would exercise the greatest influence upon the second conference, and this was indeed the case.

Although the agenda of the Mexico City Conference was specifically focused on economic issues, the conferees nevertheless addressed some purely political issues. The heart of the political matter, as raised by two much debated proposals, was the future character of the Group of 77. A small group of states led by Pakistan doggedly sought to win approval for a Group of 77 summit conference. Others, with Mexico and the Philippines in the lead, pursued the idea already advanced at Manila of a permanent secretariat for the 77.

The summit proposal was a barely veiled challenge to the political authority of the nonaligned movement. The Pakistanis argued that the growing responsibilities of the Group of 77 as the Southern negotiator justified a conference at the highest political level. Such a conference would increase the negotiating power of the developing countries by increasing the authority of the Group of 77. Pakistan's Prime Minister Ali Bhutto was eager to increase his country's role in Third World politics. Excluded from the nonaligned movement by its alliance ties (and India's insistence thereupon), Pakistan had a particular stake in seeing the Group of 77 acquire greater political stature. Bhutto reasoned that only a summit conference could transform the Group of 77 into a vehicle equivalent to the nonaligned movement. The project ran up against the conception of division of labor held by the nonaligned activists; their interest in maintaining the prevailing relationship doomed Pakistan's proposal to failure.

The most fervent backers of the secretariat proposal also were outsiders to the nonaligned movement. The Philippines, much like Pakistan, wanted to establish a reputation as a Third World leader without abandoning its U.S. military support. Mexico's situation was analogous. President Luis Echeverria had

---

same in Mexico City as in the total membership of the Group of 77, about three to one (66/86 at the conference, 85/114 in the Group as a whole at that time).

*They were Bahrein, Benin, Bhutan, Burma, Botswana, Burundi, Cameroon, Comoros, Congo, Gambia, Equatorial Guinea, Lebanon, Maldives, Malta, Seychelles, Singapore, Sao-Tomé and Principe, South Yemen, and Yemen. In addition to these nonaligned absentees, nine other members of the Group of 77 were likewise absent: Bahamas, Barbados, Chile, Colombia, Fiji, Grenada, Papua New Guinea, Paraguay, and Surinam.

given a pronounced Third World orientation to Mexican foreign policy, most prominently through the campaign for the Charter of Economic Rights and Duties of States. Mexico nevertheless hesitated to enter the nonaligned movement, a step that only the Latin American regimes most critical of the United States had taken (Allende's Chile, Velasco's Peru, Peronist Argentina, and Torrijos's Panama in addition to Cuba—Guyana and Jamaica being cases apart). Like Pakistan, Mexico and the Philippines had greater political stakes in the Group of 77, which prompted them to push for the secretariat proposal. Although this idea received a more sympathetic hearing than the summit proposal, they could not muster adequate political and financial support to implement it. The majority preferred to maintain the institutional status quo and the division of labor politically and economically that this implied.

The conference's undertakings in the realm of Third World economic cooperation also bore the stamp of the nonaligned movement. The central theme of the conference was collective self-reliance, a concept that had been most fully sanctioned by the nonaligned conferences. The two Action Programs for Economic Cooperation adopted by the fourth and fifth nonaligned summits were cited in the texts approved at Mexico City as basic models of South-South cooperation.[10] The practical effect of the Mexico City Conference was to extend the economic efforts of the nonaligned movement to the larger membership of the Group of 77 and to implicate the institutional machinery of UNCTAD in this process. Thus, for example, the Mexico City decisions directed that studies be undertaken by UNCTAD and the UN regional economic commissions on such cooperative projects as a system of intra-Third World trade preferences, a common Third World imports policy, and the exchange of information on Third World markets. They also instructed the Group of 77 to pursue several financial initiatives proposed at Colombo: a Third World commercial bank, a payments union, and a common liquidity unit. They endorsed the concept of a Council of Producers Associations that the nonaligned movement had advanced, and they called for a closer coordination between nonaligned and Group of 77 working groups in areas such as commodities policy.

The Mexico City Conference was the first full-blown articulation of the theme of collective self-reliance. As such it paved the way for some important future developments, as shall be seen in Chapter 7. For the moment, it served to associate the Group of 77 much more fully and explicitly with a program of Third World economic cooperation emanating from the nonaligned movement. The Group of 77 thereby took on a further function. To that of negotiator in North-South relations was now added that of implementer in South-South relations. This new responsibility increased the importance of the Group of 77 as a vehicle of Third World collaboration, but it did not significantly enlarge its political role relative to the nonaligned framework.*

---

*Commenting on the Mexico City meeting, the Yugoslav *Review of International*

The Third World coalition thus retained its dual organizational character. The organizational rivalry perceptible in the summit issue was one more manifestation of the perennial difficulty of managing a coalition of over 100 developing states. The Mexico City decisions temporarily resolved the question of the nature of the relationship between the two bodies.* There was no immediate prospect that the Group of 77 might displace the nonaligned movement as the major mobilizer of Third World collective diplomacy. But this settlement did nothing to exorcise the demon of bilateral disputes, which was the graver threat to the efficacy of the nonaligned movement.

The intense pace of Third World organizing and North-South negotiations that had existed since the Sixth Special Session tapered off somewhat in the closing months of 1976. As U.S. policy was a critical variable in North-South relations, there was little incentive to press issues until the U.S. elections were over, and, as matters turned out, until the new administration was in office. During this period nonetheless, the newly named nonaligned Bureau began to fulfill its enlarged mandate by organizing its activities at the United Nations. Sri Lanka assumed its acting presidency with the same verve that Algeria had shown during its tenure. The Bureau met several times during the autumn session of the General Assembly, even more frequently than the monthly schedule proposed at Colombo, and formed a number of subgroups on specific items such as disarmament, the Middle East, southern Africa, interference in internal affairs, and reorganization of the United Nations. These working groups enabled the nonaligned states to intervene with greater preparation and coordination in the debates on these items, and made the practice of working together into a regular routine. The multiplication of these consultative and organizational arrangements unmistakably established New York as the de facto headquarters of the nonaligned movement, much as Geneva served for the Group of 77. In effect they constituted a further systematization of the Third World's "majority power" in the General Assembly.

Affairs concluded that the Group of 77 "has become a forum for the elaboration and implementation of economic decisions of the nonaligned countries. This arrangement suggests that the economic activity of the nonaligned movement would in future be restricted to laying down policies and guidelines, whereas the Group of 77 would have the task of further developing and implementing these policies" (no. 637, October 20, 1976, p. 22). Obviously, Yugoslavia was predisposed to such an interpretation, but it did not seriously distort the division of labor that prevailed at Mexico City.

*Although Pakistan, seconded by Iran, renewed the summit campaign early in 1977, nothing came of it, other than an implicit condemnation by the nonaligned Bureau in an allusion to "efforts aimed at undermining the identity of the [nonaligned] Movement as well as diminishing its pivotal role in the developing world." The Bureau went on to insist upon the movement's role as the political "catalyst" of the Third World coalition. See the Communique in *Review of International Affairs*, 652 (June 5, 1977) and the commentaries on the Bureau meeting in no 650 (May 5, 1977).

The General Assembly, however, was not the critical forum for the outstanding North-South issues at this point. Even UNCTAD, where the fate of the IPC/Common Fund was still pending and where a further round of talks in March 1977 was quite inconclusive, was not the most important forum in the period following the Colombo and Mexico City conferences. This privilege was reserved for the Paris Conference on International Economic Cooperation, which the next chapter details.

The robustness of the Third World coalition was the critical variable in the power of the developing country representatives in Paris. This analysis of the evolution of the nonaligned movement and the Group of 77 through 1976 has shown that the developing states managed to keep the coalition from cracking in spite of the centrifugal forces within it. This was, in the final analysis, more a holding action than anything else. Meanwhile, the developed countries were pursuing a holding action of their own against the objectives of the poor countries in the North-South Conference.

NOTES

1. Jon McLin, "The Group of 77," *American Universities Field Staff Reports*, West Europe Series 11, no. 3 (April 1976): 1.

2. The idea of UNCTAD as an interest articulator is well developed by Robert S. Walters, "International Organizations and Political Communications: The Use of UNCTAD by Less Developed Countries," *International Organization* 25 (Autumn 1971): 818–35.

3. McLin, "The Group of 77," p. 1.

4. Ibid., p. 2.

5. "Manila Declaration and Program of Action," UN Document TD/195, Annex I, p. 10.

6. *Review of International Affairs* 623 (March 20, 1976): 7.

7. The text of Secretary Kissinger's speech appears in *Department of State Bulletin* 74, no. 1927 (May 31, 1976). The citation is on p. 660.

8. *Le Monde*, August 18, 1976.

9. *Review of International Affairs* 634 (September 5, 1976). All of the following citations from the Colombo documents come from this source. The two declarations also appear in A. W. Singham, ed., *The Nonaligned Movement in World Politics* (Westport, Conn.: Lawrence Hill, 1978).

10. The text of the Mexico City decisions appears in *Documents d'Actualité Internationale, 1976* no. 47 (November 24, 1976).

6. The North-South Conference

In the annals of North-South politics, the Paris Conference on International Economic Cooperation stands as a major episode. The idea to organize such a conference was one of the most important diplomatic responses to the international economic crisis of 1973-74. The fact that a major Northern power put its prestige behind such a forum endowed it with a political significance that was not necessarily accorded other North-South encounters. The implicit understanding that underlay CIEC was that this was the route that the North considered most conducive to progress on the outstanding issues between North and South. For this reason, diplomatic energy and attention tended to drain toward the Paris Conference as a potentially decisive event in New International Economic Order politics. For the Third World, it was imperative to make the most of the opportunity.

In Chapter 4 it was seen how this imperative led to the failure of the initial preparatory meeting in April 1975, for the Third World representatives were unwilling to sanction a conference devoted primarily to energy issues. This initial skirmish over the appropriate agenda foreshadowed many of the difficulties that lay ahead for the North-South dialogue. The developing countries wanted CIEC to open the way to substantial international economic change, while their opposite numbers wanted to restore economic peace at the lowest possible price. This fundamental conflict in political purpose was evident over the entire course of the proceedings from October 1975 to June 1977. To this extent, CIEC was a microcosm of other North-South interactions. The factor of diminished scale did not prove the key to a decisive breakthrough.

Likewise, the 19 developing countries that represented the South in CIEC were a microcosm of intra-Third World politics. Virtually all the most influential actors in the nonaligned movement and the Group of 77 were present. Most were states with important economic resources, notably oil and mineral exporters, such as Saudi Arabia, Iran, Iraq, Venezuela, Indonesia, Nigeria, and Algeria (oil), Zaire, Zambia, and Peru (copper), and Jamaica (bauxite). Brazil was also a major commodity exporter (coffee) and like Argentina one of the more industrialized Third World states. Most of the others were populous states (India, Pakistan, Mexico, and Egypt) with considerable political influence in their regions and beyond. Yugoslavia was chosen primarily for its organizational leadership in the nonaligned movement, while Cameroon was representative of the large group of relatively small francophone African states. Similar in their politicoeconomic prominence, they ranged across the Third World ideological spectrum. No less than in the Group of 77, the Paris Group of 19 had to strike its own internal accommodations before negotiating with the North.

SETTING UP CIEC: A POLITICAL OR TECHNICAL FORUM?

Such an accommodation was necessary even to launch the conference in the first place. From the outset there were conflicting conceptions within the Third World as to the very nature of the conference. These were visible during a second preparatory meeting in October 1975. Algeria was reluctant to see any conference get underway without a clear commitment to discuss the major political issues raised by the NIEO resolutions. Saudi Arabia, on the contrary, wanted to get the conference going without further delay on the basis of a simple understanding that each commission would clarify its specific terms of reference once it set to work. The issue was a further variation on the basic theme of the agenda, which had already caused the first preparatory meeting to break down.

The Saudi position was quite compatible with that of the United States, which envisaged the conference more as a technical than a political forum. The United States still wanted to talk oil prices, but was willing now to extend the talks to other matters such as product-by-product commodity accords and the handling of balance of payment deficits. It did not want broad political discussions that implied major structural changes in the international economic system. This, however, was exactly what Algeria did want. The Algerians argued, with considerable justification, that the developed countries had not yet granted the basic premises of the Third World critique of the existing economic order. They wanted guarantees that the talks could lead to genuinely new rules of the game in North-South economic relations. As the leader of the Algerian delegation expressed this position: "The industrial countries have moved their rifle to the other shoulder, but the rifle is still there. We therefore want general terms of reference which confirm the comprehensive nature of this negotiation."[1]

In insisting on the comprehensiveness of the talks, the Algerians were saying that the various issues of energy, raw materials, finance, and development
were linked in a single critique of the existing system. No single issue could be
solved satisfactorily without an overall political commitment to Third World
development. The various North-South talks to date, the Algerians contended,
had not reached the level of political agreement necessary to move on to purely
technical issues. Before entering the talks, therefore, the developing countries
should obtain a guarantee that the conference would address the large political
issues of international economic change.

The Algerian argument was vulnerable to the criticism that it presupposed
the results of a process of negotiation that had not yet taken place. It was worthwhile, the Saudis counterargued, to create a forum for further discussion on the
assumption that the talks themselves would generate progress on the various
issues in dispute. Behind this debate, of course, lay quite different Algerian and
Saudi conceptions of how much change was desirable.

However advantageous it would have been to obtain prior guarantees, none
of the developing countries wanted to push this argument to the point of another
rupture. The Northern participants remained unwilling to specify anything other
than vague mandates for the four commissions that were to be the basic working
bodies of the North-South Conference. When the chips were down, Algeria yielded
to the willingness of the other developing states to go ahead on these terms.

Thus it was agreed that the Energy Commission would seek to "facilitate
arrangements which should appear desirable between oil producers and consumers."[2] The mandates for the commissions on raw materials and on development contained the same kind of formulation. These were hardly directives at
all, let alone commitments, but rather simple designations of the issue areas to
be discussed. It was obviously not an agreement to study the idea of the New
International Economic Order; while nothing was definitively precluded by
these terms of reference, nothing was assured either. The mandate for the fourth
commission, financial affairs, contained a restriction that the Third World did
not want, but on which the United States insisted. This commission was to
examine only the financial issues "attached to the work of the three preceding
Commissions"—it was not, in other words, to engage in a full-scale reexamina-
tion of the international monetary system. In brief, on all these questions the
United States gained satisfaction.

The agreement struck at the October meeting was therefore little more
than a green light for the North-South Conference to go. Indeed it was perhaps
more accurately a yellow light, for the Final Declaration of the preparatory
meeting took note of two documents that were referred to the future commissions. These two annexes were Lists of Questions to be studied by the four commissions. One was submitted by the United States, the other emanated from
Algeria and was formally submitted by the seven developing countries. These
two appended texts revealed that the agreement to set up CIEC was not really an

accord upon the future agenda. The first question on the U.S. list was the price of oil, an item that did not appear at all on the other list; the latter, on the contrary, began with the issue of protection of the purchasing power of the oil exporters. As regarded raw materials, the U.S. list began with the matter of access to supply, the Third World list with the revaluation of commodities prices. The Third World document recommended that the conference take as its basic frame of reference the final resolution of the Seventh Special Session (which in turn referred back to the NIEO resolutions), while the U.S. list made no reference to any such general orientation. It was evident that ambiguity and conflicting expectations lay at the foundation of the CIEC edifice.

In April 1975, the Third World delegation had been united against the U.S. notion of "energy first." In October it was divided in its response to the agenda preferred by the United States. By shifting its own position, the United States placed the burden of agreement upon the developing states. Between Algeria's reservations and Saudi Arabia's strong desire to launch the conference (which, it will be recalled, was first suggested by the Saudis back in August 1974), a Third World consensus formed around the necessity to proceed on the basis of an extremely indeterminate agenda. They accepted a conference designed essentially to U.S. specifications while nonetheless expressing "a certain distrust with regard to a diplomatic machine that they [were] not sure of controlling."[3]

The actual design of the machine was as follows: 27 participants (19 of which were developing states); a negotiating process divided into four commissions; co-chairmen (one developing country and one developed country) for each of the commissions and another pair of co-chairmen for the conference as a whole.* Upon the official convocation of CIEC in December, Algeria reopened the issue of the October meeting. Hoping for greater success in the enlarged composition of the December meeting, Algeria once again argued that it was necessary to elaborate more fully the mandates of the four commissions by textual reference to such Third World objectives as indexation, the Common Fund, and debt relief. It proposed specifically that the co-chairmen of the commissions and of the plenary conference meet in January to spell out in detail the four mandates. Once again Algeria's campaign ran into the opposition of the industrial states and the irritation of Saudi Arabia and Iran, which feared that the Algerian policy would send the whole enterprise back to square one.

---

*The states holding the chairmanships were energy—Saudi Arabia and the United States; raw materials—Japan and Peru; development—Algeria and the EEC; financial affairs—Iran and the EEC. The co-chairmen of the conference as a whole were Canada (in the person of its secretary of state for foreign affairs, Allan MacEachen) and Venezuela (in the person of Manuel Perez Guerrero). Note that four of the five Third World co-chairmen were OPEC states, a fact that was not entirely appreciated by the twelve non-OPEC participants.

This time, however, Algeria was somewhat more successful in rallying support behind its strategy. In effect, the Third World newcomers to the debate (the additional 12 states selected since the October meeting) saw merit in Algeria's concerns. Upon deliberation, the 19 granted the substance of Algeria's argument and agreed to meet in early January in order to formulate directives for the Group's co-chairmen. These instructions were in turn to serve as the basis for discussion with their Northern counterparts on the terms of reference of the commissions. The 19 hesitated nonetheless to push this position to its logical conclusion, for it granted the Saudis that the commissions might begin to function in February whether or not further agreement was reached on their mandates. This compromise reflected the political split in the Group of 19 that greatly reduced the likelihood that the developing countries would get any change at all in the language of the mandates.

The cleavage between moderate and radical conceptions made it easy for the Northern Group of Eight* to refuse the essence of the Southern proposal. For the sake of appearance the Group of 8 accepted the form of the proposal while emptying it of its substance. In form the Group agreed to a meeting of the ten co-chairmen prior to the opening sessions of the commissions, but required that this meeting deliberate "in the context of the general orientations indicated in Paragraphs 10 and 14 of the Final Declaration of the second preparatory meeting."[4] The effect of this reference back to the October decisions was to confirm the original mandates as the basic point of departure for the commissions' work (Paragraph 10 setting forth these mandates, Paragraph 14 citing the two Lists of Questions). Algeria's attempt to orient the talks unambiguously toward the basic political issues of North-South relations—the principle of a new economic order and a right to development—thus failed. The "diplomatic machine" began to roll in the direction preferred by the North as sanctioned by Saudi Arabia and Iran.

Otherwise the inaugural session merely established the formal structure and timetable of CIEC. The membership of the four commissions was approved in accordance with a formula of ten developing states and five developed states per commission. The commissions were to begin to meet in February, and the conference was to reconvene in plenary session at the ministerial level some six to twelve months later. The presumption was that this timetable allowed ample working time at the commission level to analyze the issues and then to propose policy. The practice of decision making by consensus was adopted.

----

*The Group of Eight in fact represented 16 industrial states through the mechanism of a single delegation for the entire EEC. In addition to the United States and Japan, the others were Australia, Canada, Sweden, Switzerland, and Spain. For a time the British government sought a separate seat for Great Britain, but no other member of the EEC would accept such a double standard. In practice, all the major Western industrial states with the exception of Norway participated in the conference.

The basic premise underlying these ground rules was that CIEC would provide an original approach to problems that had defied solution in other forums.
As a French diplomat set forth this rationale:

> One of the assets of the conference resides in the originality of its
> methods: unencumbered by UN rhetoric, the experts will be gen-
> uinely able to discuss the heart of the matter. They will work in
> small meetings and at a reasonable pace. How many meetings have
> been doomed to failure by undue haste! The sponsors of this meet-
> ing recognize that it will have to be long.[5]

Neither rhetoric nor haste, but a statesmanlike, patient, and realistic assault on
complex issues—such was the image promoted for CIEC.

The developing countries accepted the format while entertaining doubts
about the rationale. They had no intention of dismissing the United Nations as
irrelevant to the Paris talks. On the contrary, their interest was to maintain a
political linkage between the General Assembly and the more exclusive Paris
forum. This explained one paragraph of the Final Declaration of the December
meeting: "The Conference took note of the resolution of the General Assembly
entitled 'Conference on International Economic Cooperation' (Resolution 3515
[XXX]) and agreed to communicate its reports to the General Assembly." The
explicit reference to this resolution that had just been adopted in New York was
a manner of recalling the ultimate authority, so far as the Third World was concerned, of the United Nations on international economic matters. The resolution
called upon the Paris conferees to take account of the major General Assembly
resolutions on development and to report its conclusions to the thirty-first General Assembly (the session beginning in September 1976). The significance of
these moves in New York and Paris was to assert an oversight function for the
universal organization vis-a-vis the restricted Paris Conference.

The joint contribution of the October and December sessions did not
really dissipate the ambiguities surrounding the Paris dialogue. The vagueness of
the commission mandates, the conflicting purposes evident in the two Lists of
Questions, the tension between politicized and technical conceptions of the
talks, the evocation of the ultimate supremacy of the United Nations—all were
indications that CIEC faced a rocky road.

THE GROUP OF 19 NEGOTIATES
FOR THE GROUP OF 77

From the outset, CIEC was popularly referred to as the North-South Conference or the North-South dialogue—in other words, its basically bipartite
nature was acknowledged. The selection of co-chairmen for the conference as a
whole and for each of the commissions reinforced this bicephalic character. Yet

the industrial states reasoned (or at least hoped) that the smaller scale might produce a different style of Third World diplomatic behavior, less marked by collective bargaining. The problem with this calculation was that the mere intimation that it existed triggered a defense reflex among the developing countries. The first thing that the 19 Third World participants sought to do after the December meeting was to organize themselves as the Group of 19.

Toward this end, the 19 held a consultative meeting in January. Here it drew up the List of Subjects for Discussion (already mentioned in Chapter 5) that replaced the earlier document submitted by the original seven. The new list was much longer than the earlier one, and made it evident that the developing countries would adopt a "maximum common denominator" approach. While this did not reconcile the differences within the Third World coalition, it assured that everyone had a stake in the negotiation. Throughout the talks, the South would collectively seek a package deal.*

This was the bargaining context when the commissions began to function (as foreseen, the co-chairmen were unable to reach any more specific agreement on their mandates at their January meeting). They convened in February, then in March and April, each session running about ten days. These early sessions were described as "extraordinarily serious and constructive" and much less tense than the preparatory meetings.[6] The North considered that these first months ought to constitute a period of analysis and reflection. The South granted the practicality of such an exploratory phase, but its timetable was a bit more pressed. By the end of the third session, this dissynchronization became apparent. The Group of 19 issued a statement, the gist of which was to express its "nonsatisfaction with the slow progress of the Conference." The members of the 19 contended that they had submitted concrete propositions on various items without receiving either "positive responses or constructive counterproposals." 'If we continue at this rate," declared Co-chairman Perez Guerrero, "we won't get anywhere."[7]

The April declaration was a warning sign that CIEC was generating tensions of its own, but this was not in fact its primary purpose. The essential objective of the Group of 19's declaration was to place the Paris Conference in the larger diplomatic context of UNCTAD IV. The Paris talks were not to be construed as an excuse to stall in other forums. The 19 asserted moreover that "the future of the dialogue in the framework of the Conference on International Economic Co-

---

*The essential components were already familiar: to protect the purchasing power of oil and other raw materials, to increase the capacity to transform raw materials, to improve the terms of trade through a mechanism like the Common Fund, to augment the flow of technology and financial resources, to alleviate the burden of debt. The List is summarized in *Le Monde*, January 28, 1976, and published integrally in *El Moudjahid*, February 17, 1976. The List was shortly supplemented by the Manila Declaration.

operation . . . would be compromised" in the absence of significant progress at Nairobi. For the developing states, in other words, CIEC was not a privileged instrument but rather an integral part of a larger process of North-South negotiations. By explicitly linking the concerns of the 77 at Nairobi to the attitude of the 19 in Paris, the Group of 19 was seeking to capitalize upon the North's diplomatic investment in CIEC while at the same time reaffirming their own status as agents of the larger Third World coalition.

The prompt consolidation of the Group of 19 and its explicit association with the Group of 77 established the political ground rules of the Paris Conference. The developing states were committed to a bloc strategy and insisted upon the integration of CIEC into the total environment of North-South politics. This strategy was designed to maintain the cohesion of the larger coalition as the more important long-term instrument. These early moves made it evident that the success of the conference depended upon the satisfaction of the major grievances of the developing world.

As seen in Chapter 5, UNCTAD IV fell far short of the objectives of the developing states. This led, as they had warned, to a more tense atmosphere at CIEC (which had been suspended in May while the Nairobi Conference took place). The developing states contended that CIEC ought to pick up the pieces from the last-minute compromises at Nairobi. They proposed that two issues should receive priority attention in the next "action-oriented" round of talks. One was the debt question, which the Third World proposed to discuss jointly in the commissions on development and financial affairs or, if need be, in a new commission. The developed states were opposed to any comprehensive discussion of the debt issue; they proposed instead that the most urgent cases of indebtedness be discussed in the Financial Commission and that the other cases be considered separately in the Development Commission. Behind this procedural maneuvering lay the substantive question of a package approach to the debt issue, the only approach that could give the debtor states any bargaining leverage. The United States argued that the way that the South proposed to handle the question prejudged the outcome by implicitly endorsing the concept of generalized debt relief. The other priority issue was indexation, or the maintenance of the purchasing power of the revenues of the Third World commodity exporters. The notion of some mechanism to take account of inflation in the cost of industrial goods was central to the whole debate over international commodities policy, but indexation had never been the object of an explicit North-South negotiation. The industrial states were hostile to the concept of indexation. They argued against placing it on the agenda on the grounds that the issue was essentially within the jurisdiction of UNCTAD, which had already fixed a further schedule of negotiations on the commodities issue. This pair of disputes over the agenda for the second phase of the Paris talks brought CIEC to an impasse.

The underlying problem of the ambiguity of the commission mandates, unresolved at the outset and ignored during the early sessions, now caught up with the conference. Neither a plenary session of senior officials nor the July commission meetings could resolve the agenda question. The South wanted to confront squarely the most contentious issues of North-South relations. The North did not want to venture into territory where the possibility of agreement seemed minimal. The differing conceptions of the very purpose of the conference stood in sharp relief. The North wanted to strike agreements in those domains where fundamental principles were not at stake. The South wanted to revise the basic rules of the game.

Other things being equal, CIEC might well have expired in July 1976. There was, however, a new factor that prolonged the search for a modus vivendi. This was the prospect of a change of administration in Washington. One of candidate Carter's campaign themes was the improvement of U.S. relations with the Third World. This provided an incentive to the developing countries to persist in Paris even if the immediate perspective was dim. The co-chairmen succeeded in working out a new compromise formula that allowed the commissions to resume their deliberations in September. A Program of Work was adopted in which figured the agenda items in dispute,* while the preamble of the Program specified that the decision to discuss a question by no means prejudged the outcome or implied the likelihood of agreement by the end of the conference. This was a classic instance of an agreement to disagree, which was justified so far as the Third World was concerned by the possibility of new Northern policies after the U.S. presidential election.

In these circumstances, it was not surprising that the commissions made little headway from September through November. The Group of 19 submitted a collection of detailed position papers, and requested the 8 to choose those that it preferred to discuss. The North could not agree upon a negotiating package. According to the original timetable, a ministerial meeting was to have concluded the conference in December. By the end of the November session, the conference was moribund, but in the meantime Jimmy Carter had been elected. The conferees agreed to postpone the final ministerial meeting, and to resume contact at the commission level in April 1977. The second phase of CIEC thus ended with but one hope of survival. It was apparent that only a new attitude in Washington could breathe fresh life into the body.

The stagnation of CIEC over eight months of commission sessions did not augur well for the final phase. Certainly the specific policies of the Ford adminis-

---

*The Energy Commission was to study the "maintenance of the purchasing power of energy export revenues," and a like mandate for other commodities was given to the Raw Materials Commission. The debt issue appeared as a single agenda item concerning both "the seriously affected countries and the other countries in need," and was placed before the Development Commission (*Le Monde*, September 15, 1976).

tration contributed to the standstill, but this was not a sufficient explanation. The fundamental cause of CIEC's woes resided in the conflicting conceptions of the purpose of the conference. For the North, the situation was one of bargaining as usual. As one well-informed observer put it, the North "counted on obtaining worthwhile concessions from the Less Developed Countries in return for each privilege granted or assistance pledged."[8] This style of quid pro quo bargaining, which could produce only modest reforms, ran up against the South's objective of structural change based upon a large package deal. For the developing countries, the bargain had to be substantial, because their needs were great, and wide-ranging, because their needs were diverse.

The big package deal was essentially Northern security of supply for oil and other raw materials in return for the major components of the NIEO: guarantee of a fair return for commodity exports, a commitment to a greater flow of financial resources and technology, and a debt relief scheme. The industrial states generally held such a package to be extravagant and unrealistic, and they assumed that the developing states would eventually settle for less. The developing states responded that their position was realistic, because, as Perez Guerrero put it, "the countries of the North will not be able to resolve the multiple problems which assail them without finding a solution to the problem of development and accepting a more equitable relationship with the countries of the South."[9] For the South there was little point to the whole Paris exercise if it were not aimed at a major breakthrough. To settle for less was simply to prolong the struggle.

Neither side really had a good idea of what the other side might eventually settle for. Both sides were heterogeneous, making precise diplomatic calculation difficult. Despite the tremendous weight of the U.S. position, the North was not monolithic. Sweden and the Netherlands, for example, were considerably more sympathetic to the South's proposals than the United States and West Germany. The EEC, which had to accommodate these divergent positions within its own ranks, was an uncertain actor that the South hoped to pry away from the U.S. position, perhaps under French leadership. The differences within the 8 kept open Southern hopes that the North would eventually adopt a more' flexible position. Likewise, the North counted on the diversity of the 19 to breach the Third World common front, as had occurred at the end of 1975. But the dynamics of the coalition were somewhat different once the conference was underway. The 19 acted as if it considered itself accountable to the 77, which made it difficult for the Group to depart from the grand lines of the Manila Declaration and the NIEO texts. Its own diversity in fact limited its bargaining flexibility, contrary to the calculations of the North.

To break the deadlock required a recognition of these two characteristics of the negotiating situation: the relative inflexibility of the Third World coalition and its commitment to a major package deal. But beyond this it required a willingness to concede some of the Third World's arguments. Ever since April

1976, the Group of 19 had attributed the torpor of the conference to the North's lack of "political will" to change the international economic system. So far as the 19 was concerned, the eight months of negotiations sufficed to show that only a major policy shift could resolve the tensions and frustrations of the North-South dialogue. By this point, everything turned on President Carter's "political will."

CIEC'S FINAL INVENTORY

The final phase of the conference was designed to test this will in short order. The parties agreed to the following timetable and procedures:

April 26–28: Meeting of the ten co-chairmen, and of the Groups of 19 and 8 at the level of senior civil servants

April 28–May 14: Intensive negotiation in some 15 issue-areas by newly instituted "contact groups"

May 26–27: Plenary conference of senior officials to prepare the final session

May 30–June 1: Final ministerial meeting

Meanwhile, President Carter announced before the United Nations that the United States was now ready to collaborate in a Common Fund and envisaged other measures to improve North-South relations. Yet the special conference organized by UNCTAD on the Common Fund got nowhere, each side still having different ideas of what the fund ought to be. Whether the Carter administration could really deliver the goods that the South was looking for remained in doubt as the Paris Conference resumed late in April 1977.

After a week of exchanges in the contact groups, the Group of 19 once again sounded the alarm. The Northern negotiators, the 19 contended, were not advancing proposals commensurate with the scale of the problems; the Group of 8 was reneging upon the commitment to seek "concrete results capable of producing a significant advance in international economic cooperation."[10] Perez Guerrero made it clear that time was running out on the Paris experiment, for the South was ready to return the whole matter to the General Assembly. If the North considered CIEC the best forum in which to reach an understanding, the moment of reckoning was at hand.

This Group of 19 statement was in large measure actually addressed to the summit conference of the major industrial powers (United States, Japan, West Germany, France, Great Britain, Italy, and Canada), which was about to convene in London on May 7. As this summit was devoted to the global economic situation, the Group of 19 saw fit to spell out once again the conditions of a successful conclusion to CIEC: The South would stabilize the supply of energy and other raw materials in return for implementation of the IPC/Common Fund and commitments to the preservation of their purchasing power and to debt relief. This was not the package that the North put together in London. The Northern package did include a commitment in principle to the Common Fund (but not the IPC), a $1 billion Special Action Program of aid for the neediest countries, and a more general pledge to increase the level of development aid and technical assistance. The industrial countries pledged at their London meeting "to do all in our power to assure the success of CIEC," but it was clear that the criteria of success were not the same on both sides.

The London summit incorporated everything new that the Carter administration had to offer to the North-South Conference. The new administration was willing to go a step farther than its predecessor toward the Common Fund, but for the most part it was thinking of traditional aid programs and not of new international economic structures. The hopes that the Carter presidency might inaugurate a genuinely new era in North-South relations were rapidly fading.

The final ministerial meeting of CIEC merely produced an inventory of the fruits of a year and a half of diplomatic toil. As set forth in the Report of the Conference, the inventory indicated that the participants had reached a consensus on 20 matters and had failed to come to agreement on 21 others. Was the store half-full or half-empty? On this final evaluation, the participants could not agree. The final Report was typical of much that had transpired during the Paris talks. It was an agreement to disagree in appraising the conference itself.

According to the report,[11] the developing countries

> while recognizing that progress has been made in CIEC to meet certain proposals of developing countries, noted with regret that most of the proposals for structural changes in the international economic system . . . have not been agreed upon. Therefore the Group of 19 feels that the conclusions of CIEC fall short of the objectives envisaged for a comprehensive and equitable program of action designed to establish the new international economic order.

The developed countries on the other hand

> welcomed the spirit of cooperation in which on the whole the Conference took place. . . . They regretted that it had not proved possible to reach agreement on some important areas of the dialogue such as certain aspects of energy cooperation.

These contrasting assessments summed up the distance that still separated North and South, the former concerned essentially with energy and the latter with development policy. As Jahangir Amuzegar expressed his appraisal, CIEC came to a "battered and confused end . . . on a faint and joyless note."[12]

At first glance, the Third World assessment of CIEC might appear unduly negative. Twenty items of agreement would not seem a meager result. Set against the criterion of radical change, however, the agreements were of modest significance. The most important was the commitment to the establishment of a Common Fund, but even this remained something of a question mark inasmuch as the Report stated that the "purposes, objectives, and other constituent elements were to be further negotiated in UNCTAD." Moreover, the link between the Fund and the Integrated Program of Commodities was not admitted by the North—the relationship between the two appeared on the list of disagreements. The developing states were skeptical about the extent of understanding actually reached on this item. As one Third World spokesman indicated, the Common Fund and the IPC "constitute the key elements of a profoundly innovative entire system. How much of that remains?"[13]

The second major agreement was on the subject of development aid, notably the billion dollar Special Action Program destined for the neediest countries and a pledge to increase substantially the volume of annual public developmental aid. These pledges were welcome and important, but the essential goal of the developing countries was to place development aid in the context of structural reforms. The Development Committee reached agreements on various aspects of industrialization, agriculture, and transfer of technology, in each instance following up on issues that had not been satisfactorily resolved in other forums. Here CIEC bore out the promise of gradual progress through long-term deliberations, but none of these items could be considered a major breakthrough.

All the other agreements also lay in relatively uncontroversial issue-areas: cooperation in improving the marketing and competitiveness of Third World exports; access of the developing states to international capital markets; the utility of a favorable investment climate insofar as private capital was concerned; the value of cooperation among the developing countries themselves. The agreements in the Energy Commission also fell into this category.

Energy was of course the crucial issue area for the developed countries. The accords credited to this commission amounted to a set of guidelines regarding conservation, diversification, international cooperation in research and development of alternate energy sources, and agreement upon the necessity of adequate and stable energy supplies. The United States considered that "the agreement on supply puts OPEC on record as recognizing that adequate energy supplies are necessary and that oil exporters have a responsibility of meeting energy needs."[14] These general commitments thus reassured the Northern states, but hardly exhausted the items on the Energy Commission agenda. Here, as in the other commissions, the most important were not resolved.

The main disappointment for the industrial states was the failure to gain guarantees on the price of oil. As the final session drew near without any agreed guidelines for oil pricing, the North advanced the idea of continuing the energy component of CIEC. It argued that the energy talks, unlike the other topics that would be taken up again in UNCTAD and other forums, were unique to CIEC. The industrial states wanted some form of permanent energy consultations that would make it politically more difficult for OPEC to raise prices.[15]

This Northern proposal was the only real subject of debate during the final ministerial meeting. Its effect was to bring the conference back to its point of departure. Among the OPEC participants, Algeria, Iraq, and Venezuela were firmly opposed to any arrangement that would limit their decision making power. They argued that the concessions made in CIEC by the industrial states were far from sufficient to justify the creation of such a new institution. Saudi Arabia and Iran were willing to entertain the idea, but suggested that the whole structure of CIEC, not solely the energy component, be continued. Although the United States was open to this, neither the Europeans nor the other Third World states wanted to extend CIEC. But some Third World oil importers did see benefits in ongoing energy talks, which encouraged the North to press the issue. As the dispute became more intense, the OPEC militants succeeded in rallying the rest of the Group of 19 to their position. In the face of a common Third World position, the North had no choice but to relegate the matter to the list of disagreements.

Most of the other matters recorded as disagreements in the Report represented Southern grievances. The most important were indexation, debt, and the Integrated Program of Commodities. The North was adamant on these proposals, which involved the most radical challenges to the classic liberal conception of international economic relations. On other Southern proposals, the North was looking for trade-offs: for preferential treatment of commodity exports, a pledge of "unimpaired access" to raw materials; for a code of behavior for multinational corporations, various guarantees for foreign private investment (transfer of profits, jurisdiction of disputes, compensation). These negotiations resulted in standoffs. On Third World proposals for greater participation in economic decision making (representation on commodities exchanges, in conferences on maritime shipping rates, in a study of compensatory financing), the North stood by the existing order.

If the agreements and disagreements were roughly balanced in number, the quality of the results was unsatisfactory for the developing countries. The major components of their program of international economic change (pending further developments on the Common Fund) were not approved in Paris. Despite the alleged virtues of the CIEC apparatus, the North-South Conference did not produce the breakthrough that the Third World was seeking. From its point of view, the cup was unquestionably half-empty.

In the final analysis, neither side achieved the goal that it had set for the Paris Conference. The industrial countries were looking for a respite from North-South politics, and deemed that their aid proposals and gesture toward the Common Fund justified a period of détente in North-South relations. This the South was not ready to grant. Speaking for the Group of 19, Perez Guerrero acknowledged that there were some "positive results, but of limited scope."[16] Accordingly, the Third World would now return the whole dossier of international economic reform to the United Nations.

Perhaps CIEC's greatest merit was to clarify, if need be, that the problem was not one of communication but of conflicting interests. The trimming of the ranks of 27 delegations did not transform the nature of the issues. The final phase of CIEC confirmed that the basic systemic variables had not evolved very much between September 1975 and June 1977. The North still lacked the will and the South still lacked the power to change the international economic system. The South stood by its demands, but it faced again the reality of the North's power of resistance. The problem of bringing about a change in Northern policy resumed its normal scale as the 19 reintegrated the 77.

NOTES

1. *Le Monde*, October 16, 1975.
2. The documents approved at the October conference are found in *Documents d'Actualité Internationale, 1975* 49 (December 9, 1975).
3. *Le Monde*, October 17, 1975.
4. The text of the Final Declaration of the December meeting appears in *Documents d'Actualité Internationale, 1976* 4 (January 28, 1976).
5. Bernard Peyre, "La Conférence Nord-Sud: Une opération diplomatique réussie ou un dialogue durable?" *Défense Nationale* 32 (March 1976): 43-54. A U.S. official later expressed much the same attitude: CIEC's "limited size and relative absence from public view meant that, for the most part, ideological rhetoric was eschewed, and a relatively businesslike atmosphere obtained." See the statement by Under Secretary of State for Economic Affairs Richard N. Cooper in *Department of State Bulletin* 77, no. 1986 (July 18, 1977): 93.
6. Daniel Colard, "Vers l'établissement d'un nouvel ordre économique international," *Notes et Etudes Documentaries* 4412-4414 (September 23, 1977): 65.
7. *Le Monde*, April 30, 1976.
8. Jahangir Amuzegar, "A Requiem for the North-South Conference," *Foreign Affairs* 55, no. 1 (October 1977): 148-49.
9. *Le Monde*, May 3, 1977.
10. Ibid., May 7, 1977.
11. The report appears in *Department of State Bulletin* 76, no. 1982 (June 20, 1977).
12. Amuzegar, "Requiem," p. 136.
13. *Le Monde*, June 1, 1977, quoting Ait Chaalal, co-chairman of the Development Commission.
14. Cooper, *Department of State Bulletin*, p. 95.
15. The *New York Times* quoted a "Western official who is close to this part of the conference" as follows: "An on-going energy dialogue would put the oil exporters in a moral straitjacket" (June 2, 1977).
16. *Le Monde*, June 4, 1977.

7. The Tension of Solidarity and Dispersion, 1977–79

The close of the Paris Conference marked the end of a distinctive phase in North-South politics. The period from the onset of the energy crisis and the formulation of the NIEO program to the end of CIEC can be thought of as the revolutionary era in Third World collective action. The political pressure that had been mobilized behind the NIEO demands in the spring of 1974 was largely expended by the summer of 1977. The first major thrust of Third World diplomacy, in other words, was now exhausted without achieving the bulk of its objectives. The challenge facing the Third World coalition by mid-1977 was to remobilize its forces in order to build the pressure up again.

This was no mean task, because the inherent propensity toward dispersion in so heterogeneous a body was acutely in evidence. The divisive impact of the Angolan, Western Saharan, and Lebanese crises upon the coalition in 1976 has already been seen. Other even more damaging conflicts were building up throughout 1977. They raised the specter of a return to the situation of the mid-1960s when antagonism among pro-Chinese, pro-Soviet, and pro-Western factions wrecked Bandung II and nearly buried the coalition. Some of the theaters of conflict were (more or less) new—between Somalia and Ethiopia, between Vietnam and Cambodia—while others intensified, as between Zaire and Angola, but all contained the element of great-power involvement that sapped the autonomy of the developing states. Cuba's engagement in Africa added a further dimension to these disputes, provoking additional strains within the nonaligned framework.

Changes of regime in Afghanistan and then in Iran and the dramatic shift in Egyptian foreign policy introduced yet other new variables into Third World politics. The coalition had to move, so to speak, across shifting sands. The sands were shifting under their own feet at the same time that they were changing the landscape of international politics ahead. The multitude of variables affecting the Third World coalition made it extremely difficult to chart a steady course let alone climb to new heights of solidarity. Indeed, one might well have expected the total disintegration of the coalition under these circumstances, but this did not happen.

Rather the working arrangements and practical experience developed during the first phase of NIEO politics continued to sustain the coalition. Both the nonaligned and Group of 77 frameworks had acquired enough durability by mid-1977 to withstand the centrifugal pressures. The organizational machinery was able to take the place of a waning sense of solidarity—at least over the two years following the end of the North-South Conference.

During the final stages of CIEC, the developing states decided to return the unresolved issues to the United Nations. As more and more of their collective diplomacy occurred within the UN system, the role of the Group of 77 grew in importance. More than ever before, New York became a focal point of Third World activity as the developing countries insisted upon the creation of a new General Assembly Committee of the Whole on international economic relations. The UN/UNCTAD bargaining process remained reasonably familiar and manageable at a moment when rapid change elsewhere was rendering the political landscape unfamiliar and rather unmanageable.

NEW CRISES IN THE THIRD WORLD

These changes were felt most strongly within the nonaligned movement in its self-appointed role as the political catalyst of the Third World coalition. A Yugoslav foreign ministry official acknowledged in mid-1977 that the nonaligned states now appeared to be on the defensive:

> What creates the impression of defensiveness in the nonaligned countries' action are the increasing and heightened conflicts between certain nonaligned countries. . . . This is evident in the conflict of interests over the self-determination of certain "small countries," in the obstructions to certain countries' exercising their right to free development by means of revolutionary change and also the attempts under various subterfuges to endanger the territorial integrity of certain nonaligned countries.[1]

These diplomatically veiled allusions to Western Sahara, to the separatist movements in Ogaden and Eritrea in the Horn of Africa, and to Angola and Zaire conveyed Yugoslavia's fear of a breakup of the nonaligned movement.

The threat to group cohesion posed by these conflicts was greatly exacerbated by Cuba's role in Africa. When Cuba, which had long cultivated close ties with the Marxist faction of the Angolan nationalist movement, sent troops to help establish the MPLA in power, tensions began to rise (as mentioned in Chapter 5). They escalated abruptly in March 1977 upon the first invasion of Zaire's Shaba province by rebels coming from Angola.

The Angola-Cuba-Zaire triangle reawakened the distrust that has always existed between moderate and radical regimes in Africa. The fact that Angola was willing to allow anti-Mobutu forces to mount a strike into mineral-rich Shaba province was widely interpreted as a Cuban (and hence Soviet) probe against a vulnerable Western-oriented regime. Several Third World governments—most prominently Morocco, Egypt, and Sudan—hastened to Mobutu's aid, and the insurgents withdrew almost as quickly as they had arrived. The diplomatic repercussions were of much greater consequence than the FNLC* operation itself. Reminiscent of the Congo crisis of the early 1960s, Zaire's "unending crisis" once again opened a cleavage among African states.[2]

The effect of the Shaba incursion (in which no Cuban soldiers actually participated) might have passed quickly had it not been coupled with a growing Cuban role in the Horn of Africa as well. The key change in this region was the emergence of Colonel Mengistu Haile Mariam as the strongman of the military regime in Ethiopia. Mengistu was a Marxist intent upon breaking the last of the ties of the old Haile Selassie regime (overthrown in 1974) with the United States. He was concurrently engaged in a two-front war against ethnic Somalis in Ethiopia's Ogaden region seeking union with Somalia and Eritreans seeking independence for their province. Like Angola's Agostino Neto, Mengistu called upon Cuba to provide military assistance, initially in the capacity of advisers and eventually as combat troops. Cuba's willingness to back the new regime brought it into direct conflict with Somalia and indirect conflict with Sudan, Saudi Arabia, and other Arab governments friendly to the Eritreans and uneasy about a Marxist government in Addis Ababa.

Here, as in Angola, the Cuban presence went hand-in-hand with an extension of Soviet influence in a former Western preserve. Castro no doubt had an independent commitment to support revolutionaries in Africa, but as Jorge Dominguez has put it:

> Throughout these events, Cuba has continued to coordinate policy with the U.S.S.R. in ways that make it difficult to determine who leads and who follows, even though it remains clear that neither the Angolan nor the Ethiopian operations could have been conducted in the absence of either.[3]

---

*The National Front for the Liberation of the Congo was manned principally by ex-Katanga gendarmes who fled the Congo in the 1960s and eventually fought with the MPLA in the Angolan civil war. Originally sessionists, they now aspired to spark a more generalized uprising that they hoped would topple the Mobutu government.

Cuba of course had always been at the radical end of the Third World spectrum, but this highly prominent involvement on two African fronts, each in close association with Soviet policy, strained the bounds of consensus that held the non-aligned group together. Cuba itself became an issue, all the more so because the fifth summit was scheduled for Havana.

Just as the Cuban connection was sharpening antagonisms within Africa, the new Vietnamese connection was creating intra-Asian strains. Reunited Vietnam attended the Colombo summit in 1976. The case of Vietnam raised the same kinds of objections as Cuba did in its obvious tilt toward the Soviet Union. On top of this came degenerating relations between Vietnam and Cambodia. In mid-1977, the conflict was being expressed in border clashes, but the underlying cause was ideological conflict between the Khmers Rouges and the Vietnamese communists. The geopolitics of the southeast Asian setting were such as to draw the Soviet Union and China deeply into the dispute. Here, again, the political consequences for the nonaligned group were reminiscent of the early 1960s when Soviets, Chinese, and their respective backers battled in the Afro-Asian Peoples' Solidarity Organization and over Bandung II. In brief, issues that had been fairly effectively banished over the past decade began to reappear in the nonaligned framework.

These disputes, already worrisome to the Yugoslav overseers of nonalignment in June 1977, became much worse in the following two years. First Somalia and Ethiopia went to war, later Vietnam and Cambodia did the same. The FNLC again marched into Shaba in a much bloodier and economically devastating strike. The guerrilla wars in Western Sahara and Eritrea continued to smoulder and intermittently flare up. Furthermore, new developments added yet other complications. In April 1978, a coup brought a Marxist government to power in Afghanistan. In June, communists in the ruling leftist coalition in South Yemen ousted a noncommunist president. These coups in Kabul and Aden destabilized relations with regional neighbors (Pakistan, Iran, North Yemen, Saudi Arabia) and heated up the international climate in general. As alarms sounded in Washington and Soviet-U.S. détente threatened to crumble, numerous Third World states were subjected to increasing pressure from one or the other superpower camp. Finally Egypt's sharp break with the rest of the Arab world in its approach to Israel opened up yet another arena of intragroup controversy.

UTILIZING THE UNITED NATIONS SYSTEM

This complex backdrop of rivalries and competing national interests provided the setting in which the Third World coalition had to operate as CIEC ground to a halt. The sentiment that the nonaligned framework was under siege was already quite strong in April 1977 when the Bureau held its fourth annual session in New Delhi. This is evident, for example, in the commentaries upon that meeting by Yugoslav officials who stressed that the Bureau responded to various attempts to weaken the movement and to cause rifts in it.[4]

Yugoslavia in fact perceived two slightly different threats to the non-aligned movement. One lay in the campaign to "unseat it with other parallel organizations or meetings,"[5] an allusion to the efforts discussed in Chapter 5 to convene a summit meeting of the Group of 77. None of the nonaligned activists wished to see the Group of 77 expand its political role. Yet at the same time they recognized that economic issues were more than ever the binding force in Third World relations. The New Delhi communique thus thrice reiterated the formula according to which the nonaligned states acted as the catalytic agent within the Group of 77, and called for a meeting of the Group of 77 in September when the UN General Assembly was expected to review the final report of the Paris Conference. To the extent that they saw a challenge from the Group of 77, the members of the nonaligned Bureau sought not to resist it but to flow along with it.

As they all recognized, the real threat to "unseat" the nonaligned movement stemmed not from a countermovement but from nonalignment's own internal rifts. The New Delhi meeting largely steered clear of these issues (in contrast to the case a year earlier at the Algiers Bureau meeting). The newly elected Indian government nevertheless addressed these problems indirectly. Prime Minister Morarji Desai, who had defeated Indira Gandhi in parliamentary elections just two weeks earlier, announced that India intended to pursue a conciliatory role so as to strengthen the nonaligned grouping from within. India's stand was particularly gratifying to the Yugoslavs as it promised them an ally in the task of mediating disputes and firming up the center of the movement. Desai stressed that the developing states must practice self-help, which meant not only economic cooperation but political restraint in their local disputes. Both were integral to any effective collective Third World presence in international politics.

The New Delhi meeting occurred at a moment when North-South relations were marking time, awaiting, without great optimism, the final round of the Paris Conference. Once the results were in, the focus shifted to New York where the next phase of NIEO politics began in September 1977. One can interpret the return to the General Assembly as a bid to reactivate the Third World voting majority of the Sixth Special Session. From the perspective of the developing states, that session had set a diplomatic process in motion. In the spirit of the Seventh Special Session, they had agreed to channel this process into the dialogue in Paris, a move that most now viewed as a tactical error. They intended to reopen the entire NIEO dossier, in part simply to disabuse the North of any notion that the matter be closed, in part to pursue a fresh strategy for implementing their proposals. Such a strategy seemed most promising in the context of the Third World majority in the General Assembly.

This in turn implied utilizing the Group of 77 framework to its utmost.

It has already been seen how the Third World preparations for the Sixth and Seventh Special Sessions were carried out through the Group of 77. The practice of convening the UN representatives of the Group of 77 memberstates became standard operating procedure thereafter. Nonetheless, the organizational arrangements of the Group of 77 in New York have remained minimal. The practice has been to select a chairman who serves for a year from one General Assembly session to the next. He is essentially a convenor and record keeper, acting also as Group spokesperson when appropriate. The chair rotates from Asia to South America to Africa even though it is not the practice in New York, contrary to Geneva, to hold meetings at the level of geographic subgroups. On the other hand, there is an organizational subgroup, the Group of 27 (nine from each geographic region), which acts as something of a steering committee. As in the case of its nonaligned counterpart (the Bureau), the Group of 27 is really open-ended—any member of the 77 may sit in on its meetings. Just as in the nonaligned institutional scheme, this permits a smaller group to prepare plenary meetings and ensure interim continuity without actually excluding any state from participation in the decision-making process. During the 1976-77, or thirty-first, session of the General Assembly, Pakistan held the chair and Iqbal Akhund served as chairman of the Group of 77.

The General Assembly opens a new session each September and normally adjourns a few months later, usually in December. In December 1976, however, the Group of 77 proposed not to adjourn but merely to suspend the session.* This gave the Group the option of simply reopening the Assembly (rather than convening a special session) at any moment in order to assess the results of the ongoing Paris Conference. The parliamentary device of a recess served notice that the Group of 77 considered the matter of international economic reform to be unfinished business. At the time that the decision was taken, it was expected that CIEC would conclude earlier than June; as matters turned out, the session was not "reconvened" until September. The tactic still had the effect of requiring a debate focused on international economic relations prior to the general debate that traditionally occurs upon the opening of a new General Assembly session.

This rump session, September 13-20, 1977, thus provided the occasion for the opening volley in a Third World battle to reestablish the NIEO as a priority matter in international politics. The skirmish took the form of a debate over the success of the Paris Conference. The Group of 77 submitted a draft resolution, the gist of which was to reiterate that the results of CIEC fell far short of its stated objectives. The draft also proposed that all further global

---

*Although this parliamentary device had been used three times before (in 1967, 1973, and 1974), this was the first time that the recess was explicitly linked to economic issues.

negotiations on the NIEO must be conducted within the UN system and that a special session be convened in 1980 to assess progress toward the new order by then. These latter provisions were not objectionable to the North, but the condemnation of CIEC was. The United States insisted that any resolution must recognize the concrete agreements that had been reached in Paris (essentially the Special Action Program and the commitment in principle to the Common Fund).

The stakes in this debate were mainly symbolic, and for this reason no consensus was reached. The North wanted credit for the concessions that it had made, while the South insisted that all the important matters still lay ahead. Even the Common Fund remained to be implemented, Akhund argued on behalf of the 77, and the $1 billion Special Action pledge was best measured against the $4 billion of annual debt service weighing upon the Third World. The North would not accept a resolution that did not acknowledge its view that significant progress toward meeting Third World grievances had already been made. The South was not willing to grant this point. United States Ambassador Andrew Young argued that realism dictated a compromise. The Group of 77 preferred not to dilute its assessment of the inadequacy of the North's offers.

For the moment, however, the South chose not to exercise its voting majority. Rather than pass the Group of 77 resolution over the dissenting votes of several developed countries, the Third World coalition simply let the deadlock stand. After a week of unresolved debate, the thirty-first session of the General Assembly officially closed in a diplomatically ignominious stalemate. As there were no material stakes in agreement over a dead conference, the Third World allowed stalemate to dramatize its frustrations as a prelude to the campaign that it would mount in the upcoming thirty-second session.

The basic strategy of this campaign had actually been taking shape for some time under the aegis of an ad hoc committee on restructuring the United Nations system. The ad hoc committee had been established in Part VII of the resolution adopted at the Seventh Special Session two years earlier. Its hefty mandate was to propose ways of "restructuring the United Nations system so as to make it more fully capable of dealing with problems of international economic cooperation and development." The committee labored for two years in the face of conflicting Northern and Southern conceptions of how to reorganize the United Nations. The Group of 77 submitted a proposal, the gist of which was to establish the General Assembly as the preeminent organ for setting international development policy and fixing priorities for the specialized agencies. Its goal, in brief, was "enhancing the impact of their collective majority."[6] The United States submitted a proposal, the intent of which was essentially the opposite in seeking to channel discussion of economic issues to the smaller Economic and Social Council and other limited-member consultative groups, and to preserve the broad autonomy of agencies like the World Bank and the

International Monetary Fund. The ad hoc committee assiduously worked out a compromise plan that was ultimately approved in December 1977.

The restructuring compromise contained several components that the Group of 77 considered beneficial. Perhaps the most noteworthy was the creation of a new high-level secretariat position, Director-General for Development and International Economic Cooperation.* It did not, however, institutionalize the preeminence of the General Assembly to the degree that the Group of 77 had sought. The 77 now devised a different means to a comparable end. It called for the establishment of a new General Assembly Committee of the Whole charged with overseeing and monitoring the implementation of the NIEO. Creation of the Committee of the Whole in December 1977 was the second volley in the new round of NIEO politics.

The significance of the new committee was not immediately apparent. As the idea did not figure in the restructuring proposals that had been so thoroughly discussed for over two years, it was, on the face of it, rather puzzling that such a committee should be separately instituted at the same moment that the restructuring plan was formally adopted. What did the Group of 77 have in mind? In simplest terms the establishment of the Committee of the Whole was a parliamentary maneuver to keep the entire NIEO agenda at the center of General Assembly affairs. At the minimum it was a safeguard against neglect, benign or otherwise, for it blocked closure of the issue. More ambitiously it was an instrument to stimulate progress on NIEO issues by focusing steady attention upon them. The enabling resolution called upon the committee to meet "as and when required during the intersessional periods" between regular General Assembly sessions so as to provide "a forum for facilitating and expediting agreement."[7] While there was of course no magic in such a committee to produce agreement that could not be struck elsewhere, the concept did operationalize the Third World strategy of recognizing the General Assembly as the focal point of an ongoing dialogue on development.

The committee was then an additional instrument available to the Group of 77, but one of unknown capability. It was simple to fashion (by virtue of the Third World voting majority) but more difficult to put to good use, because there was no underlying consensus between North and South as to the appropriate function of the committee. A lengthy round of procedural discussions consuming most of 1978 was necessary to clarify just what the committee might do in practice.

An initial organizational session was held at which Idriss Jazairy of Algeria was named chairman of the committee. Jazairy worked closely with Donald

---

*In March 1978, Kenneth Dadzie of Ghana, who had served as chairman of the ad hoc committee after his years of service in Geneva, was appointed to this post.

Mills of Jamaica, who was chairman of the Group of 77 in 1977–78, to legitimize a genuine substantive role for the committee. An inconclusive session was held in May, another in September. Nominally the debate was over whether the Committee of the Whole had any function other than as a forum for the exchange of views. Substantively to be sure the issue was the North's willingness to negotiate permanently on NIEO proposals. The September meeting was cut short with the matter at a total standstill. The whole debate was then bounced back to the General Assembly for "clarification." In October a modus vivendi was worked out in the form of a "statement of clarification" by the president of the General Assembly, Indalecio Lievano of Colombia.

In a carefully worded interpretation, Lievano announced that

> consultations with States had led him to conclude that the Committee would negotiate with a view to adopting guidelines on central policy questions and to achieving agreement for the solution of fundamental or crucial issues. The results of the negotiations would be expressed in action-oriented agreed conclusions addressed to states and international organizations.[8]

(If this be clarification, one might well mutter, long live obfuscation.) However obscure this clarification, it served for the moment to head off a sharp North-South confrontation. It granted the Group of 77's basic premise that the committee should conduct negotiations rather than merely record an exchange of views. It was sufficiently ambiguous about the status of the "guidelines" and "conclusions" that the committee might reach to satisfy the developed countries. The compromise "clarification" was a very modest advance for the Group of 77, but it at least held out the promise that the Committee of the Whole might yet stimulate some kind of progress in the North-South dialogue.

By October 1978, Mahmoud Mestiri of Tunisia was serving as chairman of the Group of 77. Mestiri charged that the real problem had nothing to do with the committee's terms of reference but with "the refusal of most developed countries to commit themselves seriously to the . . . restructuring of international economic relations." He professed to see a step in the right direction in the October "clarification," "because it revealed an evolution in the political attitude of the developed countries."[9] The evolution was minimal to be sure, but the Group of 77 was at least succeeding in maintaining pressure by maintaining its own organizational cohesion at the United Nations.

The bargaining situation was roughly comparable on other key NIEO fronts: The most important of these was the continuing negotiation over the Common Fund. As the Group of 77 Chairman Akhund had noted in September 1977, the developed states' agreement in principle to a commodity fund at CIEC was still a giant step away from a functioning institution. Talks on this matter resumed in Geneva in November 1977.

The Group of 77 submitted a draft scheme of what the Common Fund should look like. Its key provisions called for an initial working capital of $3 billion ($1 billion subscribed by the member-states and $2 billion in borrowing authority) that would be used to finance the anticipated commodity arrangements under the Integrated Program of Commodities, still the necessary complement of the Fund in the view of the developing states. The Fund would have authority to finance buffer stocks and other kinds of commodity-related projects (for example, diversification, productivity improvement, and marketing promotion—all new ideas in the Common Fund context). The industrial states also submitted a draft scheme, which bore little resemblance to what the Group of 77 had in mind. It envisaged merely a pool of funds siphoned off from whatever individual commodity accords that existed independently—for practical purposes virtually the opposite of what the Group of 77 wanted. The total capital would be modest in amount and in any case dependent on other agreements. As only one commodity agreement based on buffer stocks existed (in tin), the Group of 77 understandably was dubious. Furthermore, this approach precluded any investments other than regulatory stocks such as diversification projects, that is, the "second window" as this component of the Group of 77 proposal came to be called. In brief the Western position, still largely dominated by U.S. policy, had barely evolved at all from the stand taken at Nairobi, while the conception of the Group of 77 had actually become more ambitious.* The November 1977 meeting was accordingly a dismal failure.

The Common Fund appeared to languish hopelessly through much of 1978, but in fact the Group of 77 was relying upon UNCTAD processes and the gradually approaching prospect of UNCTAD V (set for May 1979) to maintain pressure. As Figure 5.1 shows, the Group of 77 maintained a working group on this issue at Geneva. Through the working group it warned that failure to get anywhere at all in the three years from UNCTAD IV to UNCTAD V on such a salient matter could severely endanger any chance for North-South détente. The Carter administration felt this pressure building up within UNCTAD, and in autumn 1978 on the eve of a further negotiating conference on the Fund, it budged a little bit. It conceded the concept of a "second window" and agreed upon financing through direct contributions rather than through separate individual commodity pacts. The amount to be contributed, the voting arrangements, and specific working mechanics of the Fund were still contentious issues, but the U.S. concessions broke the logjam.

---

*The basic reason for this expansion of the Common Fund concept was the pressure of the African group within the 77. Fearing that price stabilization alone offered little to many resource-poor African states, they pressed for the broader scheme. Although this further complicated the negotiating task, the Asians and Latin Americans had little choice but to raise the common denominator.

In two further negotiating sessions (November 1978, March 1979), the fundamental elements of the Common Fund were hammered out. The terms of the agreement revealed that the Third World made significant concessions as well. Although there were two "windows," each was small: The first was endowed with $400 million and the second with only $70 million plus a target of an additional $280 million in voluntary contributions. As the journal *The Inter Dependent* reported, "Both rich and poor countries agree that the $750 million arrangement is a far cry from the original Common Fund proposed at UNCTAD IV in 1976."[10] Second, the North prevailed on the basic operational concept of the Fund, which was to serve as a bank granting loans to the few commodity agreements with buffer stocking provisions (cocoa as well as tin by this time, with prospects likely in coffee, copper, rubber, and sugar). Although not dependent upon such individual commodity agreements as initially desired by the North, neither was the fund well enough endowed to become the master financer of an integrated program as originally proposed by the Group of 77. Finally the voting arrangements were not so favorable to the Third World as it had sought.*

The Common Fund agreement attested once again to the real but limited power of the Third World coalition. The strength was there to force bargaining upon the North but not to acquire the settlement desired. There was sufficient bargaining strength to win some concessions, but once these were offered the pressure to come to terms shifted to the South. Poor countries, as an analyst of global bargaining has argued,

> cannot afford to ignore the needs of the present. This creates enormous problems in maintaining unity, a weakness that the rich and powerful can exploit by offering slightly better terms in the existing system in exchange for abandoning challenges to the system itself.[11]

The developing countries now accepted such terms on the presumption that a mini-breakthrough toward new international economic institutions was better than none. Although the criticism that the Third World surrendered "some of its cherished ideas of economic restructuring" was valid, the Third World did

---

*The developing states began from the principle of one state, one vote, while the developed states assumed that voting weighted according to financial contribution would be instituted. A schedule of weighted voting that did give some extra weight to the Third World was worked out in March. It gave 47 percent of the votes to the developing countries whose financial contribution was 23 percent of the total. The Western industrial states got 42 percent of the votes and the East Europeans, including the Soviet Union, got 8 percent. The other 3 percent went to China. Both the United States and the Soviet Union, however, announced that they did not accept this distribution of votes, and reserved the right to reopen this question.

reinforce one of its basic premises.[12] Creation of the Fund entailed granting the Third World claim that some form of international management of commodities was necessary.

The Common Fund negotiation was not the only one between North and South during this period. A parallel negotiation took place on the other major issue of UNCTAD IV, the debt problem. Here the Third World sought outright cancellation of the public debt of the poorest countries (that is, the conversion of past loans into grants) and a formal commitment to lighten the burden of debt on other developing countries. The matter was discussed in CIEC and then at UNCTAD until March 1978 when a resolution of sorts was reached. Spurred by the example of Sweden, Holland, Canada, and Switzerland, which did cancel the public debts owed them, the other creditor states formally undertook to seek means of adjusting debt obligations. As Sweden's minister of development aid put the case, cancellation was for practical purposes a kind of "retroactive aid" that was in the general international interest.[13] Other creditor countries like the United States were not ready to adopt the Swedish solution, but they did pledge to deal with the debt problem on a case-by-case basis. The March agreement was seen as a commitment that went beyond previous policy in meeting this Third World concern.

One other issue should be noted, economic cooperation among developing countries (ECDC) or implementation of collective self-reliance. The activities of the Group of 77 in this domain were a follow-up to the Mexico City Conference. In theory, ECDC was entirely within the realm of the developing countries themselves. In practice, they needed technical expertise to improve their capacity for mutual economic cooperation, and they wanted UNCTAD to provide this technical aid. They set up a subgroup in Geneva (see Figure 5.1) to press for implementation of the various support measures requested at Mexico City. UNCTAD in turn set up a committee on ECDC that authorized a "program of work" to study the feasibility of trade preferences, joint marketing enterprises, export credit and guarantee schemes, and so on among developing countries. The developed countries were not willing to authorize officially a program of meetings by regional cooperative groupings proposed by the Group of 77. By the end of 1978, this matter had become a sticking point to be referred to UNCTAD V.

The particular significance of ECDC was the embarrassing gap between theory and practice in this field, which revealed one of the great weaknesses of the Third World coalition. There was an undeniable irony in the South arguing with the North over the amount of support that the North would give (through UNCTAD activities) to ECDC. If the developing countries cannot generate their own system of mutual economic cooperation, then a potential source of their own bargaining power erodes. The developing countries did seek to close the gap between the theory and practice of collective self-reliance at the 1979 ministerial meeting of the Group of 77 (discussed more fully below), but the dilemma remained. The long-term effectiveness of the Group of 77—whether it was bargaining on the mandate of the Committee of the Whole, the Common Fund, debt relief, or ECDC—rested upon the political and economic realities of Third World mutual cooperation that underlay their bargaining demands.

Although the coalition working as the Group of 77 was able to make some headway through 1977-78, its underlying political vitality was being sorely tested over this period. The appearance of solid political cohesion was a key variable in the capacity of the Group of 77, and this turned to a considerable degree upon the political health of the nonaligned movement. It is important now to examine how the nonaligned group was faring over this period.

CLEAVAGE IN THE NONALIGNED GROUP

The organizational machinery of the nonaligned movement was well oiled by 1977. It continued to function flawlessly, bringing the nonaligned group together at regular intervals in September 1977 at the United Nations, in May 1978 in Havana, in July 1978 in Belgrade, in January 1979 in Mozambique, and in June 1979 in Colombo. But the machine was operating, as already seen, in an overheated environment, which threatened its rapid depreciation.

The September consultations in New York were unexceptional, involving first a Bureau meeting and then a plenary meeting to fix priorities for the forthcoming General Assembly session (including the new strategy on NIEO issues). As they had done in September 1976, they again formed working groups to concentrate on specific General Assembly agenda items. In setting firm dates for the 1978 Bureau and foreign ministerial meetings, New York continued to function as the communications center of the nonaligned network.

The 1978 Bureau meeting was less routine. It was scheduled for Kabul, Afghanistan, in the first week in May. At the end of April, President Mohammed Daud, a founding member of the movement, was overthrown and killed by leftist officers who placed Nur Mohammad Taraki of the Soviet-oriented People's Democratic Party in power. The transitional turmoil in Kabul was not conducive to holding a diplomatic conference. The Bureau was obliged under very short notice to reorganize the venue and date of the meeting. Cuba, seeing an opportunity to consolidate its standing in the face of the growing challenge to its nonaligned credentials, sprang into the breach. For the second time in three years, Havana became the site of a Bureau meeting. On the one hand, the movement's capacity to improvise was commendable, but on the other the site brought some of the mounting tensions in the group to the fore.

Against this background as Yugoslavia's Assistant Foreign Minister Miljan Komatina put it:

> The Ministerial Meeting of the Coordinating Bureau was a "testing ground" of sorts, a test that had to be passed by answering a number

of questions . . . how much would mutual conflicts dominate the meeting? what degree of unity is feasible? how strong are the centrifugal forces influencing and redirecting the movement's orientation, how active are the forces espousing its further strengthening as an independent global non-bloc force?[14]

Although Komatina asserted that the movement "passed the test," the evidence is rather mixed. It is clear in any case that the "mutual conflicts" were very important at the Havana meeting.

The political atmosphere was illustrated by a report that Somalia was seeking the expulsion of Cuba from the ranks of the nonaligned.[15] Although such a move could not have won adequate support (at the best it was premature), the report was symptomatic of the malaise. So was another apparently trivial but symbolically meaningful dispute. Nonaligned declarations regularly and ritualistically included a statement to the effect that nonaligned states opposed imperialism, colonialism, neocolonialism, racism, including Zionism, apartheid, and "all other forms of foreign domination." The last phrase was understood to allude to the Soviet Union. At Havana the Cubans drafted a communique that deleted this phrase. India, Indonesia, and Yugoslavia insisted that it be restored. The Cuban maneuver, presumably backed by Angola and Vietnam, was politically maladroit, reinforcing the claims of those opposed to Cuban policy in Africa. Not only was the controversial phrase restored (with the omission nonetheless of the word "other"—how subtle, these diplomatic nuances) but the following phrase was added:

> The Bureau considered it of utmost importance to preserve all principles of nonalignment . . . and to be vigilant against any attempts to subvert these principles or compromise the Movement's role as an independent factor in international affairs.[16]

The debate over this doctrinal issue scarcely calmed the troubled waters.

The communique made no direct reference to the events underway in Zaire (Shaba II), to the recent war between Ethiopia and Somalia, or to the renewed Ethiopian offensive against the Eritreans. The latter issue was in fact the most heated. Yugoslavia made known that a Cuban engagement alongside the Ethiopian troops in Eritrea (as distinct from the earlier engagement in the Ogaden where the Somali campaign enjoyed little international sympathy) was unacceptable.[17] The communique offered only a general stock recommendation to seek peaceful solutions. Explicit reference was made, however, to Western Sahara and to the border flare-ups between Vietnam and Cambodia. Here, too, the Bureau exhorted the parties to negotiate peaceful settlements.

Such exhortations were perfunctory, and the problems continued to fester. The fundamental political threat to nonaligned cohesion lay not so much in one or another or even a series of local conflicts as in the pattern that these disputes delineated. Cuba, Angola, Ethiopia, and Vietnam, all politically associated with the Soviet Union, and Algeria, less closely tied to the Soviets but prominent in the radical wing of the nonaligned, were ranged on one side. Zaire, Morocco, Somalia, Sudan, and Egypt, informally allied on the other side of these conflicts, were all basically pro-Western in orientation. Cambodia under the Pol Pot regime was also anti-Soviet, and although diplomatically isolated except for Chinese backing, was tactically supported by other southeast Asian states fearful of Vietnam like Indonesia, Malaysia, and Singapore. The pattern of radicals versus moderates tended to produce a single line of cleavage that dominated the local conflicts. States like Yugoslavia, India, Sri Lanka, Tunisia, Nigeria, Cameroon, Zambia, and Jamaica felt as if they were sitting on a fault line.

The latter continued nonetheless to try to stave off the quake between the May Bureau meeting and the July foreign ministers meeting, exerting pressure as best they could upon the various disputants. They were able to count one success on the Angola-Zaire front. Here domestic and external pressures upon both governments led to a reconciliation agreement that was officially announced at the Belgrade foreign ministers conference. Cuba did not stand in the way of this reconciliation—on the contrary there was evidence that Cuba wished to avoid any recurrence of conflict in Shaba province; furthermore, Cuba was abstaining from direct involvement in the Ethiopian action in Eritrea, thereby respecting the view of the Yugoslavs on this matter. While these developments did not benefit Somalia or fully satisfy Zaire, they eased some of the tensions surrounding Cuban policy in Africa.

Still there was a mood of crisis at the Belgrade Conference as moderates and radicals put forth different readings of the obligations of nonalignment. Somalia led the charge against Cuba, which, in the words of the Somali foreign minister, "surely did not deserve" to belong to the nonaligned movement.[18] Morocco, Ghana, Senegal, and several Arab countries joined in the criticism of Cuban troops, while Tanzania, Benin, Congo (Brazzaville), Afghanistan, and Vietnam defended Cuba's right to come to the aid of states requesting such assistance. Egypt, Zaire, and Morocco all backed Somalia's proposal to postpone or relocate the 1979 summit scheduled for Havana, but the majority of states were satisfied at the minimum to wait and see how Cuban policy evolved.*

No state actually proposed Cuba's expulsion, but this courtesy was not extended to Vietnam. The Cambodian Foreign Minister Ieng Sary, charging Vietnamese aggression and intervention in his country, called for Hanoi's expulsion from the movement. Vietnam responded sharply, accusing Cambodia of massacring ethnic Vietnamese civilian populations in the border regions and

---

*Six states ultimately submitted formal diplomatic reservations to the decision: Zaire, Somalia, Saudi Arabia, Cambodia, Gabon, and Central African Empire.

linking Cambodia to Chinese expansionism. The rhetorical violence deepened the sense of cleavage at the conference and undermined the movement's claim to a coherent voice in international politics. As *Le Monde* editorialized on the Belgrade meeting:

> At least up until now [the nonaligned] managed to preserve a minimum of apparent cohesion. Today the conflicts are hung out for all to see. For some nonalignment is an intangible doctrine. For others nonalignment is meaningful only if it leads toward an active alliance with the "socialist countries" (in fact the Soviet Union). For yet others, it means battling against Moscow's "hegemonism." And numerous countries represented in Belgrade are totally aligned with the West.[19]

As earlier chapters have shown, there had always been varying degrees of ideological and geopolitical alignment on the part of the member-states of the nonaligned group. The situation in mid-1978 was essentially an intensified version of this perennial characteristic. For several years, radical states had prevailed in guiding the overall direction of the movement. Now, as Indonesia's foreign minister put it with a touch of irony, "The silent majority of moderates is beginning to speak up at last."[20] The divisions of 1978 had stronger overtones of superpower alignment than the previous splits, thereby sapping the intellectual rationale and the political credibility of nonalignment at one and the same time.

Could any common purpose be salvaged from this political maelstrom? The centrists believed that they could still preserve some of the movement's impact. Faith, doggedness, lack of a better alternative?—the traditional nonaligned leaders persisted in their support of the concept and the organization. Unflappable in the midst of the turbulence, the Yugoslavs turned to understatement: "Relations in the nonalignment movement are not idyllic, just as they are not, after all, in the groupings of other countries." The "sharp polemics" at Belgrade were the understandable, if regrettable, consequence of "independent countries openly confronting their particular perceptions of world problems and mutual relations." Despite the polemics, in Yugoslavia's view, the majority stood by the basic principle of nonalignment, and "attempts to reorient the nonalignment movement . . . or to convert it into anyone's reserve force were defeated."[21] The Yugoslavs were justified in arguing that neither leftists nor rightists had captured the movement. More problematic, however, was whether the center represented any real force when hobbled by pro-East and pro-West factions.

By mid-1978, the nonaligned movement no longer looked like the motor force of a driving coalition. Too many states were using it for parochial interests. Yet there was still enough of an instinct of group self-preservation to avert a complete collapse of the framework. The Vietnam-Cambodia antagonism was well beyond nonaligned influence, but Cuban policy in Africa appeared a manageable issue. Castro did not wish to throw away his opportunity to host a nonaligned summit. He was willing to keep the Cuban role in Angola and Ethiopia limited to the maintenance of those regimes and to dissociate Cuba from the Shaba and Eritrea campaigns.[22] Most nonaligned members were content to adopt a wait-and-see attitude toward Cuba. Even so, there was a sense in 1978 that the movement was living on borrowed time.

The tensions did not abate in 1979. Vietnam marched into Cambodia to install a puppet regime, while Pol Pot forces survived in pockets of resistance and abroad. At the next Bureau meeting in June 1979, the issue of Cambodian representation, shades of 1970, once again tore apart a nonaligned forum. On top of this was loaded a fierce dispute over Egyptian membership following signature of the Egyptian-Israeli peace treaty. Syria, Iraq, Algeria, and the PLO led a move to suspend Egyptian participation, which was turned back by the majority of African and Asian states. The Bureau did, however, condemn the terms of the treaty as violating previous nonaligned resolutions on the Middle East. These two issues dominated the 1979 Bureau meeting in Colombo.

Notwithstanding these debilitating disputes, several governments applied as new members for the sixth summit, indicating that the movement still served a diplomatic purpose.* More exactly the instrument was as needed as ever, but it was blunted by the cumulative effect of so many disputes. Even if the Havana summit should succeed in repairing some of the damage, the movement was weaker in 1979 than it had been for many years.

This disability prompted once again the idea that the Group of 77 might assume the major role in Third World organizing. What this implied, of course, was that solidarity was operational mainly in the realm of economic development. The Group of 77 had after all served as a rallying point during an earlier period of political disarray prior to the 1970 nonaligned renaissance. Now with the latter struggling to restore its political equilibrium, the question of whether the Group of 77 could shoulder a larger diplomatic burden was bound to arise. Not surprisingly this question was being asked among Third World representatives at the United Nations in the summer of 1979.

UNCTAD V: NEW STRESS ON COLLECTIVE SELF-RELIANCE

How was the Group of 77 organizational framework faring in 1979? On the one hand, as noted before, it could never be immune to the political prob-

---

*The new applicants were Iran (the new Ayatollah Khomeini government), Pakistan (which withdrew from Cento as did Iran), Bolivia (dropping its longstanding observer status), Grenada (where a coup had brought a more radical regime to power), and Surinam (extending its diplomatic activity after four years of independence). There were rumors also that Mexico was on the verge of becoming an active member after years of observer status.

lems that sapped the credibility of the very idea of a Third World coalition, whatever its organizational form—nonalignment, Group of 77, or a combination of the two. But its more limited mandate, focused on economic issues, gave it an incontestable raison d'etre, and it did seek to carry out its well-established role in relation to UNCTAD V.

After Algiers (1967), Lima (1971), and Manila (1976), geographic rotation led the Group of 77 back to Africa for its fourth ministerial meeting. Drawing upon a relevant symbol, the Group chose Arusha, Tanzania, as the meeting place. Site of Julius Nyerere's 1967 Arusha Declaration, in which the Tanzanian president articulated the concept of self-reliance as a national development strategy, the name Arusha was virtually synonymous with this concept. One will recall that the theme of collective self-reliance had been adopted in various nonaligned and Group of 77 documents and given specific ideological sanction at the 1976 Mexico City Conference. The potential significance of the concept was great—indeed, it was the economic counterpart of the political theme of solidarity. Yet just as it had been difficult to operationalize solidarity, so was it proving difficult to give substance to collective self-reliance.

The Arusha Conference tried to come to grips with this problem. It elevated the role of Third World self-help to the highest place in its theory of international economic reform. The developing countries, in the language of their Arusha Program:

> *Recognize* that [they] need to enhance their collective bargaining strength and exercise their countervailing power, thereby creating the compulsions which would make the developed countries willing to negotiate the desired changes in the international economic system;
>
> *Reaffirm* that such countervailing power flows from the individual and collective self-reliance of developing countries, and that the basis of collective self-reliance rests on the intensification and strengthening of economic linkages among developing countries; . . .
>
> *Resolve* therefore to give the highest priority to implementing economic cooperation among developing countries . . . as an essential element in the establishment of the New International Economic Order. . . .[23]

There followed a lengthy Program for Collective Self-Reliance, which was placed before the Framework for Negotiation in the Arusha document. The order, like the site, had a theoretical value. To place collective self-reliance before North-South negotiations was theoretically significant. To translate theory into practice was, of course, quite another matter.

The obstacles to collective self-reliance were great because it implied the most radical development strategy of all: opting out of the existing pattern of

North-South trade in favor of an austere new pattern of poor trading with poor. The infrastructure for this barely existed; at the minimum, effecting a transition would be slow, arduous work, requiring sacrifices in already strapped countries. And yet without the threat to make this radical choice, the Third World had little chance of exercising "countervailing power."

Some part of the future of North-South relations will turn upon the credibility of the Third World's choice of this option. This theme is discussed again in the final chapter. For now it is sufficient to note that the theoretical importance of the option was expressed more clearly at Arusha in February 1979 than at any previous ministerial meeting.

Although the thematic focus was on self-help at Arusha, the meeting also approved a Framework for Negotiations for UNCTAD V. Once again the problem was to identify those key issues on which the Third World considered agreement most crucial. The Arusha Framework covered the gamut of traditional UNCTAD issues (commodities, manufactures, finance, technology, shipping, ECDC, and so on), but the intent of the Group of 77 was to focus on a group of trade issues under the general heading of protectionism and industrial restructuring.

UNCTAD V met in Manila in May 1979. It will be recalled that the previous plenary conference three years earlier in Nairobi had occurred at a moment of relatively great Third World bargaining power, propelled by the Seventh Special Session. The climate was less favorable in 1979, both because of the political divisions within the coalition and because the global economy was in a severe slump. This cut the bargaining power of the Group of 77 at Manila, and it achieved little of what it set as its goals.

The resurgence of protectionist policies in the North was of great concern to the South. Protectionism threatened to nip young Third World industries in the bud. It attested to a basic defense mechanism on the part of the older industrial economies at the critical moment when they began to feel Third World competition. In a nutshell the issue was whether the North was to erect new barriers or accept an obligation to reorganize its own economies away from competition with Third World manufactures. The Group of 77 proposed establishment of a surveillance body with responsibility to recommend structural readjustment policies. As on previous occasions, the developing countries were seeking some kind of authoritative international mechanism mandated to make policy in a delicate issue area. The developed countries would not hear of such a policymaking body. All that the North would accept in this area was that the matter be remitted to UNCTAD's regular Trade and Development Board in its capacity as a general trade monitoring institution. This resolution of the issue was nothing more than a recognition that a problem existed.

Industrial restructuring was but one component of a more general debate on global restructuring. The Arusha Framework called for the secretary-general of UNCTAD to establish a "high-level intergovernmental Group of Experts" with a broad mandate to examine the world economy and recommend measures "that would ensure that the policies of the developed countries are consistent with the requirements of the structural changes . . . of the NIEO."[24] Behind this apparently all-inclusive mandate lay a more modest practical goal, namely, a strengthening of the authority of UNCTAD as an international decision maker. The debate on this item at Manila turned into an all-encompassing discussion of where the responsibility for the global economic problems of the day actually lay, which provided an opening for a reconsideration of the ever divisive energy issue.

This general "restructuring" debate was a disaster for the South. Several Latin American countries led by Costa Rica supported the North on this issue, requesting that OPEC pricing policies be placed on the agenda. After an acrimonious intra-Group of 77 discussion, Costa Rica withdrew its request only to see it raised again by the North in its draft resolution on restructuring. As a well-informed Asian journalist reported, "Some Asian negotiators felt that the energy issue was only a tactical ploy by Group B countries [the North] to be dropped at the last minute in return for a vague, essentially meaningless resolution on economic restructuring."[25] Whether a ploy or not, it demonstrated the fragility of the Group of 77 in the face of oil costs (and this before the June 1979 price increases), and it effectively destroyed the idea of the group of experts. Neither restructuring nor the UNCTAD process got the boost that the Group of 77 had set out to provide.

There were of course numerous other items discussed over the month-long conference, but these two were typical of the overall picture. As *Le Monde* concluded of the Manila Conference, "The North-South dialogue scarcely made any progress."[26] One Third World delegate added a further reaction: "The North-South dialogue has run out of words . . . [but we] may see the beginning of a true South-South dialogue. That, in the end, may be the greatest achievement from the long days and nights in Manila."[27] There were in fact some grounds for this speculation in the final acts of the Group of 77 at Manila. As it became certain that UNCTAD V would not advance North-South negotiations very far, the developing countries returned to the theme of collective self-reliance.

On the one hand, they pressed for and won approval of the matter that had been blocked in the 1978 deliberations on ECDC. Backed by some Northern countries, notably France, the Group of 77 was able to get agreement on UNCTAD financial and technical assistance support for meetings of Third World regional economic groupings. More importantly it created a 15-member committee to discuss preferential trade policies among themselves, and spur other efforts of collective self-reliance. India immediately offered to cut its own tariffs on developing country products in half.

The new committee of 15 may prove a more promising step toward mutual Third World economic cooperation than previous approaches. The idea received the blessing of Raul Prebisch, who told the Manila delegates that "their developmental solution lay in furthering the 'South-South dialogue.'"[28] As the intellectual father of the UNCTAD experience, his judgment was politically significant, and reinforced the Arusha doctrine that "countervailing power flows from . . . collective self-reliance." A further idea along these same lines was being reexamined in the summer of 1979, namely, the idea that the Group of 77 should create a secretariat of its own. Through 1976, the developing countries had hesitated to take this step. As UNCTAD V approached and unfolded, it became clear that the North was pulling in the reins on what the UNCTAD secretariat would be permitted to do. There was a growing consciousness as well that the secretariat, for all its contributions to the Group of 77 over the years, was staffed largely by Westerners and was officially responsible to the entire membership. Accordingly, the desire for a completely independent secretariat was becoming stronger. If eventually implemented, it will have considerable potential as an instrument of the Third World coalition.

In mid-1979, therefore, the coalition was at a crossroads. On the one hand, there were intimations of serious thinking about collective self-reliance. On the other, there were undeniable cracks in political solidarity. The tension between solidarity and dispersion that has marked the entire history of the Third World coalition was as highly charged as ever.

NOTES

1. *Review of International Affairs* 653 (June 20, 1977).

2. The expression is from Crawford Young, "Zaire: The Unending Crisis," *Foreign Affairs* 57, no. 1 (Fall 1978).

3. Jorge I. Dominguez, "Cuban Foreign Policy," *Foreign Affairs* 57, no. 1 (Fall 1978): 101.

4. See the articles by Miljan Komatina and Cvijeto Job in *Review of International Affairs* 650 (May 5, 1977).

5. Komatina, *Review of International Affairs*.

6. Ronald I. Meltzer, "Restructuring the United Nations System: Institutional Reform Efforts in the Context of North-South Relations," *International Organization* 32, no. 4 (Autumn 1978): 1010. This article provides an excellent review and analysis of the restructuring negotiations.

7. Resolution 32/174, the text of which appears in *United Nations Monthly Chronicle* 15, no. 1 (January 1978): 134.

8. Ibid. 15, no. 11 (December 1978): 44.

9. Ibid., p. 45.

10. "Commodity Fund: Political Success, Doubtful Impact," *The Inter Dependent* 6, no. 5 (May 1979): 3. See also Malcolm Subhan, "Developing Nations Settle for a Shadow," *Far Eastern Economic Review*, April 6, 1979.

11. Robert L. Rothstein, *Global Bargaining, UNCTAD and the Quest for a New International Economic Order* (Princeton, N.J.: Princeton University Press, 1979), p. 151.

12. This was the view of Ho Kwon Ping, economic correspondent of the *Far Eastern Economic Review* as cited in *The Inter Dependent*, "Commodity Fund."

13. *Le Monde*, March 2, 1978.

14. *Review of International Affairs* 676 (June 5, 1978): 2.

15. *New York Times*, June 11, 1978. Somalia was not in fact present at the Havana Bureau meeting. No doubt the matter was never formally raised, but Somalia was surely exploring the idea through diplomatic channels.

16. The communique appears in *Review of International Affairs* 677 (June 20, 1978).

17. *New York Times*, June 11, 1978; *Le Monde*, June 21, 1978.

18. As quoted in *Le Monde*, July 30-31, 1978.

19. Ibid.

20. *New York Times*, July 29, 1978.

21. The citations are all from an article by Miljan Komatina in *Review of International Affairs* 682 (September 5, 1978). Formerly assistant foreign minister, Komatina was about to become Yugoslavia's ambassador to the United Nations.

22. *Le Monde*, June 28, 1978.

23. *Arusha Program for Collective Self-Reliance and Framework for Negotiation*, UN Document TD/236, pp. 4-5.

24. Ibid., p. 28.

25. Ho Kwon Ping, "UNCTAD V: Bargaining to Keep Hopes Alive," *Far Eastern Economic Review*, June 8, 1979, p. 90.

26. *Le Monde*, June 5, 1979.

27. Ho Kwon Ping, "Self-Help Is Better Than No Help," *Far Eastern Economic Review*, June 15, 1979, p. 143.

28. Ping, "UNCTAD V," p. 90.

8. Third World Power and United States Policy

This study has analyzed the sources, the means, and the ends of Third World power in international politics. The political dynamics of constructing an effective coalition out of the stuff of Third World diversity has been examined, and a pattern of ebb and flow in the collective influence exercised by the developing countries has been observed. This final chapter will draw some conclusions about the nature and durability of Third World power. The power of any actor in international politics implies consequences for the other actors. This chapter gives some attention to the implications of the Third World coalition for U.S. foreign policy.

The preceding chapters have already made evident that the United States has been at the center of NIEO politics all along. While the study has focused on the other side of the bargaining table, the U.S. position has necessarily been treated. It is worthwhile now to summarize briefly the essential components of U.S. Third World policy as a preface to the concluding analysis.

THE UNITED STATES AND THE
THIRD WORLD, 1973-79

John Stoessinger has written that his old friend and Harvard classmate, Henry Kissinger, was "virtually allergic" to economics and "quite uninterested" in the United Nations and the Third World.[1] Throughout his term as President Nixon's national security advisor, Kissinger accordingly paid very little attention to North-South issues. His tenure as secretary of state (1973-76), however, coincided with the burst of Third World assertiveness that followed the OPEC revolution. Kissinger was quick to recognize that the North-South axis was assuming unprecedented significance in international politics, but he was not well prepared to deal with what were for him essentially new issues. His initial reaction was to face down the Third World in the manner of the coldest days of East-West relations.

Kissinger's confrontational style produced a period of extremely tense North-South relations through the spring of 1975. Then the style changed, but the substance of policy remained quite the same. The United States has reacted as a status quo power, seeking to neutralize the emergent power of the Third World coalition and to defend the international economic system. Both the initial hard line and the subsequent soft line stemmed from the premise that the U.S. interest was to preserve as much of the existing order as possible. Kissinger's "allergy" to economics was in fact but one symptom of the Nixon-Ford administrations' indisposition to international economic change.

Kissinger first signaled his own discomfort with the emergence of Third World power even before the oil price increases. Alluding to the Algiers nonaligned summit, Kissinger spoke testily in September 1973 of the "alignment of the nonaligned," which was assuming "the characteristics of a bloc of its own."[2] Breaking up the bloc was a U.S. policy goal from the outset.

To implement this policy, the United States moved first to organize a consumers versus producers showdown over oil prices. This maneuver was outflanked by the Third World convocation of the Sixth Special Session. According to C. Clyde Ferguson, Jr., who was a member of the U.S. delegation to the United Nations at the time, Kissinger's view of the proposed session was paternalistic: "I suppose we'll have to humor them along," the secretary is reported to have said.[3] Kissinger assumed that the way to humor the Third World was to propose emergency aid to those developing countries most seriously affected by the new oil prices. Even this gesture was blocked by the Treasury Department, which opposed any financial commitment by the United States. This bureaucratic struggle between Secretary Kissinger and Secretary of the Treasury William Simon explained the last-minute submission of the U.S. counterproposal. The U.S. proposal was maladapted in any case to the mood of the Third World coalition. The combination of paternalism and bureaucratic infighting made the session, in Ferguson's judgment, "an unmitigated debacle for the United States and the first world."[4]

The passage of the NIEO resolutions left an attitude of "bitterness at the negotiating tactics adopted by the Third World [which] persisted long after the session's conclusion."[5] For over a year, Ferguson reports, U.S. representatives to international economic conferences were instructed to abstain or vote against "any decision or resolution that referred to the New International Economic Order with the initialism NIEO."[6]

The only new order that interested the United States was a reduction in the Cost of oil States and Treasury were united in this goal, but tactical differences persisted in the Nixon administration on how to handle the Third World coalition. Kissinger began to appreciate much sooner than his cabinet colleagues that positive incentives were necessary to induce divergences inside the Group of 77. He argued that the United States should link a food and agricultural assistance program to its demands for oil price relief. Both Simon and Secretary of Agriculture Earl Butz opposed such a program as inflationary; Butz and others argued on the contrary that global food shortages gave the United States the leverage that it needed to divide the coalition. They urged that the United States wield a "food weapon" against the "oil weapon."

Upon entering office, President Ford had to choose between these two approaches. He backed Kissinger, presumably believing that food was appropriately a carrot, not a stick. Thus, in his first major foreign policy address, delivered at the United Nations in September 1974, Ford held forth the promise of new U.S. agricultural aid programs. But he completely omitted any reference to the NIEO resolutions. These the United States wished to banish from the agenda in favor of talks on energy. "Energy first," as already seen, was the essence of the Ford administration's policy.

The modest shift of tactics that occurred in May 1975 reflected a concern that the radical members of the coalition might run away with the political leadership of the Third World.[7] Stanley Hoffmann has speculated that Kissinger remained inflexible until the collapse of the April preparatory meeting so that he rather than Giscard d'Estaing would appear to unblock the diplomatic impasse.[8] Kissinger delivered three speeches in May that were heralded as a major evolution in U.S. policy, but the new line had little support in the Treasury and other departments, where resistance was more deeply rooted than at State. The task after the Kissinger speeches was to get as much diplomatic mileage as possible out of the "new look," while taking account of the opposition to change in other parts of the U.S. government.

The main difference was to modify the manner in which the United States prepared for the Seventh Special Session as compared with the Sixth. The State Department's policy planning office spent most of the summer preparing proposals, coordinating and clearing them as necessary with the other interested agencies. Thus, contrary to the performance in 1974, when the U.S. proposal was tabled at the last minute, the United States was up front in September 1975 with an overall plan that succeeded by and large in satisfying the moderate wing of the Third World coalition. This diplomatic operation was preeminently political from the outset, spurred by a desire, as Hoffmann puts it, "to dissolve artificial ideological solidarities" by bargaining more realistically.[9] The tactical shift, in other words, reflected a recognition that the United States needed to cultivate allies within the Third World coalition.

This modest step toward accommodation on international economic issues was coupled with something of a counteroffensive on other issues. The central strand of this line of policy was the denunciation of "tyranny of the majority." President Ford first articulated this theme in September 1974 and it was shortly supplemented by Daniel Patrick Moynihan's battle cry of "The United States in Opposition."[10] Moynihan's appointment as ambassador to the United Nations at once covered Kissinger's right flank and opened up a new front in the campaign to split the Third World coalition. Moynihan's term in the office, brief as it was, was aimed at "breaking up the massive blocs of nations, mostly new nations," an objective that he understood to be a "basic foreign policy goal" of his government.[11] Moynihan took on this task with such a vengeance that he quickly became an embarrassment to Kissinger. His execution of policy may well have been maladroit, but Moynihan did not misconstrue the policy goal. The United States was defending the international economic status quo by harassing the Third World coalition.

The Kissinger ploy of spring 1975 and the Moynihan fling of autumn 1975 stand out as the perturbations of a Nixon-Ford policy line that was otherwise remarkably steady from the onset of the oil crisis to the hibernation of the North-South Conference at the end of 1976. On the eve of his departure from the State Department, Secretary Kissinger summed up the outgoing administration's record in relations with the Third World. He granted that "until 1973 we did not give it systematic attention"; but, he went on to claim, if one looks at current North-South affairs, "the entire international agenda was put forward by us. There is almost no other agenda."[12] There was much hubris in this remark, but it was representative of the essence of U.S. policy from 1973 to 1976. Under Kissinger, the United States did seek to impose its notion of the agenda of North-South relations, and its enormous economic and political weight gave it some success in this endeavor. Yet in the final analysis the United States lost the battle of the agenda. At the Seventh Special Session, at UNCTAD IV, in CIEC, the United States was obliged to concede that the agenda was one of development policy and international economic change, not primarily of energy policy. The Nixon-Ford administrations did not put forward this agenda. Resistance was steady and persistent, and although the United States finally conceded the agenda, its opposition to substantive change continued to the end of the Ford presidency.

Such was the legacy to the Carter administration. Improvement of relations with the Third World was one of Carter's campaign themes. The new administration promptly announced its intention to double the amount of U.S. aid programs. After some internal debate, it also announced that the United States was ready to enter into the Geneva negotiations on the Common Fund. The desire at least to create a healthier climate in North-South relations was apparent.*

---

*The appointment of Andrew Young as ambassador to the United Nations also was seen as a positive gesture toward the Third World.

It soon became clear, however, that the new policymakers harbored many reservations about the kinds of structural changes that the developing states were proposing. Neither in the Common Fund talks nor at CIEC was the United States ready to endorse the principal elements of the NIEO. As the new under secretary of state for economic affairs, Richard Cooper, summed up the Carter administration's position: "We believe the North-South dialogue, in CIEC and other forums, should emphasize improving, rather than restructuring, the existing international economic system."[13] This meant foreign aid, trade, and investment, not generalized debt relief or indexation. The emphasis upon foreign aid proved to be the conceptual core of Carter's Third World policy.

The Carter administration did bring in critics of former policy like economist C. Fred Bergsten, who became assistant secretary of treasury. Bergsten had written that "the Third World is quite right to call for the creation of a new international economic order which more fully responds to its needs," and had called for "more positive support by the rich countries for primary policy objectives of the Third World."[14] The new policymakers thus granted that there was something to Third World grievances, but they did not accept many of the Group of 77's solutions. Bergsten explained, for example, that the new administration was unenthusiastic about the Common Fund, because it would cause problems for the market system and transfer resources in an "arbitrary" way that would not necessarily benefit the neediest countries.[15] Thus Carter's announcement in March 1977 that the United States was now ready to enter into the Common Fund talks was designed to head off an immediate confrontation rather than to endorse a Group of 77 proposal.

The way in which the Carter administration handled the Common Fund issue by moving just a bit beyond the Ford administration position was typical of its entire Third World policy. As discussed in Chapter 7, the United States stood by its own conception of the Common Fund for another year and a half. It finally abandoned its scheme (of separate commodity funds) in autumn 1978 when a high administration official acknowledged that "it's been made clear that won't fly."[16] Its policy was one of cautious incrementalism par excellence. Even in the domain of foreign aid about which it had no conceptual reservations, the Carter administration was hard pressed to deliver upon its promises. Inflation and budgetary pressure, Bergsten explained in 1979, had forced the administration to slow down the pace at which it had hoped to increase foreign aid.[17]

No doubt there were severe economic constraints operating upon the U.S. government in 1978–79. Equally pertinent was the fact that the Third World coalition was weakened by its own internal situation. The Carter administration thus did not face quite the same external pressure as its predecessor. In these circumstances, U.S. policy evolved very little from one administration to the next. The judgment expressed in 1977 by one Carter policymaker, that there was in fact "enormous continuity in American policy in this field," remained valid in 1979.[18]

The record under three presidents, then, is quite consistent. The United States has profited under the rules of the game of international economic relations established after World War II. Although the United States itself has scrapped some of these rules when its interests were thereby served, it has opposed most of the proposals of the Third World coalition to create new norms and institutions of global economic development. As the most powerful defender of the status quo, it has been the Third World's main adversary. Is this a role that the United States can or should maintain in the future? The answer to the first question may require only an assessment of Third World countervailing power, while the answer to the second obliges reflection upon some values as well.

THE NATURE OF THIRD WORLD POWER

Third World power is a fragile construct, depending as it does upon a collective cohesion that is difficult to maintain. This power has certainly grown since the 1950s and especially since 1970. It has been painstakingly constructed through the development of organizational frameworks capable of operationalizing the abstract ideal of solidarity. Although the institutional structures are extremely modest, sufficient "institutionalization" has been achieved to create an active Third World presence in international politics.

This institutionalization occurred under the leadership of several states that exercised major roles at various periods. India under Nehru was an early leader, but the first initiatives in fact had a collective character in the association of the five Colombo powers with the Bandung Conference. Egypt, Yugoslavia, and Algeria successively assumed prominent leadership roles both conceptually and organizationally. The period of Algerian leadership saw the real consolidation of the coalition and the initiation of NIEO politics. Since early 1976, the coalition has come full cycle back to a more collective form of leadership as organizational structures have thrust responsibilities upon an increasing number of states. In the past few years, Sri Lanka, Mexico, Pakistan, Jamaica, and Tunisia, for example, have all filled executive posts in nonaligned or Group of 77 offices, while others, including Cuba, Tanzania, and the Philippines, have had the responsibility for organizing major Third World conferences. This more collegial leadership situation is a positive sign for the future.

The mobilizing themes of Third World solidarity have evolved since 1955. Anticolonialism was the central bond in the early years, to be supplemented by the aspiration to genuine autonomy from the great powers. In the late 1960s, a more militant brand of anti-imperialism came to the fore, fed by the war in Indochina, the struggle for independence in southern Africa, and the setback to the Arab states in the Six Day War. From the outset, economic development was a common concern, an increasingly radical critique of global economic structures emerging in the early 1970s. The latter bond has remained the most enduring source of Third World solidarity. The passing (except in Southern Africa) of the era of anticolonial struggle has deprived the coalition of one of its sources of solidarity. In its wake has come a resurgence of old hostilities and competitive nationalism, carrying along the phenomenon of great-power involvement in proxy wars.

At Bandung, Western alliance members clashed with Soviet allies and neutralists. Twenty-three years later, in Havana and Belgrade, Western- or Chinese-oriented states clashed bitterly with pro-Soviet states. The joint non-aligned/Group of 77 framework had succeeded relatively well in banning such disputes from Third World forums during 1967–76. Their recurrence in the late 1970s has weakened the coalition. When Third World states compete with one another over local stakes such as Western Sahara or Ogaden, they are likely to look for great-power support. This in turn exacerbates the residual cleavage between moderate and radical regimes in the developing world. The cohesion of the coalition requires some measure of peaceful coexistence between its left and right wings. Otherwise diversity overwhelms solidarity, and dispersion occurs.

Dispersion can be mitigated by institutional frameworks, but ultimately institutions without underlying consensus will deteriorate. Nonaligned institutions were in danger of such deterioration by mid-1979. They were cranking out conferences that lacked a sufficient underpinning of solidarity, but there were states like the indefatigable Yugoslavia working to repair the underpinnings.

Diversity can be overcome in the final analysis only by increased mutuality. This is the nub of the concept of collective self-reliance, which implies material bases for intra-Third World cooperation. The idea of South-South economic relations has been gradually maturing in both the nonaligned and Group of 77 contexts. A fully articulated South-South strategy would entail the capacity to withhold resources from the North on a large scale. It would ultimately involve the capacity akin to the power to strike that thus far only OPEC has approximated. The developing countries as a whole are far from such mutual interdependence, but there appears to be a growing consciousness of its indispensability in any strategy of countervailing power.

One could imagine the Third World standing in 1979 at the juncture of two paths, one leading to collective self-reliance and the other to a splintered and broken coalition. The real world will not reproduce either of these models, certainly in any case not in the short term. The actual path of the coalition will continue to fluctuate between impulses toward solidarity and toward dispersion. Disputes will impair the ideal of collective power, but the special session on the NIEO scheduled for 1980 should provide a rallying point around which to re-mobilize a degree of solidarity, at least insofar as international economic issues are concerned. The Group of 77, operating under a collegial leadership, may emerge from this future special session as the new catalyst of collective diplomacy—depending in part on how Cuba exercises its presidency during and after the Havana nonaligned summit. The durability of the future coalition will also be affected by its ability to handle the repercussions of the spiraling oil prices of 1979.* Oil, ideology, and bilateral clashes will strain solidarity and place limits upon collective power, but the coalition will not collapse as an actor in the system. The strategy of empowerment through solidarity may be flawed but it is not defunct.

United States policymakers will have to continue to reckon with the coalition. It is not strong enough at present to force the U.S. hand, but it will continue to act as a developmental pressure group. Continuation of current U.S. policy may be able to hold the line against a divided and ineffectual coalition; or it may contribute to the reconsolidation of a hostile coalition as the 1974–75 policy did. Neither scenario is a very satisfying prospect for the 1980s. One need not exaggerate the immediate "threat from the Third World" (to recall Bergsten's 1973 article) to propose that the United States change its policy toward the Third World.

Rather than maneuvering to divide and weaken the coalition, rather than proceeding with a grudging incrementalism, it seems preferable to accept the Third World coalition as a genuine partner in the system. The evolution of the coalition, especially since 1970, justifies the claim that the United States must face the development issue much more squarely than it has. Despite its current divisions, the Third World has demonstrated its potential to organize and bring pressure. The goal of greater global equity that it has set does imply sacrifices for Americans and other peoples of the North, but it is not a goal that is adverse to the values that many Americans hold.

The Third World coalition has mobilized enough power to be considered a worthy adversary. The Northern choice may well be between obliging the developing countries to surmount their present disputes and recognizing the moral legitimacy of their claim to development. Between confrontation in the former case and collaboration in the latter, the choice ought to be easy.

Empowerment through solidarity has occurred. The Third World has demonstrated its potential as a collective actor in international politics. Yet solidarity is in perpetual danger of disruption. Through the 1970s, the coalition developed the foundations of organization and working routines that protect against some of the ravages of dispersion. The full edifice of operational solidarity remains a challenge calling for further, probably collegial, leadership within the Third World. The laying of foundations is nonetheless a fact that the North must recognize.

---

*The *New York Times* reported on July 4, 1979, that "Several governments that had refrained from criticizing OPEC nations for previous oil increases have begun to vent their anger now."

NOTES

1. John G. Stoessinger, *Henry Kissinger: The Anguish of Power* (New York: Norton, 1976), p. 155.

2. *Department of State Bulletin* 69, no. 1790 (October 15, 1973): 470.

3. C. Clyde Ferguson, Jr., "The Politics of the New International Economic Order," *Proceedings of the Academy of Political Science* 32, no. 4 (1977): 146.

4. Ibid., p. 148.

5. Ibid., p. 142.

6. Ibid., p. 143.

7. For a thorough account of this shift, see Richard S. Frank, "Economic Report/ U.S. Takes Steps to Meet Demands of Third World Nations," *National Journal* 7, no. 43 (October 25, 1975): 1480–89.

8. Stanley Hoffmann, "Les Etats-Unis du refus au compromis," *Revue Française de Science Politique* 26, no. 4 (August 1976): 691.

9. Ibid.

10. Moynihan's article of this title appeared in *Commentary*, March 1975. See also his *A Dangerous Place* (Boston: Little, Brown, 1978).

11. The phrases come from Moynihan's "farewell cable" as published in the *New York Times*, January 28, 1976.

12. *New York Times*, January 20, 1977.

13. Testimony to the Congressional Joint Economic Committee, *Department of State Bulletin* 77, no. 1986 (July 18, 1977): 93. See also Richard N. Cooper, "A New International Economic Order for Mutual Gain," *Foreign Policy* 26 (Spring 1977).

14. C. Fred Bergsten, "The Response to the Third World," *Foreign Policy* 17 (Winter 1974–75): 6, 25. See also Bergsten's "The Threat from the Third World," *Foreign Policy* 11 (Summer 1973).

15. *New York Times*, February 11, 1977.

16. *Washington Post*, November 16, 1978.

17. *The Inter Dependent* 6, no. 3 (March 1979).

18. Alan Tonelson, "Carter and the Third World: What's Behind the Smile?" *The Inter Dependent* 4, no. 10 (November 1977), p. 6.

9. The Politics of Stalemate, 1979–83

The *raison d'être* of the Third World coalition is to achieve change in the international economic system. This is of course a mammoth undertaking in a decentralized global economy that operates in an anarchic political setting. The anarchic international order lacks a central state to manage the kind of process of economic regulation that is implicit in the Third World call for a development-oriented world economy. The very magnitude of the undertaking, one might hypothesize, ensures frustration and deadlock. Thus one should not be surprised that the theme of stalemate recurs with nagging persistence in the literature of North-South relations.[1]

The inescapable reality of stalemate poses a serious question for any analysis of the Third World coalition as an actor in world politics. Robert Rothstein has suggested that the North-South dialogue is no more than shadowboxing for many participants in both the South and the North.[2] Shadowboxing will always end in a draw, after which the real combat will take place in some other (presumably bilateral and hence, it is often argued, more pragmatic) arena. The question is whether collective North-South bargaining over the Global Negotiation is really an important encounter. If the exercise is doomed to failure, if global structural reform is beyond the capacity of the South and alien to the will of the North, is anything significant really going on? If the record is consistently one of stalemate, is the Third World coalition really an actor worth reckoning with at all?

The premise of this chapter is that the politics of stalemate is worthy of study. However inconclusive the process of North-South bargaining may have been from 1979 to 1983, a real match was in fact going on. The issues of the dialogue entail crucial stakes for the developing countries: not solely economic development but ultimately the dignity of Third World peoples. Because the stakes are real, the outcome is genuinely important to the South. This means, moreover, that the instruments necessary to attaining a satisfactory outcome are significant to Third World governments as well. The coalition forged so painstakingly from 1955 through 1973 remains a valued tool of collective diplomacy, because collective action still constitutes an integral component of Third World strategy. This is why the member-states of the nonaligned movement grappled so earnestly with the issues of political control raised at the sixth summit in Havana in 1979. This is why the Group of 77 has further consolidated its corporate identity and decision-making procedures since UNCTAD V. The coalition has been put to the test by the very politics of stalemate since 1979, and it has survived intact. That survival is itself an important fact about contemporary international politics.

This period of stalemate in North-South relations was far from uneventful in other domains. Afghanistan, Iran, Iraq, Lebanon, southern Africa, Chad, Western Sahara, Central America, the Falkland (Malvinas) Islands—all were foyers of tension and conflict that involved states and movements that were members of the Third World coalition. Conflicting policies in these diverse conflicts provided ample opportunity for the coalition to founder. The dynamics of coalition maintenance are therefore complex. It is important to identify the techniques of intragroup diplomacy that have allowed the coalition to resist dispersion and thus to continue as an interlocutor facing the North on developmental issues (and to a lesser extent on other issues as well).

Events since 1979 have not answered definitively the question of whether the coalition is strong enough to effect substantial change through bargaining or through unilateral action. They have, however, demonstrated that Third World solidarity is not an ephemeral factor in world politics. It is a durable construct and it is maturing with diplomatic experience. To neglect this phenomenon seems increasingly perilous. To ignore that the South sees itself caught up in a struggle for the world product is a grave failure of understanding.

BLOWING SMOKE IN HAVANA

As was seen at the end of Chapter 7, both the nonaligned movement and the Group of 77 were groping for a clear-cut orientation during the summer of 1979. UNCTAD V was a major disappointment for the Group of 77. The idea of a South-South alternative to the fruitless North-South dialogue was rhetorically attractive, but it was widely perceived as a solution of last resort. Whatever might be achieved in the domain of Southern economic cooperation, the South still wished to achieve reform of international economic institutions and structures. The question was how to reopen the process of bargaining. The proposed answer turned out to be the Global Negotiation, a concept first articulated at the wildly controversial Havana nonaligned summit.

The sixth nonaligned summit in September 1979 was an extremely important turning point for the movement. The cause of all the controversy was, of course, Fidel Castro. If Castro could become chairman of the nonaligned group, the Western press widely asked, then what did "nonaligned" mean? Cuba was as aligned with the Soviet Union as South Korea was with the United States. The conclusion, for many observers, was that the idea of nonalignment was a sham.

This argument was an oversimplification of the complex nature and workings of the nonaligned grouping. It nonetheless captured an aspect of what the Havana summit was all about, for the member-states did have to address what "nonalignment" meant in the context of the late 1970s. The Cuban chairmanship did challenge the members to define the limits of the chair's prerogative and thereby to refine their own organizational procedures. These issues had to be faced, moreover, at a moment of extreme tension inside the Third World (page 126): Cambodian representation, Egyptian membership, and Cuban policy in Africa were all potentially explosive issues at the Havana summit.

The sixth summit meeting was like its predecessors in at least one regard: it continued the tradition of growing membership. Attendance as full members grew from eighty-five at Colombo to ninety-two at Havana. This figure included eighty-nine independent governments and three liberation movements (the PLO and, for the first time, the Patriotic Front of Zimbabwe and the South West African People's Organization, or SWAPO). The new members were those that had applied at the June Bureau meeting (Iran, Pakistan, Bolivia, Grenada, and Suriname) plus Nicaragua, where the Sandinista government had come to power in July 1979. This was the first participation by a Central American state other than Panama in a nonaligned conference, extending the geographic spread of the movement a bit further. Equally noteworthy was the fact that after all the talk about boycotting Havana, only one government (Saudi Arabia) actually did so.[3]

The boycott campaign had never gained any political momentum, in large measure because Yugoslavia mounted a participation campaign in order to thwart any Cuban bid for domination of the movement. The central issue in this Cuban-Yugoslav rivalry was the "natural ally" thesis, already foreshadowed at the Havana Bureau meeting in 1978.* Cuba had always been a prominent member of the radical wing of the movement; on various occasions in various forums,

---

*In fact veteran observers of nonaligned proceedings could recall a vehemently pro-Soviet speech that Castro made in his first personal appearance at a summit in Algiers in 1973. At the time, Algeria was insisting that the movement stress the dual hegemony over world affairs of the superpowers. Castro argued for recognition of Soviet assistance to anti-imperialist movements. See *Le Monde,* September 9-10, 1973.

Cuba had argued that the Soviet Union was an objective ally of the developing states in their struggle against imperialism. This Cuban position, as Peter Willetts has pointed out, was part of a long-standing and ongoing debate within the movement about what it meant to be nonaligned with regard to issues of decolonization and anti-imperialism.[4] Cuba's rise to a position of leadership and its initiative as host to the 1978 Bureau meeting (p. 123) gave extraordinary salience to this perennial question of whether or not to maintain "equidistance" from the two blocs.

In its role as host country, Cuba had the customary opportunity to prepare draft documents for the eventual approval of the full conference. In mid-July, the Cubans circulated a draft political declaration that rather ambitiously promoted the natural ally thesis. Diverse formulations of the thesis appeared at sixteen points in the draft declaration, usually in language calling for the nonaligned to struggle "together with other peaceful, democratic, and progressive forces" or in appeals for cooperation with the Soviet Union. (The expression "natural ally" was never actually used.[5]) The stage was apparently set for a dramatic encounter between Fidel Castro and the eighty-seven-year-old President Tito, who journeyed to Havana to defend his notion of equidistance.

The theatrics of the Castro-Tito clash were splendid: the fiery younger revolutionary versus the aging patriarch of "classical nonalignment." Yet the political realities were less spectacular than theatrical appearances. In fact, Cuba had already been outmaneuvered on the substantive question of the Soviet Union as a natural ally. Close observers understood that the issue was virtually predetermined by organizational moves that had been taken back in 1978. No doubt the Cubans themselves understood these diplomatic realities perfectly well. As John Graham has suggested, they finally advanced the natural ally thesis essentially as a tactical ploy in order to gain bargaining leverage on other matters, namely sharp condemnation of Western policies in Latin America and Africa and on international economic reform.[6]

The predictable rebuff to the natural ally thesis had been in the making since the 1978 Belgrade foreign ministers' meeting, which had instructed the Bureau to prepare a draft agenda for the Havana Conference by as early as December 1978. The Bureau was to do this "in closest cooperation with Cuba as the Host Country and Sri Lanka as the current Chairman."[7] The early date and the joint association of Sri Lanka (not to mention other members of the Bureau) worked to limit Cuban autonomy. Moreover, the Belgrade conference had also established a Working Group to improve the "decision-making process" within the movement. The Working Group drew up a list of twelve recommendations to promote proper debate at summit conferences. These in turn had been approved by the Colombo Bureau meeting in June 1979, coupled with an unprecedented directive to the host country to "circulate a draft final document by the first week of July 1979."[8] These organizational innovations all had the same objective: to ensure that the Cuban hosts did not play any fast tricks on their guests. They constituted clear signals to Castro that he must work within a movement-wide consensus, a constraint that he was on balance prepared to accept.

Tito's trip to Havana was thus the final episode in a meticulously planned scenario to safeguard the mainstream conception of nonalignment as a force independent of both blocs. Both leaders recognized that Yugoslavia had marshaled a clear majority on this issue, which explains why William LeoGrande later wrote that the Castro-Tito relationship at Havana was "anti-climactic" in that the natural ally "issue itself had no climax."[9] The Yugoslav delegation arrived armed with draft proposals for textual revisions that deleted most of the references to "progressive forces." Most of these revisions were eventually adopted in committee—of the original sixteen allusions, eleven were altogether omitted, and the remaining five were couched in language that barely distinguished the Soviet Union.[10]

Other states of course backed Yugoslavia in this campaign. One crucial supporter was Tanzania, thanks to Nyerere's own credibility as an independent radical. Nyerere spoke out against the natural ally doctrine on the grounds that it would severely split the movement and undermine its influence in world politics. The Tanzanian leader formulated an apt distinction: "We are a progressive movement, but we are not a movement of progressive States. We have socialists here, but we are not a movement of socialist States. We are not a bloc."[11] Nyerere in effect was arguing that it was counterproductive to act as if the member-states had identical ideological orientations. Collective diplomacy required respect for political diversity. In distinguishing the nature of the coalition from the nature of the member-states, Nyerere was claiming that the whole could be more than the sum of its parts. Other key states like Algeria, India, Panama, Peru, and Sri Lanka adopted similar positions that endorsed the Yugoslav reservations while maintaining, as an Algerian delegate put it, that nonalignment was inherently "progressive."[12] Only a few states, such as Vietnam and Ethiopia, made strong statements endorsing the notion of a natural alliance with the anti-imperialist Soviets.

That Cuba understood perfectly where the conference would come down on the natural ally thesis was evident in President Castro's keynote speech. His theme was that Cuba was at home in the diversity of the nonaligned movement.

> Yes, we are radical revolutionaries, but we don't try to impose our radicalism on anyone, much less the Non-Aligned Movement. . . . If membership in the Non-Aligned Movement depended on betraying our deepest ideas and convictions, it would not be honorable for me or for any of you to belong to it. . . . No one has ever tried to tell us what role we should play in the Movement of Non-Aligned Countries. . . . By the same token, no one except the Movement itself can determine what it should do and when and how to do it. . . . We have respected and we will continue to totally respect the rights of all members of the Movement.[13]

Castro pledged, in other words, an honest administration, and on balance he produced it over the next three and one-half years. Nevertheless, the Cubans did still have some tricks up their sleeves that agitated the Havana proceedings.

Two issues provoked allegations of Cuban manipulation. Both were matters that had already caused trouble at the previous Bureau meeting: Cambodian representation and Egyptian participation. Who should be recognized to represent Cambodia (or Kampuchea, as it was now officially called)? At Colombo three months earlier, the Pol Pot representative had been permitted to "observe" the Bureau meeting without speaking rights. As Cambodia was not a member of the Bureau in any case, this ingenious compromise was adequate for the moment, but in Havana the stakes were higher. The ousted Pol Pot regime sent its president, Khieu Samphan, to uphold its claim to be the legitimate government. The Cubans did not deny Khieu Samphan an entry visa, but they immediately whisked his delegation off to a seaside cottage fifteen miles from Havana. At the same time they invited Heng Samrin on a state visit scheduled to coincide with the nonaligned summit. Countries like Vietnam and Ethiopia argued that the representatives of the deposed and widely discredited regime should be replaced by the Heng Samrin delegation. Singapore, Indonesia, and Malaysia objected that such a decision would reward Vietnamese intervention, and they argued for perpetuating the status quo (as at the United Nations, where the old regime was still recognized). Cuba then proposed that the seat be left vacant.

The Cuban scheme advanced Heng Samrin one step forward and sent Pol Pot/Khieu Samphan one step backward. As such it was not acceptable to the Asian adversaries of Vietnam. In a special session of foreign ministers, numerous delegations, including those of Somalia, Zaire, Gabon, and Senegal—representative of Cuba's African adversaries—spoke against the vacant seat proposal. Cuban Foreign Minister Isidoro Malmierca, as presiding officer, nonetheless discerned a consensus and ruled the vacant seat resolution adopted. This episode angered many delegations; indeed, sixteen lodged a protest against Malmierca's heavy-handed abuse of the chair.[14]

On the Egyptian issue, Cuba took a prominent role in formulating a sharp condemnation of the Camp David Accords. In his opening speech, Castro called the Egyptian-Israeli agreement a "flagrant betrayal of the Arab cause . . . a Machiavellian policy."[15] He called for "moral censure" of Egypt, but not for its expulsion. Radical Arab states proposed that Egypt be suspended. Both condemnation and suspension were opposed by numerous African states wary of the precedent of censuring a member-state, and the conference was prolonged by debate over this issue. The Cuban-Arab faction finally succeeded in gaining a resolution that condemned the treaty and placed Egypt on probation pending an "examination of the damage caused to the Arab countries, particularly the Palestinian Arab people, by the conduct of the Egyptian Government."[16] Again Cuba's alignment with one group irked another group within the conference.

Divisive issues, however, were hardly new to nonaligned conferences, as we have seen. Cuba had to wrestle with internal contentiousness, just as other host countries had time and again. Cuba no more wanted the movement to "explode like a grenade" (as Castro put it in the closing session) than any other state, and it like the others sought ways to return to common interests.[17] One such issue was southern Africa—once again decolonization provided a secure rallying point. Over the previous year nonaligned meetings had accorded growing legitimacy to the Patriotic Front of Robert Mugabe and Joshua Nkomo. At Havana the Patriotic Front (which had been formed in October 1976, shortly after the fifth summit) was formally admitted as a full member on the eve of the all-important Lancaster House talks that eventually led to independence for Zimbabwe. The solid backing of the nonaligned summit was valuable to the Mugabe-Nkomo front in its final diplomatic struggle with the Ian Smith–Bishop Muzorewa "internal settlement" forces.

Economic issues were certain to provide further sustenance for healing the wounds of factional battles. The Havana summit forged a crucial link in the chain of Third World initiatives for international economic change. It was at Havana that the decision was formally taken to call for the Global Negotiation. The relevant document was Economic Resolution No. 9 on Global Negotiations Relating to International Economic Cooperation for Development. In classic form, the resolution quickly recapitulated that at the Algiers summit the nonaligned had appealed for a "new system of world economic relations" and at Colombo they had "stressed that the establishment of the New International Economic Order calls for bold initiatives, demands new, concrete and global solutions and cannot be brought about by piecemeal reforms and improvisations." The resolution further noted that "no real progress has been achieved" because of "tactics intended to divide the developing countries" and then proposed "the launching of a round of global and sustained negotiations on international economic cooperation for development, such negotiations being action-oriented, allowing for an integrated approach to the main issues involved, proceeding simultaneously on different planes and being open to universal participation."[18] The language of the resolution foreshadows future debates over the procedures to be adopted and is indicative of Third World objectives from the outset of the long struggle over this proposal.

The origins of Resolution No. 9 can be traced back to the June 1979 Bureau meeting or, more instructively, to the political context of intracoalition politics in the spring of 1979. We have already seen that oil prices were a divisive matter at UNCTAD V (p. 129). The allusion in the resolution to "tactics intended to divide the developing countries" referred essentially to the reopening of the energy question at Manila. Oil costs were of course an ever-growing burden upon the great majority of developing countries; it was incumbent upon OPEC to head off a sharp clash within the Third World between oil exporters and importers. As it had done five years earlier, Algeria once again took the lead among OPEC states in fashioning a united front.

The Algerian strategy was essentially the same, namely, to channel the energy issue into a more comprehensive negotiating framework, concurrently promising to beef up OPEC's direct aid to Third World energy importers. The task that Algeria undertook was to recreate a consensus around the notion that the oil weapon still constituted the South's best leverage upon the North and that any discussion of oil issues must be linked with the whole panoply of development issues. For the Algerians, the term "global" really meant "comprehensive." Algeria had begun to argue at Colombo right after the disappointing outcome of UNCTAD V that establishment of a new, broadly inclusive negotiating forum should become the highest priority for the South. It introduced a proposition along these lines at the Bureau meeting. The specific text adopted at Colombo reveals that the idea was still in its formative stage in June. The June document does not explicitly call for a new negotiating undertaking but rather envisages providing "the required political impulse for a forthcoming round of global and sustained negotiations."[19] The Havana summit thus became the first step in provoking such a "political impulse."

The Havana resolution laid out a blueprint for the proposed negotiations, including a specification that "the Group of 77 should, after having adopted the proposal . . . introduce it formally at the forthcoming session of the Committee of the Whole [COW]." Here one sees a further example of the official division of labor between the nonaligned movement and the Group of 77 (G-77). Having originated the idea, the nonaligned hereby turned the proposal over to the G-77 framework for implementation at the United Nations. Moreover, the resolution specifies that the eventual negotiations should be preceded by G-77 meetings, and that the COW (wherein the developing states caucus as the Group of 77) should act as the preparatory committee for the negotiations. No better example of how the Third World coalition meshed the gears of its component parts could be asked.

The call for "global and sustained negotiations" was by far the most consequential act of the Havana summit. It fixed the agenda for the following several years of debate on North-South relations. Economic Resolution No. 9 was in this regard the lineal successor of the Algiers summit's call for a New International Economic Order. Once again the politically more prominent nonaligned framework acted as a catalyst for a proposal on international economic policy that would in effect bind the Group of 77 as the Third World's bargaining agent. While it is clear that the Group of 77 did not need the nonaligned movement in order to formulate such a proposal, the political reputation of the latter added salience and credibility to the demand. More than anything else the Havana summit illustrated the crucial political function served by the nonaligned framework.

Nonaligned summits, reaching back to Belgrade (1961), have historically enjoyed a political visibility that G-77 conferences have never attained. As a political forum in which heads of state and government deliberate (forty-nine delegations were at this level at Havana, the largest number at any meeting since the Algiers summit), nonaligned summit conferences are important diplomatic events. The presence of a substantial number of Third World leaders accords legitimacy to the decisions that are taken. Even a conference marked by disputes like those over Kampuchea and Egypt can contribute positively to diplomatic mobilization around other issues like global negotiations. Indeed, the fact that these triennial summit exercises address the major political issues of the day enhances their impact as devices to focus attention upon Third World concerns.

Kampuchea and Camp David were less threatening to this mobilizational function than was the natural ally thesis. The latter was a fundamental challenge to the underlying compromise upon which the movement has rested from the outset. The doctrine was politically dysfunctional because it was likely to provoke boycotts and defections; it was diplomatically suspect because it shifted attention from Third World interests to superpower rivalry. In rejecting the natural ally thesis, the member-states acted to preserve the movement as an instrument of collective action.

That realism and pragmatism prevailed at the sixth summit was not immediately evident to some Western observers. The *New York Times*, for example, ran an editorial about the summit under the headline "Blowing Smoke in Havana."[20] According to the *Times*, the final documents of the conference set a record for "woolly silliness" and "nonsense." Such fuzzy thinking was attributable to the "bullying tutelage of Fidel Castro" and signified that "the nonaligned bloc is too diffuse to chart a coherent course." The *Times* editorial drew these conclusions by focusing on a couple of passages from the conference declarations and resolutions rather than by analyzing the political process that had actually occurred. Far from throwing up a smoke screen, the Havana proceedings cleared the air by blowing the natural ally thesis away. Havana was first and foremost a victory for Tito, not for Castro. As such it was a victory for a coherent conception of nonalignment that placed the interests of the Third World coalition first. Contrary to the view of the *Times*, the final outcome of the sixth summit demonstrated that the nonaligned grouping (which has never been a "bloc") was capable despite its diversity of charting a coherent course of organizational preservation.

The overarching objective of organizational maintenance was reflected as well in decisions on institutional matters. Whereas in the early 1970s, the task had been to create interim institutions like the Bureau, the political imperative at the end of the 1970s was to ensure the broadest possible participation in these subsidiary organs. By the end of the decade, the practice of regular Bureau meetings was well established, and gradually the Bureau had become a major decision-making body. It will be recalled that fear of the Bureau's falling under the control of its chairman or some small group of states had been one of the obstacles to its creation in the first place. By 1979, notably in the context of a Cuban chairmanship, some states were uneasy about the role that the Bureau had assumed. The summit acted to limit certain prerogatives of the Bureau and once again to expand its membership.[21] Moreover, it was agreed that "observer" states would enjoy full equality with Bureau members in arranging meetings, submitting proposals, and participating in subcommittees. In other words, the distinction between Bureau members and nonmembers was virtually erased. The effect was to maintain the capacity for nonplenary meetings while ensuring that no state could be excluded from decision making. Overall, the resistance to expanding Bureau powers signified a reassertion of the principle of the sovereign equality of the members, a principle essential to maintaining the organization.

If Algiers (1973) had been the summit of organizational consolidation, then Havana proved to be the summit of organizational preservation in the face of crisis. The potential for disaster was averted. The movement embraced the Cuban chairmanship while doctrinally and procedurally constraining it. It laid the groundwork for a major new North-South initiative. The summit guaranteed that the nonaligned framework would remain intact as a diplomatic instrument, most notably in the forthcoming drive for global negotiations on the international economic order. Havana was in the final analysis the supreme expression of the nonaligned movement's will to survive as a collective actor in international politics.

PUNCHING HOLES THROUGH SMOKE

In the immediate aftermath of Havana there were reports of a residual OPEC/non-OPEC cleavage inside the Group of 77. Assessing the mood at the United Nations, the *New York Times,* for example, found that "there is widespread agreement here that a new political fact has emerged on the world scene. The developing countries are no longer solidly lined up with the oil producers and, like the rich, are putting pressure on OPEC to grab either a smaller share of the world's resources or at least slow down the rate of their acquisition."[22] There is no doubt that oil prices had created strains in the coalition, but every effort had been made at Havana to keep these tensions under wraps. The first order of business in the fall of 1979 was to strengthen the consensus around the Global Negotiation strategy. In practice this meant an internal dialogue between OPEC and the rest of the Group of 77.

These talks were conducted behind closed doors, the coalition having no interest in publicizing its internal tensions on this matter. What was worked out was an understanding that OPEC would increase its aid fund in return for agreement on the concept of global negotiations as the only valid approach to discussing energy issues. OPEC delivered its part of the bargain at its semi-annual meeting in December 1979, at which it pledged an additional $1.6 billion in aid to Third World oil importers. This pledge helped to lay to rest Northern speculation about a shift in alliances to the detriment of OPEC. As such it was an integral component in consolidating agreement upon the Global Negotiation strategy. Once again what might be called the Algerian analysis prevailed: no discussion of energy outside a comprehensive framework, OPEC and non-OPEC united in a linkage strategy.

The importance to the South of the Global Negotiation project must be stressed. The proposal was really the culmination of five years of experience of North-South dialogue, a period that encompassed two Special Sessions, the CIEC, two UNCTAD plenaries, and the COW. It embodied the lessons of repeated frustrations and purported to identify the only constructive course to North-South cooperation. The basic lessons that the Group of 77 had learned were that negotiations must be comprehensive and that they must be conducted in a political forum like the General Assembly in order to effect any breakthrough. The reasoning was that only by linking several issues could all parties have their interests recognized. Linkage implied that the talks must at some point be centralized in a single forum and that this forum must be more political than technical, for the ultimate rationale for linked compromises was political accommodation. (This was implicitly the perennial issue of "political will" that the South had persistently evoked.) Comprehensiveness and politicization were the dual pillars of the Southern position. Only on these premises could the failing dialogue be revived.

The Group of 77 sought to incorporate these premises into the resolution on global negotiations that it drafted in the fall of 1979. Hence the language stressed the central role of the General Assembly and the concept of an integrated approach, integration serving as a codeword for linkage. We have already seen that the term "integrated approach" had appeared in Economic Resolution No. 9, which served as the model for the subsequent General Assembly resolution. The alternative to an integrated approach was a decentralized set of negotiations, each taking place in a discrete specialized forum such as the International Monetary Fund or the World Bank. While the Group of 77 did not oppose the use of multiple forums, its intention was that a central body, namely the General Assembly, where its voting majority had the highest salience, would have the final say. Both the Havana document and the subsequent United Nations resolution (No. 34/138) insisted upon "the central role of the General Assembly"—indeed the phrase appeared twice in the UN version.[23]

With the passage of Resolution 34/138 in December 1979, a new phase of diplomatic jockeying began. Ostensibly the issue was merely procedural—i.e., how should the proposed global negotiations be structured?—but procedure was the key to decision-making authority. The task of defining the procedure and the agenda for the proposed global negotiations was allocated to the Committee of the Whole. The timetable called for the COW to prepare an agreement on these matters for submission to the Eleventh Special Session, which had long been scheduled for summer 1980. The Group of 77 met in New York to adopt a draft agenda, which it submitted to the COW. It was in these rather barren pastures that the difficulty of implementing the global negotiations proposal was first encountered.

The G-77 position entailed a broad five-point agenda under the rubrics "raw materials, energy, trade, development, money and finance." Their position paper assumed that the talks should be biased in favor of "the principles guiding the establishment of a New International Economic Order, for the purpose of securing a more rapid development of developing countries and for the restructuring of international economic relations." Procedurally the G-77 paper envisaged that the Eleventh Special Session would formally convene a "United Nations conference on global negotiations" meeting at UN headquarters "at a high political level."[24] The North entered the COW with a proposed three-point agenda (food, energy, external balances), objection to the assumption of bias, and a preference for conducting negotiations within the existing specialized agencies. The latter point entailed an assumption that a specialized forum on energy needed to be created. These were the major differences among a host of minor disagreements on details.

The COW, operating in 1980 under the chairmanship of Bogdan Crnobrnja of Yugoslavia, met for three ten-to-twelve-day sessions in March–April, May, and June–July. Some progress was made toward a common position, but the fundamental question of who would ultimately be in charge of decision making—the specialized agencies or the proposed central conference—remained a sharp bone of contention. After the three rounds in the COW, India's ambassador to the United Nations, Brajesh Mishra, who was serving as chairman of the Group of 77, expressed the view that the industrialized states were concerned primarily to limit the scope and the authority of the proposed negotiations so as "to convert them into another exercise in futility." According to Mishra, the North's

> tactic has been to stall. When, after intense private consultations, a formulation was arrived at and presented in the negotiating group, they invariably suggested further changes to weaken the text even more. At the same time their own concerns were presented with varying degrees of vagueness, even dissimulation. When they are asked to concretize their suggestions, the burden of doing so was invariably transferred to us, the Group of 77. We were left with the impression that we were trying to punch holes through smoke.[25]

If smoke was rising above the field of North-South battle once again, Chairman Crnobrnja tried to hold his head above the fray. He wrote that the COW work had been useful at least in revealing expectations regarding the global negotiations project: "Some probably expect 'too much,' while others little or nothing at all."[26] For his relative equanimity, Crnobrnja was appointed head of Working Group II, which became the principal battleground during the Eleventh Special Session.

The Group of 77 had initiated the idea of the Eleventh Special Session in 1977 in the aftermath of CIEC. The session was therefore a long-awaited event on the diplomatic calendar. Its purpose at the outset had been to fix a date by which some discernible progress toward the NIEO could be marked. This original intent had by 1980 been transmuted into the goal of launching the Global Negotiation (GN), but the basic objective remained the same long-standing goal: to implement the NIEO program. The greatest significance of the 1980 Special Session lay in this long-term dimension: it was to be the culmination of the 1970s and the launching point of the 1980s. Loaded with this kind of symbolic weight, the session was very likely to collapse under the burden.

For the Group of 77, the critical objective was approval of the principle that the plenary body of the new GN forum would have the final decision-making power (this was the operational meaning of the insistence upon the central role of the General Assembly). The United States was unalterably opposed to this principle because of its implications for the specialized agencies, in which weighted voting gave the United States great power. Robert K. Olson has summarized official U.S. thinking well:

> Behind the differences lay the G-77 predisposition to centralize power in New York. The United States did not want a central, *dirigiste,* managed system, preferring, as always, a pluralistic, decentralized system that would keep economic and political forums and issues well apart. The G-77 position carried to its logical extreme would outflank the authority and autonomy of the key institutions of the IBRD, IMF, and GATT by imposing G-77 control of their activities through the conference and, ultimately, the General Assembly.[27]

As Olson suggests, the stakes were perceived as control over decision-making power, and this meant that both sides dug in their heels.

Chairman Crnobrnja searched for a formula that could satisfy both sides. After extensive consultations he introduced the "Crnobrnja paper," which outlined a three-phase approach to conducting negotiations. During the first phase, the central conference would meet for a period of up to eight weeks in order to establish objectives and provide guidance for the second round, during which specific agenda items would be negotiated in the appropriate specialized agencies. Then in phase three the central conference would reconvene to receive the results of phase two and meld them into an acceptable package agreement. The key language of the Crnobrnja proposal eventually read as follows: "The conference should have universal participation at a high political level and will be a forum for coordinating and conducting global negotiations with a view to insuring a simultaneous, coherent and integrated approach to all the issues under negotiation. The conference should result in a package agreement."[28] Most of the European countries were ready to accept this somewhat ambiguous text as sufficiently secure grounds on which to proceed into a substantive negotiation, but the United States was not.

The U.S. delegation proposed inserting the words "as appropriate" in front of the verb "conducting" as an assurance that the new conference would not preempt the role of the established specialized agencies. More generally, the United States sought assurance that phase three would not be the occasion to renegotiate agreements reached during phase two. The Group of 77 responded that the existing proposal adequately protected the role of the specialized agencies. The debate of course was not really over two words but over competing conceptions of who should decide international economic questions. The United States insisted that the Crnobrnja text failed to make clear that the central conference should not prejudice or reopen decisions taken in specialized agencies. Ambassador Joan Spero (U.S. representative to the Economic and Social Council) argued to U.S. allies that it would be a mistake to "paper over differences" that could lead to "greater difficulties in the future when the developing countries could be expected to press for adherence . . . to commitments."[29] Ambiguity, the United States feared, would impair established rules of decision making; and precommitment to a package deal might be a Pandora's box. These U.S. arguments failed to persuade most other Northern governments. They found that the United States was drawing the line at the wrong time and place, and they favored getting on to substantive talks in order to see what could be achieved. The Americans had to exert pressure on Great Britain and West Germany in order to avoid being totally isolated on their procedural reservations.*

The Group of 77 maintained tight ranks at the Eleventh Special Session with relative ease. It judged that the Crnobrnja proposal enjoyed sufficient backing to justify standing by it. Rather than incorporate the guarantees sought by the United States, the Group decided to highlight the U.S. resistance. At the final Ad Hoc Committee meeting, G-77 Chairman Mishra moved that the controversial text be adopted by consensus. This obliged the United States, the United Kingdom, and West Germany to record official objections. Mishra then moved and the Committee adopted this statement: "With the exception of three delegations, all members of the Committee expressed their readiness to accept the text contained in document A/S-11/AC. 1/L. 1/Rev. 1 as the procedural framework for the global negotiations."[30] The tactic was designed to increase the diplomatic pressure on the United States in the coming months, during which

---

*U.S. officials argue that others share their reservations but allow the United States to take the rap for blocking agreement. See, for example, the testimony to Congress of former Deputy Assistant Secretary of State Robert Hormats: "Frequently other developed countries offer compromises in the full knowledge that the United States, which tends to regard its commitments more seriously and more literally than many of them, will stand up and object. This gives the other developed country credit for having supported a compromise without ever having to deliver on its words. . . . These tactics . . . often put the United States in a difficult position of appearing alone to be blocking accommodations."[31]

several other matters would also remain to be resolved. The Group of 77 chose once again, as it had in 1977, to use failure to dramatize frustration. The Eleventh Special Session became an epitaph to the impasses of the 1970s. Mishra stressed that the North had lost an opportunity, but the Group of 77 felt cohesive and was optimistic that the global negotiations would yet be launched.

In the following months, Venezuela assumed the chairmanship of the Group in the person of a seasoned North-South expert, Manuel Perez Guerrero. The presidency of the General Assembly meanwhile fell to a new figure, Baron Rudiger von Wechmar of West Germany, who seemed determined to use informal contacts to break the deadlock. Throughout the fall of 1980 press reports indicated that a breakthrough was imminent. Von Wechmar even spirited a group of influential delegates off to the Catskill Mountains for a weekend of total immersion in informal bargaining. Yet neither the experience of Perez Guerrero nor the enthusiasm of von Wechmar sufficed to cut the knot, and the project remained in suspension when Ronald Reagan entered the White House in 1981. The Baron was well aware that this did not simplify his task, but he stoically greeted the new administration with an article on the op-ed page of the *New York Times* in which he posed the pertinent questions: "Which priority will United States relations with the Third World receive in the future? Will a Republican administration . . . grasp the political dimensions of the global round?"[32] He tactfully expressed optimism that the new administration would "see the economic benefits and the substantial political advantages of global negotiations supported by the United States" before concluding soberly that "in the end it will be the United States that can make or break the exercise." No one in the Group of 77 would have quibbled with that assessment based on the record of the previous fifteen months.

NEW CURRENTS AND THE MAINSTREAM

The election of President Reagan did have implications for the already faltering North-South dialogue, but it was perhaps more significant to the Third World in another way. Reagan had campaigned on a platform of increased military budgets and of standing up to the Soviet Union. He brought to the White House what Stanley Hoffmann called a "New Orthodoxy" that reemphasized military power as the key to coping with world problems.[33] None of this was conducive to serious reflection on North-South issues. On the contrary, the New Orthodoxy intensified East-West tensions, always a potential centrifugal force inside the Third World coalition. Reagan's victory gave a new thrust to the resurgence of cold war attitudes that had bedeviled coalition activity since the Afghanistan crisis.

The Soviet armed intervention in Afghanistan began in December 1979, some twenty months after the leftist coup that had mildly complicated nonaligned affairs in 1978 (p. 122). Now the issue exploded inside the nonaligned camp as well as upon the international system as a whole. Geopolitically Afghanistan had long constituted a buffer zone, first between British and Russian, later between U.S. and Soviet influence in Central Asia—it was in this regard a case of nonalignment or neutralism in the classic sense. The pro-Soviet coup had disturbed this classic status, but more important it had provoked internal resistance from Muslim dissidents opposed to the new regime. By the end of 1979 the rebels appeared on the verge of toppling the government. The Soviet decision to intervene to prevent the fall of the leftists thus violated the old notion of a buffer zone and gravely concerned several neighboring Muslim countries that were active in the nonaligned movement.

Third World states first had to take a position on the events in Afghanistan at the United Nations. After a Security Council resolution calling for the withdrawal of Soviet troops was defeated by a Soviet veto, the issue was transferred to the General Assembly, where a comparable resolution was passed 104–18–18. The vote among members of the nonaligned group was 56–9–17 (the remainder absent or not voting).[34] While a clear majority condemned the Soviet involvement, an important subgroup abstained—indeed, all but one of the abstentionists came from the nonaligned ranks. While these states abstained for diverse reasons (including uncertainty and lack of instructions), at least two chose to abstain largely because of concern about the implications of the issue for the nonaligned movement itself.

These were India and Algeria, whose concerns were twofold. First, a knock-down, drag-out battle in which the Cuban chair would be centrally implicated would reopen wounds that had been patchily bandaged since the Havana summit. Second, as this was an issue in which the superpowers had major stakes, it was crucial that the nonaligned avoid being utilized as an instrument of one side. While this position clearly offered solace to the Soviet Union, it also held out the possibility of extracting the Afghani problem from the superpower embrace in which the UN debate had placed it. The Algerian foreign minister traveled to New Delhi in February 1980 in order to concert the two governments' positions. They issued a joint statement that argued that "the fate of Afghanistan should not become the subject matter of discussion between great powers in terms of their respective national interests. It should rightly be decided by the Afghan people themselves," and they appealed to other nonaligned states to take heed that the movement "does not inadvertently get converted into an anti-Soviet movement."[35]

Other states, not at all inadvertently, were indeed pressing for a special ministerial session of the movement essentially to condemn Soviet policy. Yugoslavia's foreign minister made such a proposal in talks in Bangladesh, and Pakistan was also actively promoting a meeting. Meanwhile the nonaligned Bureau began a regularly scheduled session at UN headquarters at the end of February that turned into a prolonged but desultory effort to draft a group position. The inconclusive talks in New York tended to bear out the first of the Algerian-Indian concerns. The talks were divisive, and Cuba used the chair to wear down by attrition the proponents of condemnation. With the passage of time, numerous states began to drift toward the Algerian-Indian position as the best one for the nonaligned movement per se.

To some observers this implied that the movement had become "immobilized, frustrated, and uncertain," or more sardonically, "remarkably tongue-tied."[36] A more accurate assessment would be that the member-states were delineating some functional distinctions between the General Assembly and the nonaligned framework. The majority apparent in the General Assembly vote could not be readily exercised in nonaligned proceedings in which consensus was the necessary working principle. While the nonaligned movement might frequently use the General Assembly to advance its interests, the two forums could be differentiated in a case like Afghanistan. Whatever inconsistency this might reveal between General Assembly and nonaligned resolutions was diplomatically tolerable. It was a lesser cost than breaking apart the nonaligned framework.

This functional differentiation became apparent in the following months. First a compromise was struck among the nonaligned on the question of a special ministerial meeting. No such meeting was called during 1980, but it was agreed to advance the scheduling of the regular ministerial meeting from its normal late summer date to February 1981. Then the Afghanistan question was inscribed on the agenda of the fall 1980 General Assembly session. The November vote was quite similar to that of the previous January, with both sides managing to gain a few new adherents. The tally now was 111-22-12 (as against 104-18-18 in January). Both the United States and the Soviet Union had pressed abstainers among the nonaligned to pronounce on the issue and most of the new votes came from this source.[37] The breakdown of the nonaligned vote was 63-13-11. The November roll-call illustrated graphically that over two-thirds of the nonaligned member-states supported a policy of immediate withdrawal of foreign troops from Afghanistan. The political objective was clearly to condemn the use of Soviet military force (even though the resolution did not explicitly name the Soviet Union).

The UN vote set the stage for the subsequent ministerial meeting held in New Delhi in February 1981. With two strong General Assembly resolutions on the record, it became possible to formulate a nonaligned resolution in terms acceptable to a larger group by focusing upon Afghani self-determination. The nonaligned resolution did not repudiate the call for withdrawal of foreign troops but couched it in terms of a political settlement on the basis of "full respect for the independence, sovereignty, territorial integrity, and nonaligned status of Afghanistan and strict observance of the principle of non-intervention and non-interference."[38] The gist was close enough to the General Assembly resolution to satisfy Pakistan and other strongly committed Islamic states, while the general reference to intervention and interference could be interpreted to include support of the rebel forces as well.[39] Although the Kabul government itself denounced any discussion of its internal affairs, the resolution was eventually approved. The primary function of the nonaligned resolution was to reconcile divergent partners, a different purpose from that of the General Assembly vote.

The debate on Afghanistan rippled over to affect the Kampuchea debate as well. The states of the Association of South East Asian Nations (ASEAN), backed by other regional governments like Bangladesh and Nepal, compared the situation in Kampuchea to that in Afghanistan. They urged a comparable resolution calling for withdrawal of foreign forces from Kampuchea. Although the New Delhi Conference did follow the Havana precedent of the vacant seat, it broke with the Havana documents by adding a statement of urgent need for a "comprehensive political solution that would provide for the withdrawal of all foreign forces."[40] This language offended Vietnam, but reconciled the Asian states unhappy over the empty-seat approach to Kampuchean representation. In this instance as well, one can note a difference from what was happening at the United Nations, where the majority of nonaligned states joined the larger General Assembly majority in favor of seating the Pol Pot delegation. The New Delhi decision took account of a different constellation of forces and arrived at a different outcome.

In differentiating nonaligned and UN decisions, the member-states were acting pragmatically to preserve the nonaligned framework. At the same time one can see that the new nonaligned consensus (from which only Vietnam and Afghanistan formally absented themselves) was closer to the UN resolutions than previous nonaligned policies had been. A centrist consensus that the Yugoslavs referred to as "the mainstream" had reasserted control at New Delhi.[41] This mainstream position reflected the cumulative experience of an organization that was now twenty years old. A process of organizational learning and adaptation had occurred over these two decades that had perfected the art of elaborating a consensus anchored in the mainstream. The New Delhi consensus took account of the position expressed at the United Nations and adapted it to a form that maximized the cohesion of the nonaligned grouping. This mode of adaptation implicitly acknowledged that, rhetoric to the contrary, nonalignment was less a movement than a diplomatic instrument of the developing states' coalition.

Demarcating the mainstream was all the more desirable in the face of yet another crosscurrent, the six-month-old war between Iraq and Iran. The conference gamely decided to sponsor a "peace panel," which was active in mediation efforts over the next several months to no avail.[42] The Iran-Iraq war, however, did not create any sharp cleavage through the rest of the membership. The conflict was relatively limited in its implications and local in its impact. Moreover, the growth in the very numbers of the organization meant that it could absorb some local conflict without shattering. Experience had demonstrated that a considerable amount of business as usual could be conducted even when some member-states were bilaterally engaged in nasty struggles. The

Iran-Iraq war did pose a procedural dilemma nonetheless, because the next summit was scheduled for Baghdad. For the time being, the conference reiterated the commitment to meet in Baghdad in 1982, perhaps providing the Iraqis an incentive to seek a settlement.

The decisions at New Delhi had a stabilizing effect at a moment when the developing states, like others, needed time to assess the new administration in the United States. President Reagan appeared likely to provide the sharpest break with continuity in U.S. foreign policy in some time. Both the pronounced anticommunism and the free market orthodoxy of the Reagan campaign clashed sharply with basic premises of the nonaligned grouping. In this period of new assessments, the nonaligned framework needed a firmer foundation for its own future strategy. The mainstream position charted at New Delhi served this end.

Several other developments during 1980 also contributed to this need for a fresh assessment by the Third World. One was the outcome of the UNIDO conference held in January-February. Successor to the 1975 Lima Conference (p. 62), the 1980 version was a real donnybrook. The stage had been set in December 1979, when the Group of 77 met in Havana and adopted a platform of dubious realism. The G-77 document had two provocative features. It called first for creation of a mammoth new fund to promote industrial development ($300 billion over ten years, twice that over twenty years), which was to be managed by the developing countries themselves. This was a quantum jump beyond anything that the North had ever contemplated. Second, the financial demands were accompanied by a political declaration that condemned capitalism and its support of colonialism, imperialism, and racism.* Needless to say, this was not what the industrial powers of the North had come to discuss.

The conference promptly bogged down as the North denounced the South for submitting a "political tract" while the South insisted that it had made a realistic appraisal of the overall problem of industrialization in a capitalist world economy. As the allotted conference period drew to a close, host country India announced that it had a compromise to avert a debacle. The proposed Indian text turned out to be a recapitulation of the G-77's maximalist financial demands minus the political references to South Africa, Palestine, Zionism, and the like. This approach did not mollify the North, which was concerned as much about the funding propositions as about the polemics. The North rejected the Indian initiative, and the Group of 77 stubbornly put its original document to a vote, bringing the conference to a close on a discordant note of confrontation. (The

---

*This G-77 document was a merger of two drafts, one prepared by a G-77 body working in Vienna (seat of UNIDO) and the other by the host country, Cuba.[43] The political flavor of the document was attributable to this Cuban input, which most of the other developing states presumably considered negotiable.

vote was 83-22-1, the entire Organisation of Economic Co-operation and Development (OECD) group voting against, a pyrrhic victory if ever there was one, as the program had no possibility of implementation.)

This spectacular failure caused some misgivings within the Group of 77. An opportunity had been wasted by the insertion of gratuitous issues into the industrialization debate. Here was an example of a counterproductive linkage of political and economic issue areas that tended to undermine other attempts at linkage. The argument that the Group of 77 should distinguish itself quite sharply from certain nonaligned issues gained currency. The tactics of the Group of 77 at UNIDO III were largely conjunctural, however. Attention had already shifted early in 1980 to that summer's Eleventh Special Session. As one delegate interpreted the fiasco in New Delhi, "Each party wanted to place himself in what he judged to be the best position for New York."[44] According to this analysis, a failure at UNIDO would increase pressure for a subsequent agreement on the Global Negotiation. The summer's events disproved this hypothesis.

Tactical questions were raised also by the publication in February 1980 of the Brandt Commission Report. The report stemmed from a novel initiative first sponsored by Robert McNamara, president of the World Bank. McNamara's idea was that an independent commission of eminent persons from North and South ought to be able to bring some enlightenment to the sound and the fury of the NIEO debate. Willy Brandt, former chancellor of West Germany and author of the *Ostpolitik* that had calmed tensions in Europe, agreed to chair such a panel, on which such dignitaries as Eduardo Frei (former president of Chile), Edward Heath (former prime minister of Great Britain), Olof Palme (former prime minister of Sweden), Pierre Mendès-France (former prime minister of France, who was later replaced on the commission by Edgard Pisani), Shridith Ramphal (secretary-general of the Commonwealth), and others agreed to serve.[45] The endeavor was preeminently political, its objective being to enlarge the Northern constituency for international economic reform. McNamara and Brandt sought to provide a reasoned argument, stripped of some of the customary rhetoric and endorsed by respected public figures on both sides of the North-South divide, that would encourage leaders on both sides to moderate their positions.

The report did contain an eloquent appeal for cooperation in development based upon "the idea of a global community, or at least a global responsibility" and the "thesis that there are growing mutual interests."[46] It called for greater resource transfers to be effected through a system of "international taxation," including levies on trade and arms sales. The details of the commission's proposals were less significant than the intended public impact. In this regard the timing was unfortunate. Brandt signed his introduction on December 20, 1979, barely a week before Soviet forces entered Afghanistan. The report thus fell upon rather barren soil and never bore the desired fruit, especially in U.S. public opinion. Yet it did contain one short-term recommendation, its call for a "summit for survival," that aroused a tactical debate among the developing countries.

Mexico seized upon the summit proposal as a valuable concrete initiative. Much as his predecessor Luis Echeverria had championed the Charter of Economic Rights and Duties of States, President Jose Lopez Portillo embraced the commission project of a summit "to include only a limited number of heads of states or governments."[47] The rationale of this elite summit was the same one that had been advanced on behalf of CIEC—manageable numbers, serious deliberations behind closed doors. The argument was suspect, however, to other states with skeptical recollections of the CIEC experience. These states had misgivings about endorsing the summit proposal. Lopez Portillo therefore enlisted the aid of Austrian Chancellor Bruno Kreisky, close associate of Brandt in the Socialist International, who invited delegates from ten governments (five Northern and five Southern) of varying views to Vienna for consultations. The Southern representatives were Algeria, India, Mexico, Nigeria, and Yugoslavia, but Algeria requested that Tanzania also be invited to participate as a representative of the least developed countries. The Northern invitees were Canada, France, West Germany, and Sweden, along with Austria. The issue at Vienna, in a nutshell, was summit versus Global Negotiations.

Algeria's fear was that the summit might be used to sidetrack the Global Negotiation enterprise. Mexico was the only one of the Southern states that was not a member of the nonaligned as well as of the Group of 77. It had therefore not been involved in the original call for global negotiations and did not vest them with the same significance that Algeria did. While Yugoslavia and Nigeria were very close to the Algerian position, India was as open to a summit meeting as to the UN talks. This explained Algeria's insistence upon the inclusion of Tanzania, which it knew to be committed primarily to global negotiations. With four of the six Southern countries of this persuasion, they were in a good position to safeguard their priorities. They were willing to cosponsor the Mexican summit so long as it was clearly specified that this was an auxiliary exercise which by no means could replace the larger project. Such was the understanding that emerged from the Vienna consultation: the global negotiations were the priority framework, the summit an informal means to help them along.

This then was the origin of the eventual Cancun summit. From the perspective of the Third World coalition, it is important to underline, Cancun was a project outside ordinary channels. The Group of 77 did not formally discuss the Mexican initiative, much less its Austrian counterpart. The operation did not fit the model of collective diplomacy that the coalition had developed as its basic approach to North-South relations. Later, once the summit was firmly scheduled, the Group of 77 formulated some substantive advice about what it should achieve, but otherwise the Group regarded the event as an experiment. Summitry in fact had never been directly applied to North-South relations. No one could argue that the established methods were working so well that the experiment was not worth trying.

Indeed, this was the much larger issue facing the South in the early part of

1981. Despite intensive negotiating efforts, the formula for launching the Global Negotiation had not been discovered. The Carter administration had not budged, and now the Third World faced an administration even more hostile to the notion of a managed global economy. Moreover, the world was slipping back into a recession that made the prospect of a global bargain even more distant. Hard times began to weigh upon the cohesion of the coalition.

INDIAN INFLUENCE AND THE
DUAL-TRACK STRATEGY

Economic recession on the one hand, Reaganomics on the other—these two factors presented the developing countries with an intractable environment in which to contemplate global economic change. The early decision of the Reagan administration to back out of the long-standing Law of the Sea negotiations raised grave doubts about the likelihood of coaxing or pressuring the Reaganites into global negotiations. Some states began to question the realism of fixing such talks as the primary goal of their collective diplomacy. Questions of strategy and tactics arose within the Third World in the face of the prospect of long-term stalemate.

The most radical strategic move would have been to shift sharply away from global negotiations into collective self-reliance, in the terms of the 1979 Arusha Program. There was, however, no consensus within the Group of 77 on a genuine delinking of Southern economies from the North. Still, the concept of collective self-reliance, or economic cooperation among developing countries (ECDC) in its less radical formulation, was worth keeping alive, in part as a potential alternative, in part as a way of strengthening Southern cooperation.

The Group of 77 thus organized a conference in Caracas on South-South cooperation both to enhance intragroup relations and to examine further the perennial idea of a G-77 secretariat. The toughest issue in the former domain was, as always, energy cooperation. Oil importers again pressed oil exporters for assistance on a larger scale. Venezuela and Algeria, the prime boosters of aid programs inside OPEC, had both initiated preferential pricing policies to selected states. Venezuela in conjunction with Mexico was supplying oil to Caribbean and Central American states. Algeria had worked out a plan with Libya, Nigeria, and Gabon to sell to other African states at some discount. The May 1981 conference was not able to transform these pilot projects into an OPEC-wide commitment, nor was an alternative proposal to transform the OPEC Fund into a full-scale development bank approved. The major capital-holding state, Saudi Arabia, agreed only to increase the volume of its loans.

The Caracas conference inched forward on the organizational issue. Venezuela argued for creation of a permanent secretariat. Kuwait favored instead an elected "bureau" on the model of the nonaligned organ, an interim body rather than a permanent staff. Neither of these options was finally endorsed, but establishment of a mini-secretariat in New York was authorized. The new arrangement was essentially an extension of the office of the G-77 chairman at UN headquarters. In recognition of the chair's responsibility for disseminating information and coordinating activities, he was authorized to engage six persons for assistance in this task. The initial conception was to fund these positions through voluntary contributions; in practice governments chose to release experts on temporary assignment to the chairman's office.[48] However modest this secretariat, it was a commitment to greater organizational efficiency. At the same time, it was a commitment to the Group of 77 as a bargaining agent with the North, not an instrument of collective self-reliance.

What the South should aim for at Cancun was the tactical question in mid-1981. As originally envisaged, the Mexican summit was to take place in June 1981 before the annual economic summit of the major industrial powers. The idea was that the Northern summit would act to implement the decisions of the North-South summit. President Reagan did not like this ordering of events. He requested delay of Cancun until the fall. Not only was the scheduling tailored to U.S. preferences, so was the agenda. The United States fixed four preconditions to its participation: no preparatory documents, no formal negotiations or concrete agreements, no final communique, no Cuba. President Reagan wanted an informal chat, not a decision-making forum, and he did not want any rabble-rousers. All these conditions were accepted in order to insure U.S. participation. But toward what end?

The Group of 77, thirteen of whose members were invited to Cancun,[49] published a declaration early in October. The Group's mandate to its "delegation" was simple and straightforward. The objective of the summit was to open the way to the Global Negotiation. One government, according to the G-77 declaration, stood in the way. The purpose of Cancun was to persuade the United States to change its position. The Group of 77 was not the only source to address a message to the summit. Willy Brandt and Commonwealth Secretary-General Ramphal also wrote to the Cancun heads of state suggesting that the summit's first goal should be to enable the global negotiations to begin. France's new president, François Mitterrand, whose foreign minister had recently proclaimed at the United Nations, "We belong to the South," was strongly committed to launching the global round.[50] The test of the summitry experiment was its capacity to influence Ronald Reagan.

By this standard Cancun was a colossal flop. The Western press emphasized the cordial atmosphere at the Mexican resort, but Brandt later more aptly observed that the meeting had produced "millimetric progress."[51] Although Julius Nyerere was reported to have convinced Reagan that concessional aid rather than private investment was appropriate for constructing basic infrastructure, no one swayed his position on the central substantive issue.[52] Rather Reagan used Cancun as an opportunity to reiterate his faith in the free market as an allocator of global wealth. He expressed his confidence in existing international agencies as the appropriate forum for discussing economic development. The ambiance of summitry had no impact upon the U.S. position. Although Cancun has been called Reagan's "greatest triumph in north-south diplomacy," it was undeniably a failure for everyone else concerned.[53] Moreover, it was a hollow triumph, if one at all, for the United States: to hold firm without reshaping the diplomatic context is a modest achievement.

In a final statement the conference chairmen announced that the twenty-two heads of state had "confirmed the desirability of supporting at the United Nations a consensus to begin Global Negotiations on a basis to be mutually agreed and in circumstances offering the prospects of meaningful progress."[54] The tortuous language revealed that Cancun had produced only a consensus about the desirability of a consensus heretofore quite elusive. The entire debate was shifted back to the United Nations, whence it had come, and the Group of 77 continued to advance its notion of "circumstances offering prospects of progress." No more blunt an epitaph to Cancun could be found than the remark three weeks later of U.S. Ambassador to the United Nations Jeane Kirkpatrick: "We are stuck with the same problem this body has been stuck with for the last two years."[55]

If the United Nations was stuck, that of course meant that the Group of 77 was stuck. The matter of Third World morale had to be taken into account. No doubt some G-77 states "accept the idea," as a *New York Times* journalist wrote, "that the United States and others cannot be moved."[56] These states reportedly wanted to shift the focus of North-South relations directly to the specialized agencies, where the United States was more comfortable and hence perhaps more forthcoming. During this post-Cancun period, however, the chairmanship of the Group of 77 had passed to Algeria, probably the most committed advocate of global talks in the entire group. Algeria's ambassador to the United Nations, moreover, was Mohammed Bedjaoui, author of a book entitled *Towards a New International Economic Order.* Bedjaoui was not one to let matters drop, and he saw to it that the Group of 77 came up with a new "blueprint" for comprehensive talks in December 1981. The new plan sought to address certain U.S. objections and concurrently served notice that the Group of 77 had not abandoned its basic concept.[57] Yet more than a firm G-77 consensus, it represented the capacity of a strong chair to guide the group, for the Algerians were warding off a growing sentiment in favor of a shift in tactics.

The discussion within the Third World became more apparent in the course of ad hoc consultations organized by India in February 1982. One group, led by India and Pakistan, argued that the time had come to engage in talks on the decentralized procedural basis preferred by the United States. The Algerian-led camp responded that any "deglobalization" would compromise the developing countries' ability to achieve significant reform. A shaky middle ground was constituted around the formula "firm on principles, supple on tactics."[58] As the matter of tactics was becoming more and more central, one could discern an emergent trend toward a flexible bargaining position.

U.S. steadfastness was not the only factor that underlay this trend. Implications of the changing situation in the world oil market were also affecting national calculations. By 1982 oil prices had peaked and were now on the decline. In the long term, this decline undermined Third World bargaining power, for it diminished one Northern incentive to seek a deal. Moreover, OPEC countries like Algeria had been the parties most willing to delay talks for the sake of future bargaining advantage. As OPEC's own global position weakened, so did the Southern incentive to stand fast by a strategy that had originally emanated from an OPEC perspective. The fact that Saudi Arabia declined to attend the consultations in New Delhi cast a further shadow upon G-77 unity: the most important financial surplus state was distancing itself from the common enterprise.

Moreover, the general sluggishness of the world economy was discouraging. The debt issue was becoming daily more threatening, and protectionism was growing. Interest rates were high, currency exchange rates ever more volatile, and financial markets ever less certain. Given a mood of impending crisis and urgent needs, the inducement to get talks started on any basis was growing.

Meanwhile, the North was in the same leaky boat. U.S. partners took another crack at bailing out the negotiations as the June 1982 industrial powers' summit approached. Canada circulated a draft that contained an understanding that the central conference would not have authority to create bodies that would duplicate the role of the existing specialized agencies. The United States came under considerable pressure at the Versailles summit to accept this formulation. In mid-June the United States officially endorsed the document as a basis for beginning the Global Negotiation, but the Group of 77 then rejected the text. Diplomats reported that most G-77 states were prepared to accept the Canadian compromise, but others objected that it contradicted the original conception of negotiations essentially mandated by the central conference. In the absence of a consensus to alter the G-77 position, the stand-off could not be broken.[59] This decision to reject a Northern offer acceptable to the majority increased the strains inside the Southern coalition, and numerous states began to drift away from the Global Negotiation proposal—at least as a practical priority.

The summer of 1982 was an unmarked turning point for the Third World coalition. On the organizational level, the chairmanship of the Group of 77 in New York rotated from Algeria on to Bangladesh, "full circle" from India's active role under Brajesh Mishra at the beginning of the Global Negotiation project. Substantively Bangladesh was close to India on matters of international economic policy, and India, as we have seen, was becoming increasingly skeptical of the realism of a project that had advanced so little over three years. By the same token the passage of three years meant new opportunities on the diplomatic calendar, most notably UNCTAD VI. The regular quadrennial conference was a bird in hand at a moment when there was no guarantee that the global negotiations were even in the bush. Three years of frustrations, divisions over the Canadian compromise, OPEC's fading capacity, pessimism over global economic conditions—all contributed to an unheralded shift away from Global Negotiation as a priority.

In principle the Group of 77 stood by its project. Forty-seven states working in Manila as a "committee" during the summer drafted a report that they submitted to the full Group in New York. It contained another revised bid to initiate the talks, which the annual ministerial meeting duly endorsed in October. In practice, however, no one really expected the Global Negotiation format to prevail, and practical attention turned toward planning strategy for UNCTAD VI, scheduled for Belgrade in June 1983. The official position became to conduct talks on urgent issues without waiting for the start of global negotiations. In effect this was an admission that the time was not ripe for the ambitious scenario envisaged at Havana. The Indian position was gradually displacing the Algerian position as the G-77 norm.

Whether this displacement would hold or not would be determined by the seventh nonaligned summit. As the Iran-Iraq war ground on, the plausibility of Baghdad as a site waned. As late as June 1982, when the nonaligned Bureau held its regular ministerial-level meeting, Baghdad had been retained. There was considerable reluctance to admit that an internal dispute could force a change of venue; moreover the Saddam Hussein government had already made a massive investment in preparations for the conference. In mid-July, however, the Iranians launched a major new offensive into Iraqi territory that discouraged even the hardiest souls from venturing to Baghdad. Ayatollah Khomeini thus deprived Hussein of the prestige of hosting a summit. The highest imperative was to find a ready-made site where the meeting could be remounted with minimal delay. The obvious candidate was New Delhi, veteran of international conferences but never previously host to a nonaligned summit. The rescheduling could only enhance India's already formidable influence.

The Indians set out to make the delayed seventh summit a model of political maturity. Despite the relatively short lead time, their task was simplified by several factors. Foremost was the fact that no new radically divisive issue had arisen since the 1981 ministerial meeting. It was as if the previous New Delhi conference had been a dress rehearsal for 1983: the states had already dealt with Kampuchea, Afghanistan, the Iran-Iraq war. Although acrimony still surrounded these issues, the formulas hammered out two years earlier still constituted tolerable positions. The Indians were able to contain the most rancorous of the debates—namely over Kampuchea, in which the ASEAN states tried to overturn the empty-seat compromise—in the foreign ministers' meeting preceding the actual summit. Prime Minister Gandhi thus had the opportunity to focus on other matters. She chose to return to some of the basics of the early nonaligned movement, notably disarmament and development.

Gandhi's keynote address stressed the fundamental linkage between ending the arms race and getting on with economic development. Pointing out that one nuclear aircraft carrier costs more ($4 billion) than the GNP of 53 countries, she recalled Nehru's plea that without peace "all our dreams of development turn to ashes." "The hood of the cobra is spread. Humankind watches in frozen fear, hoping against hope that it will not strike. Never before has the earth faced so much death and danger."[60] The ashes of annihilation, the ashes of charred dreams—such were the traces that the world of the 1980s threatened to leave if it could not turn away from arms races to development.

The evidence since 1979, Gandhi recalled, was discouraging:

> Since Havana, there have been four consecutive years of stagnation or decline in the world economy . . . balance of payments deficits of the developing countries and their debt burdens have doubled to US dollars 180 billion and 680 billion respectively. . . . Concessional assistance has rapidly declined. . . . Commodity prices, which were declining, have collapsed. . . . In spite of Ottawa, Cancun, and Versailles, the dialogue between the developed and the developing has not even begun and only a few in the North realize that the sustained social and economic development of the South is in its own interest.[61]

At this point, she reiterated the nonaligned commitment to a "thorough-going restructuring of international economic relations," but she also implicitly indicated a new set of priorities. "Long range solutions," Gandhi said, "need time and preparation. Immediate problems brook no delay." She suggested two responses to these urgent problems: enhancing collective self-reliance and redirecting the focus of North-South relations to the forthcoming session of UNCTAD.

For once it was the conference's Economic Committee that housed the most lively discussion. Two competing approaches, Algeria's emphasis on the Global Negotiation and India's stress upon immediate measures, were placed on the table. Prime Minister Gandhi's inaugural speech was of course perfectly compatible with the tone of the draft economic document prepared by India. The Indians submitted a second draft that took account of some of Algeria's misgivings, whereupon the Algerians submitted a draft document entitled "Collective Action for Global Prosperity." Each submission represented a slightly different emphasis; on the other hand, the competing approaches were not strictly incompatible. The differences were not so much eliminated as surmounted by a cumulative process that produced an unusually long economic document, which the assembled diplomats "considered to be the most important achievement of the conference."[62] In brief, the Algerian camp won sanction for what might be called a dual-track conception, while the Indian camp was satisfied that this permitted prompt attention to immediate issues.

This internal balancing can be discerned in three major chapters of the final economic declaration.[63] Chapter III is entitled "Negotiations for the Establishment of the New International Economic Order," and it is subdivided into two parts on "Assessment" and "Strategies for Forthcoming International Economic Negotiations." The explicit emphasis on strategy is novel in a nonaligned document. Here the heads of state call for "constructive interaction between steps to promote world economic recovery and the restructuring of existing international economic relations."

Chapter IV is headed "Global Negotiations Relating to International Economic Cooperation for Development." It contains a paragraph (numbered 28 bis) that was added to the draft text in the course of the committee proceedings. An Algerian initiative, the paragraph envisages a two-step approach to the Global Negotiation. The new formulation was

> to launch Global Negotiations in early 1984 by taking up in the first phase those issues on the formulation and allocation of which agreement would have been reached. During the first phase, parallel efforts should be made through a working group of the conference for expanding the Global Negotiations to include in the second phase other issues, particularly those effecting [sic] the structure of the international economic system and institutions.

This two-phase conception was an effort to ensure that the GN project not be abandoned in the process of initiating a second track of talks on immediate measures. In adopting a step-by-step approach, the partisans of the GN strategy were in effect incorporating an element of the immediate measures strategy into their own approach.

Chapter V authorizes the new second track under the heading "Program of Immediate Measures in Areas of Critical Importance to Developing Countries." As Chapter IV incorporated the concerns of the Algerian camp, Chapter V belongs to the Indians and begins by echoing Gandhi's opening speech: "In the meantime, the solution of the immediate problems of the developing countries brooks no delay." A lengthy chapter, it contains a catalogue of thirty-nine items for urgent attention under the familiar rubrics of monetary and financial issues (including indebtedness, IMF, World Bank, development assistance), trade and raw materials, energy, food, and agriculture. It ends with a new proposal, which also came directly from the Gandhi speech, to convene "an international conference on money and finance for development." The summit added a Chapter V bis on procedures "to organize the necessary political support" to enact the various immediate measures, which in turn referred to the declaration on "Collective Action for Global Prosperity" that the Algerians succeeded in appending to the summit documents. Here one can read again that "the approach of Global Negotiations remains the most appropriate instrument for dealing with current economic problems in a comprehensive and effective manner," but that "in the meantime, the solution of immediate problems . . . brooks no delay."[64]

This meticulous balancing act perfectly captures a crucial component of collective diplomacy. The coalition must accommodate as amply as feasible the competing policy preferences of its most active members. The dual-track notion that emerged from New Delhi served this function admirably. On the one track, the Global Negotiation project was preserved, albeit in a new two-phase format; on the other track, the coalition authorized the pragmatists to pursue immediate measures through existing channels, notably at UNCTAD VI (to which Chapter VIII of the declaration was devoted). The second track nonetheless did represent a redistribution of influence within the coalition.

The predominance of economic issues and strategies at New Delhi was conjunctural, prompted by the depressed state of the world economy. The focus upon economics did not mean that the nonaligned and G-77 frameworks were becoming redundant, as one might be tempted to conclude. The nonaligned organization retained its function as the articulator of a Third World voice in global politics. Stagnancy and global depression were the highest-priority concerns in 1983, and the nonaligned states used their organization to define a policy strategy on these issues. Beneath the process of the normal ebb and flow of influence among member-states, where a new Indian pattern was defined, lay a fundamental continuity of purpose in the utilization of the nonaligned instrument.

The process of organizational evolution continued at New Delhi also. Membership pursued its steady upward trend to reach ninety-nine full participants (including the PLO and SWAPO).* Although the normal cycle of meetings had been perturbed by Afghanistan (early convocation of the foreign ministers' meeting) and by the Iran-Iraq war (postponement of the summit), which in turn disrupted the customary schedule of the Coordinating Bureau, the organization had managed to operate fairly smoothly through Bureau and ministerial meetings at the United Nations. Well-established working practices existed, in other words, but there was still a lingering doubt about the proper composition of the Coordinating Bureau. The summit resolved the question of Bureau membership by approving a new arrangement by which self-selection replaced election. Any state that submitted a formal request to serve would be appointed to the Bureau at the conclusion of the summit; moreover, in accordance with the existing practice, all meetings of the Bureau were to remain open in any case. In this manner, a Bureau of sixty-six volunteers was constituted.[65] This was a bureau in name alone, but it did preserve the practice of frequent interim meetings that

---

*There were six new member-states at New Delhi: Colombia, Ecuador, Barbados, Bahamas, and newly independent Belize and Vanuatu. The first three were former observer states, and Belize had enjoyed a special status. Chad and Saudi Arabia, absent at Havana, were also present, but one state, Burma, had left the ranks after the Havana Conference. Burma is the only state formally to have renounced membership in the organization.

was the essence of the bureau concept. That fully two-thirds of the member-states wished to participate was a sign of organizational vitality (as much as an assertion of sovereign prerogatives).

This voluntaristic conception of the Coordinating Bureau essentially codified what had become the working practice of open meetings. It signified narrowly that all member-states enjoyed equal rights in nonaligned decision making. More broadly this new institutional arrangement underscored the members' conceptualization of the nonaligned framework as an international organization. The experience of the past few years had clarified the understanding that nonalignment designated something closer to a conventional international organization than to a movement. Like other international organizations, it had to respect the prerogatives of sovereignty in a state system. Like others, it was an instrument of states, not an authority in its own right. The states assembled in New Delhi understood that they were using the instrument to define a new policy.

The essence of the new policy orientation was the effective shift in priorities from long-term to short-term negotiations. This new emphasis in turn reflected an awareness that nonalignment as a Third World "movement" had failed since Havana to force the North into the Global Negotiation. The new strategy implemented a widely held conviction that a more limited, more pragmatic set of goals was needed in the face of global recession and an unyielding U.S. government. The seventh summit with its focus in the bargaining inside the Economic Committee consummated the transition to a new set of priorities that had been under way for some time. The dual-track formulation served notice that the longer-term goal of structural change through a global conference had not been abandoned, but New Delhi did reorder the items on the North-South agenda.

MODERATION AND REBUFF

The economic focus of the New Delhi summit might lead one to conclude that the nonaligned and G-77 frameworks had become redundant. The nonaligned conference on the contrary clearly envisaged a tandem operation. The two component instruments of the Third World coalition were to collaborate to prepare for UNCTAD VI and what lay beyond. The summit instructed Prime Minister Gandhi as the new chairperson to organize a series of consultations to build political support for the New Delhi economic declaration. Her first action under this mandate was to convene a meeting of nine key members (Algeria, Tanzania, Yugoslavia, Cuba, Sri Lanka, Indonesia, India, Bangladesh, as the current chair, and Argentina, primarily in its capacity as host to the G-77 preparatory meeting). This officially "informal consultation" insured a continuing nonaligned surveillance of events and in turn called for the dispatch of messages to the upcoming Williamsburg and Council for Mutual Economic Assistance (COMECON) summits of the major industrial powers of West and East. The gesture underscored the significance attached to the next round of international economic talks.

So too did the April ministerial meeting of the Group of 77 in Buenos Aires, called as usual in preparation for the UNCTAD plenary. Buenos Aires substantively implemented the revised priorities established at New Delhi. The Western press quickly identified a new tone in the Southern bargaining position. The *New York Times*, for example, reported "signs of an emerging mood of moderation in their demands on the industrialized world," and the *Financial Times* headlined its account "How the Third World Is Changing Its Strategy."[66] The *Inter Dependent* moreover reported that officials in Washington "were well aware of the increasingly moderate tone of the developing countries."[67] The central theme of the Buenos Aires platform was mutual need. In this it was very close in spirit to the second Brandt Commission report, *Common Crisis*, which appeared about the same time. The key idea was that the North needed Southern markets to revitalize their own economies. North and South thus shared an interest in measures to stimulate the Southern economies. In muting the language of structural inequality and stressing ameliorative measures, the Group of 77 sought to encourage a joint rescue of the world economy.

The specific proposals contained in the G-77 paper included a new IMF allocation of 15 billion Special Drawing Rights linked to development financing, an increase in the developing-country share in IMF quotas, and relaxation of the conditions surrounding IMF loans. These were standard expansionary measures basically within the framework of the existing institutional structure. While the document did repeat the New Delhi proposal for an international monetary conference, this in itself was a more limited project than the Global Negotiation (to which the G-77 document essentially paid lip service). There were also several debt relief proposals, but the accent was placed upon a cooperative common . roach to this area of obviously shared interests. (No threat of debt renunciation as a possible weapon was intimated.) In the crucial area of commodities, the document merely urged ratification of the Common Fund Treaty, which had finally been signed in 1980 but was still awaiting implementation pending the required number of ratifications. (This was for all practical purposes an appeal to the United States, whose failure to ratify the treaty was the main obstacle to implementation.*) There were stock proposals regarding resource transfers—exhortations to achieve the goal of 0.7 percent of GNP, notably by increasing contributions to the World Bank's subsidiary, the International

---

*By mid-1983, China, thirty-seven Third World states, and eleven developed states had ratified the treaty, which required ninety ratifications in all. The assessed U.S. contribution was critical to raising the prescribed $314 million (two-thirds of the total $470 million) needed to initiate Fund operations. Five more ratifications were recorded during UNCTAD VI, but the U.S. administration did not announce an intention even to submit the treaty to the Senate.

Development Association (IDA). Nothing in this was inflammatory, the Group of 77 seeking to promote an atmosphere of cooperation in a common cause. The mood was captured by the deputy secretary-general of UNCTAD, Jan Pronk, who declared, "The period of North-South polarization is behind us. Yet it must not happen that the hopes of the developing countries be disappointed again, for they are expecting a great deal from UNCTAD VI."[68]

Thus the developing countries formulated at Buenos Aires a moderate program inspired by the notion of "common crisis" elaborated in the second Brandt Commission report. The inner dynamics of the coalition produced a triumph of the moderates akin to that of the summer of 1975. The prevailing assumption was that sufficient common ground finally existed between North and South—equally concerned to stimulate global economic recovery—to permit a nonconfrontational UNCTAD plenary finally to take place. Rendezvous was fixed for Belgrade in June.

Once again Third World hopes were dashed. The hackneyed scenario of dispute and stalemate was replayed. As Henry Kissinger had ignored the G-77 platform in 1976, Deputy Secretary of State Kenneth Dam, who headed the U.S. delegation, made no mention of the Buenos Aires platform. Rather he reiterated the familiar homilies of the Reagan administration about recovery in the North as the motor to get development going in the South. He offered the South trade with the North rather than any direct aid stimulus, in effect questioning the basic premise of the Southern position. This new instance of the two sides' talking past one another was a discouraging start to UNCTAD VI.

The G-77 proposal for an SDR allocation was turned down; the issues of quotas and conditionality were likewise evaded by the argument that these were not proper UNCTAD issues. The insistence upon IMF jurisdiction simply threw back at the Group of 77 the whole wrangle over appropriate forums that had caused so much grief. The proposal to authorize an international monetary conference was also stricken from the final resolution because of U.S. opposition. On debt relief the North refused to endorse any obligation. The United States resisted pressure not only from the South but from most of its European allies on the matter of the Common Fund. On IDA replenishment also the United States refused any new commitment.

In brief, the tone of the G-77 position paper had little observable impact upon U.S. policy at UNCTAD VI. This inflexibility irked both the South and several U.S. partners in the North. The French were particularly annoyed at the unwillingness of the United States to make a gesture of political accommodation. French Foreign Minister Claude Cheysson criticized U.S. policy as a constraint upon the North as a whole; nor did he spare his Common Market partners in remarking that "the Europeans are rarely courageous when the Americans are at the bargaining table."[69] Observers discerned the emergence of a French-Swedish-Austrian axis in contention with a British-German-U.S. axis inside the Northern group, but the former had little ultimate impact upon the latter.

Corresponding tensions arose within the Third World coalition in the face of yet another disillusioning stalemate. Angry delegates, arguing that the developing states "were the only ones making any concessions," proposed that the whole session be adjourned as a failure.[70] Yugoslavia was loathe to permit such an outcome, and its foreign minister labored to produce a final package of resolutions acceptable to both sides. Many G-77 states reportedly felt that they were being forced to choose between unsatisfactory resolutions and none at all.[71] After some discussion, the Group of 77 agreed to go along with the Yugoslav package deal, which placed the kindest possible interpretation upon the meager results of four weeks of talks. In other words, a consensus upon moderation was maintained all the way to the bitter end of UNCTAD VI.

The events of 1983 from New Delhi to Buenos Aires through Belgrade demonstrated the capacity of the Third World coalition to shape, modify, and defend a collective position. During this period, influence within the coalition was redistributed to favor the preferences of the moderates, and the Group of 77 maintained discipline around that position in the face of widespread disaffection. The entire exercise was quite impressive in its mastery of the techniques of collective diplomacy. Notwithstanding this achievement, the operation failed: it did not break the stalemate.

POWER AND POLICY

The disappointing outcome of UNCTAD VI from the point of view of the Group of 77 cannot be attributed to lack of unity—at least at the tactical level. Nor, as some suggested afterward, should it be attributed to ineffective preparation on the part of the UNCTAD secretariat. Rather the conclusion must be drawn that despite an admirable effort of coherent collective diplomacy behind a pragmatic platform, the Third World coalition was thwarted by the greater power of the defenders of the status quo. In the realm of international economic relations, it is easier to defend the existing order than to institute a new one. Although the Third World has in fact increased its power through effective organization, that additional increment of power has not sufficed to achieve the intended objective.

In the international system, power runs up against countervailing power, and stalemate can become a way of life for extended periods of time. The situation of the Third World coalition in mid-1983, after a decade of organization-building, was in the final analysis little different from that of other important actors in a multipolar distribution of power. It had to operate in a context of constraints imposed by the power of others. The balance of power in North-South relations was the balance of a stand-off.

Acting in a state system, a coalition as a multistate actor does face some inherent limitations. The most powerful actors in the state system are the governments of states, and coalitions are not governments. This basic insight has led Carol Geldart and Peter Lyon to conclude that the Group of 77 "must be classified as illustrating the diplomacy of influence rather than of power." They argue with good reason that in the state system "there are still no satisfactory available substitutes for governmental policy which involves harnessed resources, applied power."[72] Yet acting in concert, as the members of a coalition strive to do, is a mode of harnessing resources. For this reason, I would argue that the Third World coalition is in fact engaged in the "diplomacy of power," but Geldart and Lyon still have a basic point. To the extent that national differences prevent sustained, concerted policy, Third World power is less than it might become.

The question remains whether the United States has acted wisely in choosing to check Third World power. There is no doubt whatsoever that U.S. policy has been the only insurmountable obstacle to the initiation of the Global Negotiation. Much more broadly, the United States is the leader of resistance to change in the global economic order. Although the United States has succeeded in blocking this Third World project, success has come at the price of anger and resentment.

Sometimes the exercise of power commands respect. In the domain of North-South relations, however, the United States has appeared as a stubborn defender of institutions and practices that have patently failed to bring welfare to the world's majority. This posture invites hostility, not respect; the long-term consequence is likely to be alienation from U.S. purposes among more and more of the world's people. The defense of a particular economic and decision-making structure at this cost cannot in the long run serve U.S. interests.

There was some recognition of this risk during the Carter administration, particularly during the tenure of Secretary of State Cyrus Vance. The impulse to acknowledge Third World grievances was then overwhelmed by the Iranian hostage-taking and by Soviet involvement in Afghanistan. Since the 1980 election, there has been virtually no recognition of the resentment that the United States is incurring. If, as Richard Feinberg has written, "Reagan's decision to attend the Cancun Summit ultimately gave the administration its greatest triumph in north-south diplomacy," then the record through UNCTAD VI must be adjudged a costly diplomatic failure.[73]

The case for cooperation between North and South has been well made elsewhere. The second Brandt Commission report, *Common Crisis,* amply elaborates the rationale. What is needed here is not to restate that case, but to spell out a single policy implication of the existence of the Third World coalition as an actor, however constrained, in world politics. The coalition has created an issue on which the United States has become increasingly isolated and resented. In a world of interdependence, that is not an enviable status.

NOTES

1. Note, for example, Roger Hansen's influential *Beyond the North-South Stalemate* (New York: McGraw-Hill, 1979) and Michael Doyle's analysis four years later, "Stalemate in the North-South Debate: Strategies and the New International Economic Order," *World Politics* 35, no. 3 (April 1983): 426–64.

2. Robert L. Rothstein, *The Third World and U.S. Foreign Policy: Cooperation and Conflict in the 1980s* (Boulder, Colo.: Westview Press, 1981), p. 31.

3. One might note that Chad, beset by civil war, was unable to send a delegation to Havana. This absence was balanced by the presence of Malawi, which participated again for the first time since 1964. One other new member actually admitted in 1978 was Djibouti, independent only since 1977. A composite chart of attendance at nonaligned summits can be found in Peter Willetts, *The Non-Aligned in Havana: Documents of the Sixth Summit Conference and an Analysis of Their Significance for the Global Political System* (New York: St. Martin's Press, 1981), pp. 65–67.

4. Ibid., p. 11.

5. Ibid., p. 13.

6. John A. Graham, "The Non-Aligned Movement After Havana," *Journal of International Affairs* 34, no. 1 (Spring-Summer 1980): 157.

7. Cited in Willetts, *Non-Aligned in Havana*, p. 12.

8. Ibid., p. 12.

9. William M. LeoGrande, "Evolution of the Nonaligned Movement," *Problems of Communism* 29 (January-February 1980): 47.

10. Willetts, *Non-Aligned in Havana*, p. 13. For example, one paragraph "recognized the role that the non-aligned countries, the United Nations, the Organization of African Unity, the socialist countries, the Scandinavian countries and other democratic and progressive forces play in supporting . . . the peoples of Zimbabwe, Namibia, and South Africa." Ibid., p. 87.

11. Cited in Gerard Viratelle, "A propos du VIe sommet des non alignés," *Maghreb-Machreq* 86 (October-December 1979): 7.

12. Ibid.

13. The text of Castro's speech appears in Willetts, *Non-Aligned in Havana*, pp. 216–27.

14. Ibid., p. 53. See also the account in LeoGrande, "Evolution of the Nonaligned Movement," pp. 48–49; and the *New York Times*, September 8, 1979.

15. Willetts, *Non-Aligned in Havana*, p. 220.

16. Paragraphs 108 and 109 of the Political Declaration, as found in ibid., p. 101.

17. *New York Times*, September 10, 1979.

18. The text of the resolution appears in Willetts, *Non-Aligned in Havana*, pp. 204–5.

19. See paragraphs 33–39 of the Declaration on Economic Matters in *Review of International Affairs* 702-703 (July 5-20, 1979): 41. The citation is from paragraph 37.

20. *New York Times*, September 11, 1979.

21. Formal Bureau membership was increased to thirty-six states. The right to issue communiques was withdrawn, and the authority to convene an annual ministerial-level meeting of the Bureau was abolished. Nor was any authority granted, as some states sought, to take on a peaceful settlement-of-disputes function. The details of the institutional decisions are meticulously analyzed by Willetts, *Non-Aligned in Havana*, pp. 34–41. See also Willetts's institutional chart, p. 70.

22. *New York Times*, September 18, 1979.

23. The text of the United Nations resolution appears in the *Yearbook of the United Nations 1979*, p. 468.

24. The full text of the G-77 submission appears in UN Document A/S-11/1, pp. 31–36.

25. Ibid., pp. 60–61.

26. *Review of International Affairs* 728–729 (August 5–20, 1980): 10.

27. Robert K. Olson, *U.S. Foreign Policy and the New International Economic Order: Negotiating Global Problems 1974–1981* (Boulder, Colo.: Westview Press, 1981), p. 112.

28. Cited in U.S. Congress, House, Committee on Foreign Affairs, Subcommittees on International Economic Policy and Trade and on International Organizations, *U.N. Special Session on Development: A Review*, Hearings, 96th Congress, 2nd Session, November 19, 1980 (Washington, D.C.: Government Printing Office, 1981), 71–72.

29. Report of Congressman Benjamin Gilman to the House Committee on Foreign Affairs, in U.S. Congress, House, Committee on Foreign Affairs, 96th Congress, 2nd Session, *United Nations 11th Special Session on Economic Development and Cooperation* (Washington, D.C.: Government Printing Office, 1981), p. 7.

30. UN Document A/S-11/AC. 1/SR 5, p. 7.

31. *U.N. Special Session on Development: A Review*, p. 3.

32. *New York Times*, January 24, 1981.

33. *New York Review of Books*, April 16, 1981.

34. The roll-call of the vote appears in the *New York Times*, January 15, 1980. Members of the nonaligned movement voting against the resolution were Afghanistan, Angola, Cuba, Ethiopia, Grenada, Laos, Mozambique, South Yemen, and Vietnam.

35. *New York Times*, February 28, 1980.

36. Graham, "Non-Aligned Movement After Havana," p. 159; *New York Times*, April 19, 1980.

37. New votes in favor of the call for withdrawal of foreign troops included Burundi, Central African Republic, Comoros, Equatorial Guinea, Guinea, Uganda, Sudan, and Zambia; new votes against the resolution came from Madagascar, Sao Tome and Principe, Seychelles, and Syria. One other new vote was cast for the resolution by Solomon Islands, but two January supporters (Bolivia, Iraq) failed to vote in November, thus producing a total of seven new yes votes. The roll-call appears in the *New York Times*, November 21, 1980.

38. *Review of International Affairs* 741 (February 20, 1981): 27.

39. See the account in *India News*, February 16, 1981, of lengthy discussions in the drafting committee. The draft "mentioned not the Soviet action alone but also other types of interventions, which tend to destabilize conditions in the region. . . . Pakistan's amendment did not find favor with committee as it referred only to Soviet action and not to other factors. The drafting group also rejected the amendments proposed by Afghanistan and South Yemen asking for deletion of any reference to Soviet intervention."

40. *Review of International Affairs* 741 (February 20, 1981): 27.

41. As Miljan Komatina put it in ibid., p. 3.

42. The panel was composed of Cuba, India, Zambia, and the Palestine Liberation Organization.

43. Karl P. Sauvant, *The Group of 77: Evolution, Structure, Organization* (New York: Oceana, 1981), p. 56.

44. *Le Monde*, February 12, 1980.

45. The complete membership of the commission is listed in the report, which was published as *North-South: A Program for Survival* (Cambridge, Mass.: MIT Press, 1980; and London: Pan Books, 1980.)

46. Ibid., pp. 12–13, 20.

47. Ibid., p. 27.

48. A summary of the Caracas "Program of Economic Cooperation" appears in "North-South Monitor," *Third World Quarterly* 3, no. 4 (October 1981). The chairmanship of the Group of 77 in New York passed from Manuel Perez Guerrero of Venezuela to Mohammed Bedjaoui of Algeria in September 1981. The stature of Perez Guerrero added weight to the argument for a secretariat; Bedjaoui became the first to direct such a staff.

49. In addition to the United States and the eleven countries at the Vienna meetings, the participants were Bangladesh, Brazil, Guyana, Ivory Coast, Philippines, Saudi Arabia, and Venezuela from the Group of 77 and Britain, Japan, and China. The Soviet Union declined an invitation to attend.

50. *Le Monde*, September 25, 1981.

51. Cited in Pedro-Pablo Kuczynski, "Action Steps After Cancun," *Foreign Affairs* 60, no. 5 (Summer 1982): 1022.

52. Richard E. Feinberg, "Reaganomics and the Third World," in Kenneth A. Oye, Robert J. Lieber, and Donald Rothchild, eds., *Eagle Defiant: United States Foreign Policy in the 1980s* (Boston: Little, Brown, 1983), p. 135.

53. Ibid., p. 134.

54. *New York Times*, October 24, 1981.

55. Ibid., November 14, 1981.

56. Bernard Nossiter (in the *New York Times*, November 4, 1981), of whom one might ask, "Which others?"

57. For example, the December proposal explicitly incorporated consensus as the mode of decision making in the central conference (giving the United States—and everyone else—the equivalent of veto power) and inserted the word "appropriate" (as the United States had earlier proposed) into the language about directives from the central conference to the specialized agencies. *New York Times*, December 6, 1981.

58. See the account in *Le Monde*, February 26, 1982. A much more

circumspect Yugoslav account that nonetheless acknowledges "differences in the developing countries' stands" appears in *Review of International Affairs* 767 (March 20, 1982): 5-7.

59. Donald Puchala, ed., *Issues Before the 37th General Assembly of the United Nations, 1982-1983* (New York: United Nations Association of the United States of America, 1982), p. 70.

60. The text of the speech appears in *India News*, March 14, 1983.

61. Ibid.

62. *New York Times*, March 13, 1983.

63. The text appears in *Review of International Affairs* 792 (April 5, 1983): 40-60.

64. Ibid., p. 68.

65. This contrasted with the thirty-six member Bureau formed at Havana. The "List of Members Who Have Communicated a Request to Serve on the Bureau" and the relevant report appear in ibid., pp. 70-71.

66. *New York Times*, April 6, 1983; *Financial Times*, April 5, 1983.

67. Robert A. Manning, "UNCTAD: The Poor Man's Summit," *Inter Dependent*, May-June 1983. This issue of the *Inter Dependent* also features an article entitled "Is the NIEO Dead?"

68. *Le Monde*, June 7, 1983.

69. Ibid., July 2, 1983.

70. Ibid., June 28, 1983.

71. Ibid., July 3-4, 1983.

72. Carol Geldart and Peter Lyon, "The Group of 77: A Perspective View," *International Affairs* 57, no. 1 (Winter 1980-81): 98.

73. Feinberg, "Reaganomics and the Third World," p. 134.

Appendix: Chronology of Major Third World and North-South Conferences

Date	Nonaligned	Group of 77	UNCTAD	Other
April 1955	–	–	–	Asian-African Conference, Bandung
December 1957	–	–	–	AAPSO (Cairo)
September 1961	Belgrade Summit	–	–	–
July 1962	Cairo Economic Conference	–	–	–
March–June 1964	–	–	Geneva	–
October 1964	Cairo Summit	–	–	–
October 1967	–	Algiers	–	–
February–March 1968	–	–	New Delhi	–
April 1970	Dar es Salaam, Foreign Ministers	–	–	–
September 1970	Lusaka Summit	–	–	–
November 1971	–	Lima	–	–
April–May 1972	–	–	Santiago	–
August 1972	Georgetown Foreign Ministers	–	–	–
September 1973	Algiers Summit	–	–	–
March 1974	Algiers (Bureau)	–	–	–
April 1974	–	–	–	Sixth Special Session, New York
February 1975	–	Algiers (UNIDO)	–	Raw Materials, Dakar
March 1975	Havana (Bureau)	–	–	OPEC Summit, Algiers
April 1975	–	–	–	CIEC Preparatory Meeting, Paris
August 1975	Lima, Foreign Ministers	–	–	–
September 1975	–	–	–	Seventh Special Session, New York
October 1975	–	–	–	CIEC Second Preparatory Meeting, Paris
December 1975	–	–	–	CIEC, Paris
February 1976	–	Manila	–	
May 1976	–	–	Nairobi	
June 1976	Algiers (Bureau)	–	–	
August 1976	Colombo Summit	–	–	
September 1976	–	Mexico City (ECDC)	–	

(continued)

Date	Nonaligned	Group of 77	UNCTAD	Other
March 1977	–	–	Common Fund Negotiation, Geneva (continued 11/77, 11/78, 3/79,	
April 1977	New Delhi (Bureau)	–	–	
June 1977	–	–	–	End of CIEC
May 1978	Havana (Bureau)	–	–	–
July 1978	Belgrade, Foreign Ministers	–	–	–
February 1979	–	Arusha	–	–
May 1979	–	–	Manila	–
June 1979	Colombo (Bureau)	–	–	–
September 1979	Havana Summit	–	–	–
December 1979	–	Havana (UNIDO)	–	–
February 1980	–	–	–	UNIDO
September 1980	–	–	–	Eleventh Special Session
February 1981	New Delhi, Foreign Ministers	–	–	–
April 1981	Algiers (Bureau), Namibia	–	–	–
May 1981	–	Caracas (ECDC)	–	–
October 1981	–	–	–	Cancun
June 1982	Havana (Bureau)	–	–	–
August 1982	–	Manila (ECDC)	–	–
December 1982	–	–	–	Law of the Sea (treaty signature)
January 1983	Managua (Bureau)	–	–	–
March 1983	New Delhi Summit	–	–	–
April 1983	–	Buenos Aires	–	–
June 1983	–	–	Belgrade	–

Bibliography

BOOKS

Atlantic Council Working Group. *The United States and the Developing Countries.* Boulder, Colo.: Westview Press, 1977.

Bedjaoui, Mohammed. *Towards a New International Economic Order.* New York: Holmes and Meier (for UNESCO), 1979.

Berg, Eugene. *Non alignement et nouvel ordre mondial.* Paris: Presses Universitaires de France, 1982.

Bergesen, Helge Ole; Hans Henrik Holm; and Robert D. McKinlay, eds. *The Recalcitrant Rich.* New York: St. Martin's Press, 1982.

Brecher, Michael. *New States of Asia.* New York: Oxford University Press, 1966.

Brzezinski, Zbigniew, ed. *Africa and the Communist World.* Stanford, Calif.: Stanford University Press, 1963.

Colard, Daniel. "Vers l'établissement d'un nouvel ordre économique internationale." *Notes et Etudes Documentaires,* 4412–14. Paris: La Documentation Française, 1977.

Common Crisis North-South: Co-operation for World Recovery. The Brandt Commission 1983. Cambridge, Mass.: MIT Press, 1983.

Conte, Arthur, *Bandoung tournant de l'histoire.* Paris: Laffont, 1965.

First, Ruth. *Libya, The Elusive Revolution.* Baltimore: Penguin, 1974.

Goodwin, Geoffrey, and James Mayall, eds. *A New International Commodity Regime.* New York: St. Martin's Press, 1980.

Gosovic, Branislav. *UNCTAD: Conflict and Compromise.* Leiden: A. W. Sijthoff, 1972.

Handel, Michael. *Weak States in the International System.* London: Frank Cass, 1981.

Hansen, Roger D., et al. *U.S. Foreign Policy and the Third World, Agenda 1982.* New York: Praeger Publishers (for the Overseas Development Council), 1982.

Hansen, Roger D., ed. *The "Global Negotiation" and Beyond.* Austin, Tex.: Lyndon B. Johnson School of Public Affairs, 1981.

_____. *The U.S. and World Development: Agenda for Action, 1976.* New York: Praeger Publishers (for the Overseas Development Council), 1976.

Haq, Mahbub ul. *The Poverty Curtain.* New York: Columbia University Press, 1976.

Jankowitsch, Odette, and Karl P. Sauvant, eds. *The Third World Without Superpowers: The Collected Documents of the Nonaligned Countries.* Dobbs Ferry, N.Y.: Oceana, 1978.

Kahin, George McTurnan. *The Asian-African Conference.* Ithaca, N.Y.: Cornell University Press, 1956.

Kay, David A., ed. *The Changing United Nations: Options for the United States.* Proceedings of the Academy of Political Science, 32, 4. New York: 1975-77.

_____. *The New Nations in the United Nations, 1960-1967.* New York: Columbia University Press, 1970.

Kegley, Charles W., Jr., and Pat McGowan, eds. *The Political Economy of Foreign Policy Behavior.* Sage International Yearbook of Foreign Policy Studies, Vol. 6. Beverly Hills and London: Sage Publications, 1981.

Kimche, David. *The Afro-Asian Movement.* New York: Halsted Press, 1973.

Laszlo, Ervin; Robert Baker, Jr.; Elliot Eisenberg; and Venkata Paman. *The Objectives of the New International Economic Order.* New York: Pergamon Press, 1978.

Letelier, Orlando, and Michael Moffitt. *The International Economic Order.* Washington, D.C.: Transnational Institute, 1977.

Lyon, Peter. *Neutralism.* Leicester, England: Leicester University Press, 1963.

Moss, Alfred George, and Harry N. M. Winton, eds. *A New International Economic Order, Selected Documents 1945-1975,* 2 vols. New York: United Nations Institute for Training and Research, 1976.

Neuhauser, Charles. *Third World Politics, China and the Afro-Asian People's Solidarity Organization, 1957-1967,* East Asian Monographs no. 27. Cambridge, Mass.: Harvard University Press, 1968.

North-South: A Program for Survival. Report of the Independent Commission on International Development Issues Under the Chairmanship of Willy Brandt. Cambridge, Mass.: MIT Press, 1980; and London: Pan Books, 1980.

Olson, Robert K. *U.S. Foreign Policy and the New International Economic Order: Negotiating Global Problems 1974-1981.* Boulder, Colo.: Westview Press, 1981.

Oye, Kenneth A.; Robert J. Lieber; and Donald Rothchild, eds. *Eagle Defiant: United States Foreign Policy in the 1980s.* Boston: Little, Brown, 1983.

Puchala, Donald, ed. *Issues Before the 37th General Assembly of the United Nations, 1982-1983.* New York: United Nations Association of the United States of America, 1982.

Reubens, Edwin P. *The Challenge of the New International Economic Order.* Boulder, Colo.: Westview Press, 1981.

Rothstein, Robert L. *Global Bargaining, UNCTAD and the Quest for a New Economic Order.* Princeton, N.J.: Princeton University Press, 1979.

_____. *The Third World and U.S. Foreign Policy: Cooperation and Conflict in the 1980s.* Boulder, Colo.: Westview Press, 1981.

_____. *The Weak in the World of the Strong.* New York: Columbia University Press, 1977.

Rubinstein, Alvin Z. *Yugoslavia and the Nonaligned World.* Princeton, N.J.: Princeton University Press, 1970.

Sauvant, Karl P. *Changing Priorities on the International Agenda: The New International Economic Order.* New York: Pergamon Press, 1981.

_____. *The Group of 77: Evolution, Structure, Organization.* New York: Oceana, 1981.

Singham, A. W., ed. *The Nonaligned Movement in World Politics.* Westport, Conn.: Lawrence Hill, 1978.

Singham, A. W., and Tran Van Dinh, eds. *From Bandung to Colombo.* New York: Third Press Review Books, 1976.

Stoessinger, John G. *Henry Kissinger: The Anguish of Power.* New York: Norton, 1976.

Stremlau, John J., ed. *The Foreign Policy Priorities of Third World States.* Boulder, Colo.: Westview Press, 1982.

Taylor, Phillip, and Gregory A. Raymond, eds. *Third World Policies of Industrialized Nations.* Westport, Conn.: Greenwood Press, 1982.

Thompson, W. Scott, ed. *The Third World: Premises of U.S. Policy.* Rev. ed. San Francisco: Institute for Contemporary Studies, 1983.

Towards a New International Economic and Social Order. Autumn 1976 issue of *International Social Science Journal* 28, no. 4.

Tyler, William G., ed. *Issues and Prospects for the New International Economic Order.* Lexington, Mass.: Heath, 1977.

United Nations. *Report of the Committee of the Whole Established Under General Assembly Resolution 32/174.* Document A/S-11/1. New York, 1981.

U.S. Congress, House, Committee on Foreign Affairs, *United Nations 11th Special Session on Economic Development and Cooperation.* Report, 96th Congress, 2nd Session. Washington, D.C.: Government Printing Office, 1981.

U.S. Congress, House, Committee on Foreign Affairs, Subcommittees on International Economic Policy and Trade and on International Organizations, *North-South Dialog: Progress and Prospects.* Hearings, 96th Congress, 2nd session. Washington, D.C.: Government Printing Office, 1980.

_____. *U.N. Special Session on Development: A Review.* Hearings, 96th Congress, 2nd session. Washington, D.C.: Government Printing Office, 1981.

Willetts, Peter. *The Non-Aligned in Havana: Documents of the Sixth Summit Conference and an Analysis of Their Significance for the Global Political System.* New York: St. Martin's Press, 1981.

_____. *The Non-Aligned Movement.* London: Frances Pinter, 1978.

Williams, Gwyneth. *Third-World Political Organizations.* Montclair, N.J.: Allanheld Osmun, 1981.

ARTICLES

Addo, Herb. "Foreign Policy Strategies for Achieving the New International Economic Order: A Third World Perspective." Pp. 233-53 in Charles W. Kegley, Jr., and Pat McGowan, eds., *The Political Economy of Foreign Policy Behavior*. Sage International Yearbook of Foreign Policy Studies, Vol. 6. Beverly Hills and London: Sage Publications, 1981.

Akins, James. "The Oil Crisis: This Time the Wolf Is Here." *Foreign Affairs* 51 (April 1973).

Amuzegar, Jahangir. "A Requiem for the North-South Conference." *Foreign Affairs* 55 (October 1977).

Bergsten, J. Fred. "The Response to the Third World." *Foreign Policy* 17 (Winter 1974-75).

Castaneda, Jorge. "La Charte des droits et des devoirs économiques." *Annuaire Français de Droit International*. 1974.

"La CNUCED à l'heure du 'pacte libéral.' " *Le Monde Diplomatique*, June 1983, pp. 9-15.

Cox, Robert W. "Ideologies and the New International Economic Order: Reflections on Some Recent Literature." *International Organization* 33 (Spring 1979).

Doyle, Michael W. "Stalemate in the North-South Debate: Strategies and the New International Economic Order." *World Politics* 35, no. 3 (April 1983): 426-64.

Erb, Guy F. "Africa and the International Economy: A U.S. Response." In *Africa and the United States*, edited by Jennifer Seymour Whitaker. New York: New York University Press, 1978.

Frank, Richard S. "Economic Report: U.S. Takes Steps to Meet Demands of Third World Nations." *National Journal Reports* 7 (October 25, 1975).

Geldart, Carol, and Peter Lyon, "The Group of 77: A Perspective View." *International Affairs* 57, no. 1 (Winter 1980-81): 79-101.

Graham, John A. "The Non-Aligned Movement After Havana." *Journal of International Affairs* 34, no. 1 (Spring-Summer 1980): 153-60.

Hoffmann, Stanley. "Les Etats-Unis du refus au compromise." *Revue Française de Science Politique* 26 (August 1976).

Jacobson, Harold K.; Dusan Sidjanski; Jeffrey Rodamas; and Alic Hougassian-Rudovich. "Revolutionaries or Bargainers? Negotiators for a New International Economic Order." *World Politics* 35, no. 3 (April 1983): 335-67.

Krasner, Stephen D. "North-South Economic Relations." In *Eagle Entangled, U.S. Foreign Policy in a Complex World*, edited by Kenneth A. Oye, Donald Rothchild, and Robert Lieber. New York: Longman, 1979.

Kuczynski, Pedro-Pablo. "Action Steps After Cancun." *Foreign Affairs* 60, no. 5 (Summer 1982): 1022-37.

LeoGrande, William M. "Evolution of the Nonaligned Movement." *Problems of Communism* 29 (January-February 1980): 35-52.

McLin, Jon. "The Group of 77." *American Universities Field Staff Reports*. West Europe Series 11 (April 1976).

Meltzer, Ronald I. "Restructuring the United Nations System: Institutional Reform Efforts in the Context of North-South Relations." *International Organization* 32 (Autumn 1978).

Moynihan, Daniel P. "The United States in Opposition." *Commentary* 59 (March 1975).

Peyre, Bernard. "La Conferénce Nord-Sud: Une opération diplomatique réussie ou un dialogue durable?" *Défense Nationale* 32 (March 1976).

Rifai, Taki. "La crise petrolière internationale (1970–1971), Essai d'interprétation." *Revue Française de Science Politique* 22 (December 1972).

Shaplen, Robert. "The Paradox of Non-alignment." *New Yorker* 59, no. 14 (May 23, 1983).

Smyth, Douglas C. "The Global Economy and the Third World: Coalition or Cleavage?" *World Politics* 29 (July 1977).

Tonelson, Alan. "Havana: A Rude Slap for U.S. Policy." *Inter-Dependent* 6, no. 9 (November 1979).

Viratelle, Gerard. "A propos du VIe sommet des non alignés." *Maghreb-Machreq* 86 (October-December 1979): 5–8.

List of Abbreviations

AAPSO	Afro-Asian Peoples' Solidarity Organization
ASEAN	Association of South East Asian Nations
CENTO	Central Treaty Organization
CIEC	Conference on International Economic Cooperation
COMECON	Council for Mutual Economic Assistance
COW	Committee of the Whole
CRESM	Centre de Recherches et d'Etudes sur les Sociétés Méditerranéennes
ECDC	Economic cooperation among developing countries
ECLA	United Nations Economic Commission for Latin America
ECOSOC	United Nations Economic and Social Council
EEC	European Economic Community
FNLA	Angolan National Liberation Front
FNLC	National Front for the Liberation of the Congo
G-77	Group of 77
GATT	General Agreement on Tariffs and Trade
GN	Global Negotiation
GPRA	Provisional Government of the Algerian Republic
GRAE	Angolan Revolutionary Government in Exile
GRP	Vietnamese Provisional Revolutionary Government
GRUNK	Royal Government of the Khmer National Union
IDA	International Development Association
IEA	International Energy Agency
IMF	International Monetary Fund
IPC	Integrated Program of Commodities
MPLA	Popular Movement for the Liberation of Angola
NATO	North Atlantic Treaty Organization
NIEO	New International Economic Order
OAPEC	Organization of Arab Petroleum Exporting Countries
OAU	Organization of African Unity
OECD	Organisation of Economic Co-operation and Development

OPEC	Organization of Petroleum Exporting Countries
PLO	Palestine Liberation Organization
SDR	Special drawing right
SEATO	Southeast Asia Treaty Organization
SELA	Latin American Economic System
SWAPO	South West African People's Association
UNCTAD	United Nations Conference on Trade and Development
UNIDO	United Nations Industrial Development Organization

Index

AAPSO. *See* Afro-Asian People's
  Solidarity Organization
Abu Dhabi, 44
Action Program of Economic
  Cooperation, 37–38, 50, 63, 79, 88,
  92
Addis-Ababa conference, 16
Adoula, Cyril, 13
Afghanistan, 8, 12, 42(n7), 89, 110, 113,
  122, 142, 155–157, 176(n34),
  177(n39)
Afro-Asianism, 8, 10, 11, 12, 15, 18–22
Afro-Asian Peoples' Solidarity
  Conference, 10
Afro-Asian Peoples' Solidarity
  Organization (AAPSO), 10–12, 21
Akhund, Iqbal, 115, 116, 118
Akins, James E., 47
Algeria, 1, 11, 13, 19, 20–22, 25–27,
  29–30, 33, 34, 36, 37, 38–41,
  42(n7), 44, 45, 46, 49, 50, 52,
  61–65, 73(n27), 79, 85, 86, 89, 93,
  96–99, 137, 145, 147–148, 156,
  161, 162, 164, 167–168, 170
Algiers Charter, 28–29, 34, 35, 54
Algiers Nonaligned Summit, 38–41, 44,
  51, 53, 67, 70, 88
Ali, Mohammed, 7
Allende, Salvador, 34, 86
Amuzegar, Jahangir, 71, 106
Angola, 1, 19, 31, 72(n23), 75, 84–85,
  86, 89, 90, 110, 123, 124, 176(n34)
  triangle with Zaire-Cuba, 112
Arafat, Yasir, 58
Argentina, 38, 79, 92, 96, 170
ASEAN. *See* Association of South East
  Asian Nations
Asian Solidarity Committee, 10
Assad, Hafez, 39

Association of South East Asian
  Nations (ASEAN), 158
Australia, 99
Austria, 59, 161

Bahamas, 91, 169
Bahrein, 39, 91
Bandaranaike, Simimavo, 15, 18, 39
Bandung Conference, 6–9, 22, 39
Bandung II, 6, 20–21, 22, 25
  Jakarta preparatory meeting, 18–19
Bangladesh, 39, 89, 158, 165, 170,
  177(n49)
Barbados, 91, 169
Bedjaoui, Mohammed, 164, 177(n48)
Belgium, 49, 59
Belgrade Conference (foreign ministers),
  124–125, 144
Belgrade nonaligned summit, 12–15, 88
Belize, 169
Ben Bella, Ahmed, 20, 21, 24, 25
Benin, 91
Bergsten, C. Fred, 136, 139
Bhutan, 39, 91
Bhutto, Ali, 91
Bolivia, 16, 90, 126, 176(n37)
Botswana, 42(n7), 89, 91
Boumediene, Houari, 21, 25–27, 30, 39,
  40, 49, 50, 52, 54–55, 58
Bourguiba, Habib, 15, 39
Bouteflika, Abdelaziz, 21–22, 28, 37, 39,
  57, 58
Brandt Commission reports, 160, 171,
  172, 174
Brandt, Willy, 160, 163
Brazil, 16, 62, 64, 68, 79, 83, 90, 96,
  177(n49)
Brazzaville Group, 13
Brezhnev, Leonid, 41

Brillantes, Hortensio, 76, 79
Burma, 7, 8, 12, 38, 91, 169
Burundi, 19, 34, 40, 92, 176(n37)
Butz, Earl, 134

Cairo conference, 10–11, 13
Cairo Economic Conference, 16
Cairo nonaligned summit, 18–20, 31, 33, 88
Cambodia (Kampuchea), 1, 8, 12, 19, 30–31, 38, 87, 110, 113, 146, 166
Royal Government of the Khmer National Union (GRUNK), 30–31, 36
Cameroon, 11, 19, 79, 91, 96
Canada, 49, 59, 98, 99, 105, 121, 161, 165
Cancun summit, 161, 163–164, 167, 176
Cape Verde, 86
Carter, Jimmy, 103, 105, 135–137
Casablanca bloc, 13
Castro, Fidel, 14, 15, 39, 143–145
Central African Republic, 13, 19, 42(n7), 176(n37)
Central Treaty Organization, 12
Chad, 19, 89, 142, 169, 176(n3)
Charter of Economic Rights and Duties of States, 92
Cheysson, Claude, 176
Chile, 16, 34, 37, 38, 83, 86, 91, 92
China, 8, 9, 10, 11, 13, 15, 18, 20–22, 32, 41, 52, 87, 113, 171, 177(n49)
CIEC. See Conference on International Economic Cooperation
Clark, Akporode, 76
Colombia, 83, 91, 169
Colombo nonaligned summit, 86–91, 93, 94
Colombo Powers, 7, 137
COMECON. See Council for Mutual Economic Assistance
. Committee of the Whole (COW). See under United Nations
Common Fund. See Integrated Program of Commodities/Common Fund
Comoros, 86, 91, 176(n37)
Conference on International Economic Cooperation (CIEC), 57, 66, 75, 79, 95, 100–109, 116
Paris preparatory meeting (April), 64–65, 98
Paris preparatory meeting (October), 94–100, 101, 108
Special Action program, 106, 107
Congo-Brazzaville, 13, 19, 42(n7), 91
Cooper, Richard, 136
Corea, Gamani, 68, 71, 75, 82–83
Costa Rica, 90, 129
Council for Mutual Economic Assistance (COMECON), 170
Council of Producers Associations, 88, 92

COW. See United Nations, Committee of the Whole
Crnobrnja, Bogdan, 152, 153
Cuba, 12, 13, 14, 33, 34, 40, 42(n7), 85, 89, 92, 110, 123, 137, 138, 170, 176(n34), 177(n42)
policy at Havana summit, 143–147
Cyprus, 13, 19, 87

Dadzie, Kenneth, 76, 117
Dahomey, 13, 19, 38
Dakar Conference on raw materials, 61, 84
Dakar Declaration, 61
Dam, Kenneth, 172
Daud, Mohammed, 122
Debt problem, 121. See also UNCTAD IV
Decolonization, 4, 9, 19, 20, 22
Denmark, 49, 59
Desai, Morarji, 114
Détente, 39
Djibouti, 175(n3)
Dominguez, Jorge, 112
Dominican Republic, 90
Dorticos, Osvaldo, 15

ECDC. See Economic Cooperation among Developing Countries
Echeverria, Luis, 58, 91, 161
Economic Cooperation among Developing Countries (ECDC), 80–81, 121, 129, 162–163
Mexico City Conference, 81, 88, 90–94
Ecuador, 16, 90, 169
EEC. See European Economic Community
Egypt, 8, 9, 12, 13, 18, 19, 20, 21, 34, 38, 40, 42(n7), 43, 79, 85, 96, 110, 112, 113, 137, 146
Eleventh Special Session (UN), 151–155, 160
El Salvador, 90
Enders, Thomas, 64, 69
Equatorial Guinea, 176(n37)
Ethiopia, 1, 8, 12, 14, 34, 40, 110, 113, 123, 145, 146, 176(n34)
Eritrea, 111, 113, 123
Ogaden, 111
European Economic Community (EEC), 62, 65, 98, 99, 104

Faisal, King, 7, 39
Falkland (Malvinas) Islands, 142
Feinberg, Richard, 176
Ferguson, C. Clyde, Jr., 133
Fiji, 91
Ford, Gerald, 57, 134
France, 13, 19, 31, 48–50, 52, 57, 59, 62, 76–65, 83, 104, 105, 161
Frei, Eduardo, 160

Gabon, 13, 38, 146, 162

Gambia, 38, 91
Gandhi, Indira, 39, 114, 166, 167
Geldart, Carol, 174
Geneva Conference on Trade and
    Development. *See* United Nations
    Conference on Trade and
    Development, UNCTAD I
Georgetown nonaligned conference
    (foreign ministers), 34, 36–38
    Georgetown declaration, 36–37, 52
Ghana, 7, 8, 11, 12, 13, 14, 19, 42(n7)
Gilman, Benjamin, 176(n29)
Giscard d'Estaing, Valery, 61, 62, 64,
    134
Gizenga, Antoine, 13
Global Negotiation, 141, 143, 147–155,
    161, 163–165, 167–169
Gowon, Yakubu, 39
Graham, John, 144
Great Britain. *See* United Kingdom
Grenada, 91, 126, 176(n34)
Group of Eight, 99
Group of 19, 79–80, 96, 99, 100–109
Group of 24, 76
Group of 75, 17
Group of 77 (G-77), 2, 3, 6, 16–18, 24,
    28, 29, 30, 32, 33–34, 35, 38, 41,
    48, 50–56, 59, 61–62, 66, 67–71,
    74–84, 85, 87–88, 90–94, 96, 102,
    104, 109, 114–115, 151–152,
    163–166
    Algiers conference, 25–29, 76
    Algiers conference (preparatory to
        UNIDO), 61–62, 64
    Arusha conference, 127–128
    Buenos Aires conference, 171–172
    Lima conference, 34–35, 76
    Lima Declaration, 34, 38, 69
    Manila conference, 78–81
    Manila Declaration, 79, 82, 104
GRP. *See* Vietnamese Provisional
    Revolutionary Government
G-77. *See* Group of 77
GRUNK. *See* Cambodia, Royal
    Government of the Khmer
    National Union
Guatemala, 90
Guinea, 11, 13, 14, 19, 42(n7), 89, 90,
    91, 176(n37)
Guinea-Bissau, 86
Guyana, 33, 34, 40, 72(n5), 89, 92,
    177(n49)

Haile Selassie, 15, 39
Haiti, 90
Hansen, Roger, 66
Haq, Mahbub ul, 5(n1)
Hassan, King, 15
Havana nonaligned summit, 143–150
Heath, Edward, 160
Heng Samrin, 146
Hoffmann, Stanley, 134, 155
Honduras, 90
Hormats, Robert, 154

Houphouet-Boigny, Felix, 39
Hussein, Saddam, 166

IMF. *See* International Monetary Fund
India, 1, 7, 8, 10, 12, 18, 20, 21, 34,
    38, 40, 42(n7), 51, 52, 62, 64, 79,
    89, 91, 96, 114, 123, 145, 156, 161,
    164–170, 177(n42)
Indochina, 36, 72(n23), 86
Indonesia, 6, 7, 8, 12, 14, 18, 21, 30,
    34, 36, 40, 42(n7), 44, 79, 89, 96,
    123, 146, 170
Information Center on Transnational
    Corporations, 88
Integrated Program of Commodities
    (IPC)/Common Fund, 81–84, 94,
    98, 105–108, 119–120, 136, 171
International Bank for Reconstruction
    and Development. *See* World Bank
International Development Association.
    See under World Bank
International Energy Agency, 49, 50
International Finance Corporation. *See
    under* World Bank
International Monetary Fund (IMF), 35,
    68, 117, 151, 168, 171, 172
International Resources Bank, 82, 83
IPC. *See* Integrated Program of
    Commodities/Common Fund
Iran, 8, 44, 47, 48, 52, 62, 63, 68, 79,
    80, 90, 93, 96, 98, 108, 110, 113,
    126, 142, 174
Iran-Iraq war, 158–159, 166
Iraq, 8, 12, 16, 33, 34, 40, 42(n7), 44,
    45, 73(n27), 79, 85, 89, 90, 96,
    108, 142, 176(n37)
Ireland, 49, 59
Israel, 7, 8, 37, 43, 47, 59, 71
Italy, 31, 49, 59, 105
Ivory Coast, 13, 29, 38, 177(n49)

Jamaica, 34, 79, 89, 92, 96, 137
Japan, 8, 9, 13, 31, 42, 46, 47, 49, 59,
    62, 98, 99, 105, 177(n49)
Jazairy, Idriss, 117
Joint Declaration, 16–17
Jordan, 8, 13, 19

Kasavubu, Joseph, 13
Kaunda, Kenneth, 31–32, 39, 40
Keita, Modibo, 15
Kenya, 17, 19, 42(n7)
Khane, Abdelrahman, 62
Khieu Samphan, 146
Khmers Rouges, 113
Khomeini, Ruhollah (Ayatollah), 126,
    166
Kimche, David, 9
Kirkpatrick, Jeane, 164
Kissinger, Henry, 41, 50, 52, 54–55, 58,
    66, 67, 82, 132–135
Komatina, Miljan, 122, 131(n21)
Kreisky, Bruno, 161
Kuwait, 16, 19, 40, 42(n7), 44, 89

Lacouture, Jean, 41
Lai, Peter, 76
Laos, 8, 12, 13, 19, 30, 36, 42(n7), 87,
    176(n34)
Lebanon, 8, 12, 85, 91, 142
    civil war, 75
LeoGrande, William, 145
Lesotho, 42(n7)
Liberia, 8, 13, 19, 40, 42(n7), 72(n5),
    89
Libya, 8, 13, 16, 19, 42(n7), 44–45, 46,
    73(n27), 85, 162
Lievano, Indalecio, 118
Lima Declaration. *See under* Group of
    77
Lima nonaligned conference (foreign
    ministers), 67, 70–71
London summit of Western
    industrialized countries, 106
Lon Nol, 30–31
Lopez Portillo, Jose, 161
Lumumba, Patrice, 13
Lusaka nonaligned summit, 29–33, 36,
    88
    Dar es Salaam preparatory meeting,
        30, 34, 36
    Lusaka Declaration, 31–32, 33, 37, 52
Luxemburg, 49, 59
Lyon, Peter, 174

MacEachen, Allan, 98
McLin, Jon, 74
McNamara, Robert, 160
Madagascar, 38, 176(n37)
Makarios (Archbishop), 15, 39
Malawi, 19, 90, 175(n3)
Malaysia (Malaya), 16, 19, 21, 30, 34,
    36, 40, 42(n7), 89, 146
Maldives, 86, 91
Mali, 13, 42(n7), 51, 89
Malmierca, Isidoro, 146
Malta, 39, 91
Manila Declaration. *See under* Group
    of 77
Mauritania, 19, 42(n7), 85, 86
Mauritius, 38
Martinez, Gabriel, 76
Mendès-France, Pierre, 160
Mengistu Haile Mariam, 112
Mestiri, Mahmoud, 118
Mexico, 16, 73(n27), 79, 83, 90, 91–92,
    96, 137, 161
Mills, Donald, 118
Mishra, Brajesh, 152, 154, 155
Mitterrand, François, 163
Mobutu Sese Seko, 39, 112
Mongolia, 11
Morocco, 4, 13, 34, 40, 42(n7), 85, 86,
    112
Moynihan, Daniel Patrick, 68, 135
Mozambique, 31, 72(n23), 86, 176(n34)
Mugabe, Robert, 147
Muzorewa, Abel, 147

Namibia, 31
Nasser, Gamal Abdul, 7, 9–15, 18, 20
NATO. *See* North Atlantic Treaty
    Organization
Natural ally thesis, 143–145
Nehru, Jawaharlal, 7, 8, 9–10, 14, 15,
    20
Nepal, 8, 12, 16, 40, 72(n5), 89, 158
Netherlands, 49, 59, 83, 104, 121
Neto, Agostino, 112
New Delhi conference. *See* UNCTAD
    II
New Delhi nonaligned conference
    (foreign ministers), 157–159
New Delhi nonaligned summit,
    166–170
New International Economic Order
    (NIEO), 2, 3, 43–58, 62, 64, 68–69,
    79, 88, 95, 96–98, 104, 110,
    114–118, 147, 153
    U.S. policy toward, 53–56, 69,
        133–136
New Zealand, 17
Nicaragua, 143
NIEO. *See* New International Economic
    Order
Niger, 13, 38, 89
Nigeria, 19, 44, 46, 79, 85, 89, 96, 161,
    162
Nixon, Richard, 48, 57, 133
Nkomo, Joshua, 147
Nkrumah, Kwame, 14, 15, 24
Nonaligned Bureau, 40, 41, 67, 80,
    88–90, 93, 149–150, 156, 169–170
    Algiers meeting, 49–51
    Colombo meeting, 126, 144, 147
    Havana meeting, 122–124, 143
    New Delhi meeting, 113–114
Nonaligned movement, 2, 3, 6, 8, 9,
    11–12, 14–15, 18–20, 22, 29–41,
    49–56, 61, 70, 71, 74, 76, 80,
    85–94, 96, 122–126
    foreign ministers conferences. *See*
        under Belgrade; Georgetown; Lima;
        New Delhi
    summit conferences. *See under*
        Algiers; Belgrade; Cairo; Colombo;
        Havana; Lusaka; New Delhi
North Atlantic Treaty Organization
    (NATO), 8, 12
North Korea, 7, 8, 11, 86, 87
North Vietnam, 8, 13
Norway, 49, 59, 99
Nuclear issue, 14
Nyerere, Julius, 37, 39, 127, 145, 163

OAPEC. *See* Organization of Arab
    Petroleum Exporting Countries
OAU. *See* Organization of African
    Unity
Olson, Robert, 153
Oman, 39
OPEC. *See* Organization of Petroleum
    Exporting Countries

Organization of African Unity (OAU), 16, 19, 49, 57, 78, 86, 90
Organization of Arab Petroleum Exporting Countries (OAPEC), 47, 50
Organization of Petroleum Exporting Countries (OPEC), 3, 41, 43–49, 50, 52–53, 55–61, 63, 64, 66, 75, 85, 98, 107–108, 150, 162, 165
  Algiers summit, 63, 64
  Caracus meeting, 45–46
  Teheran negotiation, 46
  Ottawa summit, 167

Pakistan, 1, 7, 8, 16, 18, 20, 68, 79, 80, 90, 91–92, 93, 96, 113, 126, 137, 156, 164, 177(n39)
Palestine Liberation Organization (PLO), 58, 74, 85, 86, 89, 90, 143, 169, 177(n42)
  Palestinian issue, 4, 37, 58
Palme, Olof, 160
Panama, 37, 86, 92, 143, 145
Papua New Guinea, 91
Paraguay, 91
Patriotic Front, 143, 147
Perez Guerrero, Manuel, 75, 79, 98, 101, 104, 105, 108, 155, 177(n48)
Peru, 34, 37, 38, 40, 79, 89, 92, 96, 98, 145
Philippines, 8, 68, 80, 90, 91–92, 137, 177(n49)
Pisani, Edgard, 160
PLO. See Palestine Liberation Organization
Polisario Front, 85
Pol Pot, 146, 158
Portugal, 31
Prebisch, Raul, 16, 25, 75, 129
Pronk, Jan, 172

Qaddafi, Muammar, 39, 41, 45, 71(n1)
Qatar, 39, 44

Ramphal, Shridath, 160, 163
Reagan, Ronald, 155, 159, 163, 174
Rhodesia, 31
Robinson, Charles, 64
Romulo, Carlos, 7
Rothstein, Robert, 141
Royal Government of the Khmer National Union. See under Cambodia
Rumania, 90

Sadat, Anwar, 10, 39
São Tomé and Principe, 86, 91, 176(n37)
Sary, Ieng, 124
Sastroamidjojo, Ali, 7
Saudi Arabia, 8, 12, 14, 38, 44, 47, 60–64, 79, 85, 96–99, 108, 112, 113, 143, 162, 165, 169, 177(n49)
Scali, John, 52, 56, 60

Scandinavia, 83
Schlesinger, James, 50
SEATO. See Southeast Asia Treaty Organization
Senegal, 13, 19, 35, 40, 85, 89, 146
Senghor, Leopold, 39
Seventh Special Session (UN), 44, 66–71, 75, 79, 98
Seychelles, 86, 91, 176(n37)
Sibai, Yussuf, 11
Sierra Leone, 19
Sihanouk, Norodom, 7, 15, 30, 31, 39
Simon, William, 133
Singapore, 16, 42(n7), 91, 146
Sino-Soviet split, 11, 12
Sixth Special Session (UN), 1, 2, 24, 44, 48–56, 57, 59, 63, 65, 79, 93
Smith, Ian, 147
Solidarity Fund, 88
Solomon Islands, 176(n37)
Somalia, 1, 13, 40, 42(n7), 89, 110, 113, 123, 124, 146
South Africa, 7, 8, 31, 58
Southeast Asia Treaty Organization (SEATO), 12
South Korea, 7, 8, 17, 27, 87, 90
South Vietnam, 8, 13, 17, 27, 30, 38
South West African People's Organization (SWAPO), 143, 169
South Yemen, 42(n7), 91, 113, 176(n34), 177(n39)
Soviet bloc, 8, 10
Soviet Union, 10, 11, 14, 19, 20–21, 22, 41, 50, 87, 113, 144, 155–157, 177(n39,49)
Spain, 59, 99
Spero, Joan, 154
Sri Lanka (Ceylon), 7, 8, 12, 34, 40, 42(n7), 72(n5), 89, 93, 137, 144, 145, 170
Stoessinger, John, 132
Sudan, 7, 8, 12, 34, 40, 42(n7), 89, 112, 176(n37)
Suez Canal, 45
Suez crisis, 9, 10, 47
Sukarno, Ahmed, 7, 10, 14, 15, 18, 21, 24
Sulzberger, C. L., 41
Surinam, 91, 126
SWAPO. See South West African People's Organization
Swaziland, 42(n7)
Sweden, 99, 104, 121, 161
Switzerland, 99, 121
Syria, 8, 12, 19, 40, 42(n7), 43, 73(n27), 85, 89, 176(n37)

Taiwan, 7, 8
Tanzania, 11, 16, 18, 19, 33, 34, 40, 42(n7), 89, 137, 161, 170
Taraki, Nur Mohammed, 122
Thailand, 8, 90
Tito, Josip Broz, 9–15, 16, 18, 19, 20, 24, 29–30, 33, 39, 86, 144–145

Togo, 19, 42(n7)
Touré, Sekou, 15
Trinidad, 34
Tshombe, Moise, 21
Tunisia, 13, 42(n7), 137
Turkey, 8, 9

Uganda, 19, 42(n7), 176(n37)
UNCTAD. *See* United Nations
  Conference on Trade and
  Development
UNIDO. *See* United Nations Industrial
  Development Organization
United Arab Emirates, 39, 85
United Arab Republic, 12
United Kingdom, 31, 49, 52, 59, 84,
  99, 105, 154, 177(n49)
United Nations, 4, 6, 15, 31, 32, 33,
  49, 51, 53, 59, 69, 70–71, 87, 93,
  100, 105, 109, 111
  central role of General Assembly,
    151, 153
  Committee of the Whole (COW),
    117–118, 148
  restructuring of, 116–117
  See also Eleventh Special Session;
    Seventh Special Session; Sixth
    Special Session
United Nations Conference on Trade
  and Development (UNCTAD), 4,
  15, 16, 17, 24, 25, 35, 37, 74,
  75–81, 84, 88, 92, 94, 102, 105,
  107, 108
  UNCTAD I, 15–18, 20, 24, 27, 75
  UNCTAD II, 27–29, 35, 36, 54
  UNCTAD III, 32, 33–36, 38, 54, 58
  UNCTAD IV, 78–79, 81–84, 101–102
  UNCTAD V, 128–130
  UNCTAD VI, 172–173
United Nations Industrial Development
  Organization (UNIDO), 57, 61–62,
  69
  Lima conference, 62
  New Delhi conference, 159–160
United States, 4, 5, 10, 14, 19, 26, 29,
  31, 35, 37, 41, 43, 46, 47, 48–56,
  57–60, 62, 64–66, 68–71, 82–83,
  92, 93, 96–98, 99, 102, 103–107,
  132–137, 153–155, 157, 164, 174

U Nu, 7, 10, 15
Upper Volta, 13, 38
Uruguay, 16, 90

Vance, Cyrus, 174
Vanuatu, 169
Velasco, Juan, 34
Venezuela, 16, 44, 62, 73(n27), 79, 85,
  90, 96, 98, 108, 155, 162, 177(n49)
Versailles summit, 165, 167
Vietnam, 1, 19, 26, 29, 86, 87, 89, 90,
  110, 113, 123, 145, 146, 158,
  176(n34)
Vietnamese National Liberation Front,
  29
Vietnamese Provisional Revolutionary
  Government (GRP), 30–31, 36,
  86–87
von Wechmar, Rudiger, 155

Waldheim, Kurt, 50, 58
Walker, Herbert, 76
Warsaw Pact, 12, 90
Washington Conference on Energy, 49,
  50, 53
West Germany, 31, 49, 52, 59, 84, 104,
  105, 154, 161
Western Sahara, 75, 85, 86, 110, 111,
  113, 123, 142
Willetts, Peter, 144
World Bank, 26, 68, 116, 151, 168
  International Development
    Association, 68, 171–172
  International Finance Corporation, 68

Yamani, Zaki, 60
Yemen, 8, 12, 42(n7), 91, 113
Yom Kippur War, 3, 43
Young, Andrew, 116, 135
Yugoslavia, 9, 10, 11, 13, 15, 18, 20,
  29–30, 33, 34, 38, 40, 42(n), 52,
  79, 80, 89, 90, 93, 96, 114, 123,
  137, 138, 143, 161, 170

Zaire (Congo), 1, 12, 13, 19, 21, 40,
  42(n7), 62, 64, 65, 79, 85, 89, 96,
  110, 124, 146
Zambia, 19, 31–33, 34, 40, 79, 89, 96,
  176(n37), 177(n42)
Zimbabwe. *See* Patriotic Front

Titles in This Series

The Exclusive Economic Zone: A Latin American Perspective, edited by Francisco Orrego Vicuña

† *The Third World Coalition in International Politics,* Second, Updated Edition, Robert A. Mortimer

† *Latin American Nations in World Politics,* edited by Heraldo Muñoz and Joseph S. Tulchin

Militarization and the International Arms Race in Latin America, Augusto Varas

Other Titles of Interest from Westview Press

Bibliography on Economic Cooperation Among Developing Countries, 1981-1982: With Annotations, Research Centre for Co-operation with Developing Countries

Comparative Development Perspectives, edited by Gustav Ranis, Robert L. West, Cynthia Taft Morris, and Mark Leiserson

The Emergence of the NIEO Ideology, Craig Murphy

The Challenges of South-South Cooperation, edited by Breda Pavlič, Raúl R. Uranga, Boris Cizelj, and Marjan Svetličič

† *Threat to Development: Pitfalls of the NIEO,* William Loehr and John P. Powelson

U.S. Foreign Policy and the New International Economic Order: Negotiating Global Problems, 1974-1981, Robert K. Olson

† *International Financial Cooperation: A Framework for Change,* Frances Stewart and Arjun Sengupta, edited by Salah Al-Shaikhly

† *From Dependency to Development: Strategies to Overcome Underdevelopment and Inequality,* edited by Heraldo Muñoz

† *The Foreign Policy Priorities of Third World States,* edited by John J. Stremlau

† *The Third World and U.S. Foreign Policy: Cooperation and Conflict in the 1980s,* Robert L. Rothstein

† Available in hardcover and paperback.

About the Book and Author

The Third World Coalition in International Politics
SECOND, UPDATED EDITION
Robert A. Mortimer

In this second, updated edition of *The Third World Coalition in International Politics,* Professor Mortimer expands his comprehensive analysis of the emergence and maintenance of the nonaligned movement and the Group of 77 with new material that provides students with a clear account of developments in Third World collective diplomacy through the recent North-South negotiations at UNCTAD VI in 1983. The book examines the process by which a heterogeneous group of states launched the call for greater equity through a New International Economic Order; analyzes the political and organizational techniques by which the durable Third World coalition has held itself together during times of economic recession and political turmoil; and concludes with reflections on U.S. policy toward the reality of poverty that lies at the root of the very existence of a Third World coalition.

Robert A. Mortimer is professor of political science at Haverford College, Haverford, Pennsylvania. In 1974–75 he served as Fulbright Professor at the Institut d'Etudes Politiques of the University of Algiers in Algeria.